GREAT SIOUX WAR ORDERS OF BATTLE

GREAT SIOUX WAR ORDERS OF BATTLE

How the United States Army Waged War on the Northern Plains, 1876–1877

Paul L. Hedren

UNIVERSITY OF OKLAHOMA PRESS
Norman

Also by Paul L. Hedren

First Scalp for Custer: The Skirmish at Warbonnet Creek, Nebraska, July 17, 1876 (Glendale, 1980)

With Crook in the Black Hills: Stanley J. Morrow's 1876 Photographic Legacy (Boulder, 1985)

Fort Laramie in 1876: Chronicle of a Frontier Post at War (Lincoln, 1988)

(ed.) *The Great Sioux War 1876–77: The Best from* Montana The Magazine of Western History (Helena, 1991)

(ed.) *Campaigning with King: Charles King, Chronicler of the Old Army* (Lincoln, 1991)

Traveler's Guide to the Great Sioux War: The Battlefields, Forts, and Related Sites of America's Greatest Indian War (Helena, 1996)

We Trailed the Sioux: Enlisted Men Speak on Custer, Crook, and the Great Sioux War (Mechanicsburg, 2003)

Library of Congress Cataloging-in-Publication Data

Hedren, Paul L.

Great Sioux War orders of battle : how the United States Army waged war on the Northern Plains, 1876–1877 / Paul L. Hedren.

p. cm. —

Includes bibliographical references and index.

ISBN 978-0-8061-4322-4 (paperback)

1. Dakota Indians—Wars, 1876. 2. Cheyenne Indians—Wars, 1876. 3. United States. Army. Cavalry—History—19th century. 4. United States. Army. Infantry—History—19th century. I. Title. II. Series.

E83.876.H415 2011

973.8'2—dc22

2010026868

Great Sioux War Orders of Battle: How the United States Army Waged War on the Northern Plains, 1876–1877 is Volume 31 in the Frontier Military Series.

Manufactured in the U.S.A.

Paperback edition published 2012.

To Connie, with all my love

Contents

Preface

Historians are at once captivated and bedeviled by the Great Sioux War of 1876–77, the Indian war in which George Armstrong Custer was killed. In its nearly two-year-long course this grueling conflict pitted almost one-third of the U.S. Army against Lakota Sioux and Northern Cheyennes over issues such as access to the new goldfields of the Black Hills, construction of a northern transcontinental railroad, and fundamental treaty rights that ran counter to any manner of white settlement of the northern plains. Before it ended, the war had played out on twenty-seven different battlefields scattered across a five-state region, cost hundreds of killed and wounded and millions of dollars, and had immediate and lingering transformative impacts on the landscape and on survivors on both sides.

Great Sioux War Orders of Battle is a new look at this compelling saga and the product of my own lifelong fascination with the orthodoxies and intriguing characters of the Indian fighting army, coupled with an especially intense interest in this specific Indian war. Some students of the Great Sioux War postulate that the U.S. Army was not at all well suited for this extraordinary conflict, contending that too many of its officers were untested, that company ranks were filled with inexperienced recruits and the dregs of society, and that it had no formal doctrine for unconventional warfare—all elements of this war's supposed bedevilment. But the historical record reveals quite a different story. Instead of the litany of presumptive shortcomings that apologists use to explain questionable conduct at Powder River, Rosebud Creek, and especially Little Big Horn, quite a different army emerges from contemporary sources. This army was very well led and equipped, of sound composition, and with an orthodoxy, albeit unwritten, quite well suited to the mission at hand. Certainly this army of 1876 was not fighting a conventional war and was not the American Army of Empire, a notion virtually unfathomable at the time. But this was an army appropriate for the American West in 1876. While it did lose at Powder River and Little Big Horn, it did not lose the Great Sioux War.

In presenting and analyzing the U.S. Army and Great Sioux War, I use the concept "order of battle" (or its plural), which has several subtly different meanings. Military dictionaries define "order of battle" rather consistently. At its most basic, the term identifies the command structure, strength, and disposition of personnel, equipment, and units of an armed force. One dictionary parses it as the arrangement or disposition of the different component parts of an army on the brink of engagement, and that rather simple concept is embraced and reflected in this book. Typically, of course, an order of battle defines the forces on both sides of an engagement or conflict. The many extant orders of battle for Gettysburg, for instance, conventionally detail Union and Confederate force structures to the regimental level. The availability of information of this sort before the engagement was keenly useful to commanders and helped predict movements and gauge success or disaster. Historians use orders of battle to frame and understand military orchestrations, movements, and consequences, whether interpreting a Civil War battle, the Normandy invasion, or, in this instance, a fascinating and consequential Indian war.[1]

To be sure, constructing an order of battle for an Indian campaign or war has its own peculiarities. Indian warfare was purely unconventional, and the army's responses were often happenstance. *Great Sioux War Orders of Battle* is admittedly and necessarily a one-sided look at this war. Readers interested in how Sioux and Northern Cheyennes repeatedly reacted and engaged for two years (whether individually or driven by influential personalities) have access to a number of stellar books that probe that side of the story. Especially recommended are Robert M. Utley's biography of Sitting Bull, *The Lance and the Shield*; Kingsley M. Bray's *Crazy Horse*; Robert W. Larson's *Gall*; and Peter J. Powell's *Sweet Medicine.*

In all of my work I am concerned with the entire war and not merely any one part. Like many who study and write on the Great Sioux War, I was hooked as a kid by "Custer's Last Stand." This book has much to say about Custer and the Seventh Cavalry and their phenomenal battle on the banks of the Little Big Horn River. But I am as deeply interested

---

[1] Boatner, *The Civil War Dictionary,* 610; Wilhelm, *A Military Dictionary and Gazetteer,* 370; Farrow, *Farrow's Military Encyclopedia,* 2:440. For comparison, see recent examples of orders of battle for Gettysburg in Sears, *Gettysburg;* and Trudeau, *Gettysburg.*

in the war's opening movements at places like Fort Pease and Powder River, its languishing middle, and its closing gasps as I am in the Little Big Horn and offer considerable analysis and reflection on those aspects of the conflict as well.

Great Sioux War Orders of Battle has three parts. Part I explores doctrine, training, culture, and matériel to understand and contextualize the American Army and this particular Indian war. I look at an array of variables, some familiar and many that are new, in developing and defending the premise that this army was in fact much better suited for Indian warfare in 1876 than is commonly supposed, particularly in light of the stunning defeat at Little Big Horn. I specifically explore the army's aptitude and preparedness for classic unconventional warfare and document a well-practiced body of tactics perfectly suited for these conflicts on the plains and this particular war with the Sioux. I analyze the organizations of Phil Sheridan, Alfred Terry, George Crook, Nelson Miles, Wesley Merritt, and Ranald Mackenzie, who commanded the largest and most significant deployments of the war. I look closely at the officer class as a whole to achieve a greater understanding of both its individual and collective capacity to wage war. *Great Sioux War Orders of Battle* is not a narrative history of this Indian war in the conventional sense: I do presume readers' familiarity with the story and especially its complex undergirding. I also commend the fine studies by Jerome A. Greene, Robert M. Utley, Paul Andrew Hutton, and Charles M. Robinson III, among others, which are cited repeatedly herein and upon which this work is grounded.

Part II uniquely dissects the Great Sioux War and identifies twenty-eight deployments that I believe constitute the conflict from its start, when troops relieved a besieged trading post, Fort Pease, in February 1876, through the anticlimactic Little Missouri Expedition in the mid- and late summer of 1877. Several of these orchestrations (the second iteration of George Crook's Big Horn and Yellowstone Expedition, Alfred H. Terry's and John Gibbon's combined movement in midsummer 1876, Crook's Powder River Expedition, and the Little Missouri Expedition) were substantial in scope. Their brigades and multiple battalions resembled equivalents of the great army orchestrations so consequential in the Civil War, though certainly on a Great Plains, postwar, Regular Army scale. At the same time, some deployments were small, achieving their purposes with a few troops maneuvering in a short time frame. Many more involved regimental-strength orchestrations spanning weeks in the field. The twenty-eight deployments in *Great Sioux War Orders of Battle* are presented in chronological order, from the first recognized day of the respective movement.

In this book I look for commonalities as well as differences in the various deployments of this Sioux war. Consistent with the premise of an order of battle, I document command structures, regiments and companies deployed, and all 452 officers and physicians who could one day call themselves Great Sioux War veterans. I also carefully introduce each of the individual deployments and offer observations on its peculiarities, relationships to other actions, engagements if any, and consequences or outcomes of the movement. To be sure, the legacy of the American Indian wars includes nothing as phenomenal as the Great Sioux War, and such a broad, multifaceted, deeply impacting orchestration was never again repeated in the West.

Central to my definition of what constitutes a Sioux War deployment is that each respective movement had to occur on the northern plains within the time frame of 1876–77 (during the war's so-called active phase) and beyond the discernible security of a military post. A deployment had to expose soldiers to a chance or purposeful encounter with Sioux or Northern Cheyenne warriors and the inherent prospect of death, whether on a formal campaign, escorting freight or steamboats, or standing duty at a field cantonment or way station. Within these simple limitations, movements of any scale beyond Fort Abraham Lincoln, Fort Buford, Fort Fetterman, or any of the other posts on the margins of the war zones that could have resulted in an encounter with Sioux or Northern Cheyennes are identified as deployments. Episodes like Terry's peace mission to Fort Walsh, the botched arrest of Crazy Horse at Camp Robinson, and the poignant surrender of Sitting Bull at Fort Buford, however, while central to the story of the Great Sioux War, are not deemed deployments. They occurred under the unique mantle of North-West Mounted Police protection or within the army's realm of close control and did not involve a campaign-like orchestration. Under those circumstances, the prospect of bloodshed or death in a hostile encounter was unlikely, even when emotions ran nearly unchecked, as during the Crazy Horse arrest and killing frenzy.

Included in my tally of twenty-eight orchestrations are two unique consolidated deployments, one on the Yellowstone River and the other on the southern margins of the Black Hills. Each of these deployments involved dozens of small movements like freight and steamboat protection, camp or depot duty, road patrol, and small engagements on the order of Orlando H. Moore's encounter with Sioux at the abandoned Powder River Depot site on the Yellowstone or Company K, Second Cavalry's sharp little fight on Richard Creek, south of Fort Laramie. By themselves, these small actions in no way compare to any of the major deployments; but collectively they represent considerable effort by the army to manage tasks or obligations within two separate geographic regions that were directly associated with the major movements of the Great Sioux War and accordingly contributed to the outcome of the war itself.

Finally, part III addresses the issue of how an otherwise sound American Army failed on several of this war's battlefields. While the army of 1876 did not lose the Great Sioux War, it lost embarrassingly at Powder River and astonishingly at Little Big Horn. But I delve into the consequences suffered and lessons learned along the way as I grapple with yet another compelling dimension of this unique Indian war.

In researching and writing *Great Sioux War Orders of Battle* I particularly exploited an unheralded but extraordinarily rich body of primary source material in the National Archives in Washington, D.C. The regiments, companies, and names in the twenty-eight Great Sioux War deployments described in this book are derived largely from the army's Regimental Returns for each of the units engaged. Regimental Returns were oversized two-page reports generated monthly at regimental headquarters and transmitted to the Adjutant General's Office in the War Department. These specific returns documented the garrison assignments of the headquarters, band, and each of the companies of the given unit; the status of every officer assigned to the regiment; the deployments of the companies that month (if any); the strengths of the individual companies; the separation of men and arrival of recruits; and any special action or accomplishment warranting mention. In all, I examined some 185 monthly Regimental Returns applicable to this story.

I also examined Post Returns for certain forts prominent in the war and especially Cantonment Reno, Tongue River Cantonment, and Big Horn Post, because the founding and early existence of these installations themselves were critical Great Sioux War deployments. Like Regimental Returns, Post Returns were also monthly oversized two-page reports generated at post headquarters and transmitted to the Adjutant General's Office. They accounted for companies and officers on duty at the post, officers casually present, the deployments of the companies present (if any), the medical staff present for duty, and similar matters. Many of these details are different from those provided on Regimental Returns.

I also examined a wide array of primary reports, diaries, and narratives related to the war, which often reported on or confirmed the functional order of the various columns and the specific dates of the movements. And I benefited as well from the substantial body of secondary source material on the Great Sioux War, particularly the works of Jerome A. Greene and the late James Willert, two master historians of this Indian war and devotees of narrative history drawn from primary sources. *Great Sioux War Orders of Battle* rests solidly on their foundation but substantially expands the story.

Long ago I called the Great Sioux War America's greatest Indian war. I based that conclusion on my lifelong study of this intriguing conflict and an intimate understanding of the war's geography, its battlefields, and its dramatic impacts on participants and successors. I stand by that pronouncement but also believe that this book strengthens my case substantially. This was indeed a unique Indian war calling for an unprecedented response and orchestration by the United States Army. It remains a deeply significant and enthralling period whose full story has yet to be told.

Acknowledgments

Great Sioux War Orders of Battle began as a small diversion following my move from O'Neill, Nebraska, to Omaha in October 2007. I had just retired from the National Park Service and fully intended in early retirement to complete a book project begun some seven or eight years ago. As I idled away the days unboxing books and outfitting a new study, I was reminded of a topic that occasionally piqued my curiosity. I started exploring the manner in which the U.S. Army organized itself for the campaigns of the Great Sioux War. I imagined similarities in Crook's and Terry's early orchestrations and increasing complexities when more and more troops came to the field as the war raged on. I drew out an order of battle for Crook's and Joseph Reynolds's Big Horn Expedition of March 1876, believing that Jesse Vaughn's book *The Reynolds Campaign on Powder River* provided a good outline (which it does). In detailing that expedition and associated Powder River fight I developed a usable format for outlining and analyzing the handful of other campaigns that I then rather automatically assumed constituted this Indian war. At that time I hardly foresaw analyses of twenty-eight distinct deployments or substantial interpretations attempting to explain it all in the context of not only the Great Sioux War but other Plains Indian wars preceding it.

In the excitement of discovery as the project blossomed, I started playing observations, notions, hunches, and conclusions off a handful of steadfast friends. I am especially grateful for the responses and insights provided by Jerry Greene, Arvada, Colorado; Eli Paul, Kansas City, Missouri; Tom Buecker, Crawford, Nebraska; and Doug McChristian, Tucson, Arizona. These colleagues also read portions of the manuscript before it was tendered to the Arthur H. Clark Company, and their comments sharpened my analyses and broadened my perspectives.

An array of other good friends also assisted along the way, variously providing encouragement, advice, access, or source material. They include

Sandra Lowry and Baird Todd, Fort Laramie National Historic Site, Fort Laramie, Wyoming; Tom Heski, Cannon Falls, Minnesota; David Hayes, University of Colorado at Boulder Libraries; Marv Kaiser, Prescott, Arizona; Warren Arganbright, Valentine, Nebraska; Jim Potter, Chadron, Nebraska; C. Lee Noyes, Morrisonville, New York; Randy Kane, Fort Union Trading Post National Historic Site, Williston, North Dakota; Mark Sundlov, Fort Buford State Historic Site, Williston, North Dakota; Ephriam Dickson, Fort Douglas Museum, Salt Lake City, Utah; Gil Bollinger, Buffalo, Wyoming; John Gavin, Jim Gatchell Memorial Museum, Buffalo, Wyoming; Jeff Barnes, Omaha, Nebraska; Carla Kelly, Valley City, North Dakota; Jack McDermott, Rapid City, South Dakota; Marc Abrams, Brooklyn, New York; B. William Henry, Jr., Florence, Oregon; Chuck Rankin, University of Oklahoma Press, Norman; James A. Hanson, Museum of the Fur Trade, Chadron, Nebraska; and Bob Clark of the Arthur H. Clark Company, Norman, Oklahoma.

I must especially acknowledge the courtesies extended by the many public servants of all stripes at the National Archives and Records Service and U.S. Army Military History Institute. Having devoted my own life to public service for nearly thirty-seven years, I have boundless appreciation and admiration for the men and women who so selflessly serve us all. These archivists know their collections inside and out, are eager to assist, and brim with useful suggestions: Lori Cox-Paul, National Archives, Kansas City, Missouri; Jill M. D'Andrea and Trevor Plante, National Archives, Washington, D.C.; and Richard J. Sommers, Clif Hyatt, and Richard Baker, U.S. Army Military History Institute, Carlisle Barracks, Pennsylvania.

David Roth, editor of *Blue & Gray Magazine,* was indefatigable in helping me chase the source of an extraordinary tribute allegedly paid to Regular Army infantry troops engaged at Gettysburg by a Pennsylvania Volunteer: "for two years the U.S. Regulars taught us how to be soldiers; in the Wheatfield at Gettysburg, they taught us how to die like soldiers." He connected me with Tim Reese, author of a significant history of the Regular regiments serving in the Army of the Potomac, many of which later fought in the Great Sioux War. To our great collective chagrin, this incredible, oft-repeated quotation proved to be spurious and, while capturing an apt sentiment of exceptional valor at Gettysburg, originated only a decade or so ago. But Roth and Reese directed me to legitimate contemporary praise paid to these Regulars, including one shining tribute that found its way into my story.

In all of my book projects I relish acknowledging the unflinching kindness and support given me by my family, including my wife, Connie; daughters Ethne and Whitney; and son-in-law Shaun Denham, who bear with my single-mindedness when I am lost in the events of 1876. Connie's daughter Alicia and son-in-law David Larrick and their girls Gabriella and Sophia got caught up in this effort too, and Richard Simons, a British member of my extended family, read much of the manuscript while bluntly assuring me that if I made sense to him the project had hope. The list of these supporters, nay sufferers, continues to grow. Little granddaughters Emma and Kate Denham do not quite yet "get" Custer or Crook but do like pawing through Grandpa's books. I am told that they are already eager for their own first visit to the Warbonnet skirmish site, a special family adventure.

To all of you, please accept my warmest thanks. Richard, I sure hope there's some plain talk and good sense here, and perhaps even some new thinking.

Part I

Waging the Great Sioux War

The American Army of 1876

A notion persists in twenty-first-century America that the army unleashed in 1876 by President Ulysses Grant on the Sioux Indians of the northern plains was a force broadly unsuited for this heady challenge. To some, this was an army and particularly a senior officer corps still preparing for conventional war, as evident in its political relations and its war-making doctrine, weaponry, and tactics. Certainly a disproportionate percentage of the army's officers were veterans of the nation's most recent conventional war, the Civil War, and that template for warfare and war-making still dominated the army's psyche. This army had fared poorly against the Sioux in the calamitous Red Cloud or Bozeman Trail War of the middle and late 1860s and had struggled against them for three years running on the Yellowstone River in the early 1870s.

But outward appearances were deceiving at all levels. In the main, the line regiments of the American Army of 1876 were in fact rather capably led by a cadre of well-educated and well-seasoned officers, as plainly evidenced in the record. And this army had recovered materially from the excesses of the Civil War and was now more than adequately armed and outfitted. Most importantly, this was an army that evinced an evolving if indeed still unwritten war-making orthodoxy quite well suited to Indian warfare. Though the Great Sioux War began ominously for Lieutenant General Philip Henry Sheridan, the army's chief strategist for this inevitable and unavoidable conflict, he deployed a compelling array of intelligent and adaptable officers who led capable troops and ultimately prevailed on the northern plains. In the end, Sheridan's Army earned a hard-fought victory by its resolve, achieving repetitive battlefield successes and waging a war of harassment and attrition that allowed the northern Indians no recourse but to accept the abandonment of a highly evolved buffalo culture for the constraints of the Great Sioux Reservation.

General William Tecumseh Sherman had commanded the U.S. Army from the War Department in Washington, District of Columbia, since March 1869. Joining him in the confines of the Old War Department Building on Pennsylvania Avenue,[1] located immediately west of the White House, was an array of staff bureaus and chiefs, including the Quartermaster, Subsistence, Medical, and Ordnance departments. Much to Sherman's annoyance, the army's staff chiefs reported not to him but to James D. Cameron, the secretary of war from May 1876 to March 1877. Sherman's lack of direct control over all aspects of the American Army was a matter of continuing friction among the commanding general, the bureau chiefs, and the secretary that went unresolved until the creation of the General Staff at the turn of the twentieth century. But Sherman did exercise line authority over the army's four geographic divisions (three after June 26, 1876), each commanded by a major or lieutenant general.[2]

For administrative purposes, the army segmented the nation into geographic divisions and departments. The Great Sioux War was fought wholly within the bounds of the Military Division of the Missouri, commanded by forty-five-year-old Philip Sheridan. Headquartered in Chicago, Sheridan's division spanned the heartland of the nation from the Gulf of Mexico to Canada and the western Great Lakes and Mississippi River to the Great Basin, including the entire Great Plains. Across the division were five administrative departments (Dakota, Gulf, Missouri, Platte, and Texas), each commanded by a brigadier general. Troops from throughout Sheridan's division heeded his call to the Great Sioux War during its nineteen-month course, as did select infantry and artillery units from the divisions of the Atlantic and Pacific.[3]

The Great Sioux War most directly impacted the departments of Dakota and Platte, commanded respectively by brigadier generals Alfred Howe Terry and George Crook. Terry's Department of Dakota, headquartered in St. Paul, Minnesota, spanned Minnesota, Dakota Territory, and Montana Territory. Within its bounds were the entire Great Sioux

[1] The Old War Department Building occupied in 1876 is not to be confused with the ornate State, War, and Navy Building constructed wing-by-wing on the same general site beginning in 1871, to which the War Department finally relocated in 1879.

[2] White, *The Republican Era*, 140–46; Thain, *Notes Illustrating the Military Geography of the United States*, 4; Wooster, *The Military and United States Indian Policy*, 20–21.

[3] Thain, *Notes Illustrating the Military Geography of the United States*, 24–25; Wooster, *The Military and United States Indian Policy*, 19–20.

Reservation, a vast landscape spanning Dakota Territory west of the Missouri River and south of the forty-sixth parallel of north latitude (more or less today's South Dakota west of the Missouri River), and three of its five agencies: Standing Rock, Cheyenne River, and Lower Brule, all situated on the Missouri River. Also located within this department was the revered buffalo-hunting country along Montana's Yellowstone River and the tumbling prairie of the Big Open north of the river and reaching to the Missouri. In part, this was the landscape prescribed by the Fort Laramie Treaty of 1868 as the unceded territory where Sioux could hunt and whites could not settle. The treaty did not specify a northern boundary for the unceded territory.[4]

Of even greater interest to the nation in the mid-1870s, and of paramount interest to the Lakota Sioux, was the mineral-rich area of the Black Hills, lying almost entirely within the Dakota Department and Great Sioux Reservation. To white America, the announcement of gold in the Black Hills was an irresistible lure, drawing thousands to its rich placer streams. To Indian America, the Black Hills provided fresh mountain water, lodge poles for tipis, and medicine plants. And for the Northern Cheyennes and Sioux the Black Hills were a holy place: the site where vision quests occurred and home to Wakan Tanta, the Great Spirit, the sum of all that was powerful, sacred, and full of mystery. Terry would grapple with burdens and responsibilities stemming from these diametrically countering interests throughout the long course of the Great Sioux War.[5]

General Crook's Department of the Platte, headquartered in Omaha, Nebraska, spanned the states of Iowa and Nebraska, Wyoming and Utah territories, and the southeastern quarter of Idaho Territory. Located within these bounds were two rich buffalo-hunting areas prescribed by the Fort Laramie Treaty: contiguous lands in Nebraska along the North

---

[4] Thain, *Notes Illustrating the Military Geography of the United States*, 58; Kappler, *Indian Affairs*, 998, 1002–1003.

[5] Lazarus, *Black Hills/White Justice*, 7; Sundstrom, "The Sacred Black Hills"; Ostler, *The Plains Sioux and U.S. Colonialism from Lewis and Clark to Wounded Knee*, 58–60. Interestingly, some scholars express the view that nineteenth-century Lakotas saw only the economic value of the Black Hills. This contention is particularly championed by James A. Hanson of the Museum of the Fur Trade, Chadron, Nebraska, who argues that the embrace of the Black Hills by the Sioux is largely rooted in the twentieth century, citing the relative ease with which Red Cloud and Spotted Tail would have sold the Black Hills in the mid-1870s but for an agreement on price, the lack of any recognition of the Black Hills in early Lakota oral traditions and histories, and the relatively late arrival of the Sioux on the plains from central Minnesota, where they previously had viewed the Mille Lacs Lake countryside as the center of their universe.

Platte River and on the Republican Fork of the Smoky Hill River and the southern portions of the vast unceded territory in Wyoming, north of the North Platte River and east of the summits of the Big Horn Mountains. The two most important avenues to the Black Hills goldfields crossed portions of Crook's department. The Sidney–Black Hills Road originated on the Union Pacific Railroad at Sidney, Nebraska. The more heavily traveled Cheyenne–Black Hills Road, also originating on the Union Pacific, made use of a critical bridge spanning the North Platte River midway at Fort Laramie. Although the Black Hills themselves lay in Terry's department, Crook wrestled with greater burdens than did his counterpart in St. Paul, because the principal avenues to the goldfields originated in his department. As well, two tumultuous agencies serving the Sioux, Red Cloud and Spotted Tail, located on the White River in northwestern Nebraska, figured conspicuously in the day-to-day affairs of the department. These agencies were located near the Great Sioux Reservation but not on it, a matter of great contention in Nebraska because the Fort Laramie Treaty had prescribed agencies within the bounds of the reservation, not outside of it.[6]

❧ ❧ ❧

Throughout the nineteenth century, the United States Military Academy at West Point, New York, educated the army's officer corps, providing its cadets with an excellent technical education. The academy's four-, sometimes five-year curriculum emphasized engineering. Its graduates were all capable civil and military engineers, and top graduates served in the army's Engineer Corps. In addition to being able mathematicians, graduates were well versed in American and military history, good grammarians, knowledgeable in civil and military law, competent geographers, and proficient in chemistry, mineralogy, geology, French, Spanish, draftsmanship, drawing, and other classical subjects. The academy also provided a solid understanding of weapons and army routines, and graduates were adept at map reading, drill, and small-unit tactics. As one of its own noted, a West Pointer was an "all-around well-informed man, and especially so in all that appertains to his profession." Graduates received appointments as second lieutenants and were dispersed to the

---

[6] Thain, *Notes Illustrating the Military Geography of the United States,* 89; Kappler, *Indian Affairs,* 1002; Hedren, *Fort Laramie in 1876,* 37.

line regiments, where they generally rounded out their formative educations with Regular Army service. Company captains taught these subalterns the skills necessary to lead troops, manage logistics, and handle small-unit staff duties. One-third of the officers engaged in the Great Sioux War were West Point graduates, nine more attended the academy but did not graduate, and one, First Lieutenant Henry J. Nowlan of the Seventh Cavalry, was a graduate of Sandhurst, England's elite military academy.[7]

Commissioned veterans of Civil War volunteer regiments also filled post–Civil War Regular Army officer ranks, having demonstrated a requisite two years of distinguished wartime service and passed an examination by a board of officers. As a class, these were experienced men who embraced careers in the army and ultimately performed admirably on the frontier and in the Great Sioux War. At the company grades at the time of the Great Sioux War, non–West Pointers outnumbered academy graduates by more than three to one. At the field grades, however, that difference was reversed, with West Pointers substantially outnumbering civilian appointees. Still, nongraduates like James S. Brisbin, Orlando H. Moore, William B. Royall, and Nelson A. Miles acquitted themselves with extraordinary distinction during this Indian war.[8]

Combat experience during the Civil War substantially enhanced the leadership prowess exhibited by the officers engaged in the Great Sioux War. Sixty-one percent of all Sioux War officers were Civil War veterans, including every general and field-grade officer engaged. The worth of Civil War service cannot be overstated: that great conflict provided common learning experiences and bonding. And the scale of operations and relative size of United States forces gave even company-grade officers opportunities to gain perspectives on operations and enabled them to appreciate the grand tactics of battles. Of considerable significance as well, more than fifty-six percent of these Civil War veterans received brevets for valorous acts in combat, including action in some of the war's most terrifying engagements, such as Antietam and Gettysburg. The tabulations in appendices B and C only include brevets for gallant and meritorious service (suggesting combat recognition) as opposed to brevets also awarded at the time for faithful and meritorious service (implying

[7] Hattaway and Jones, *How the North Won*, 11; Forsyth, *The Story of a Soldier*, 34 (quotation); Donovan, *A Terrible Glory*, 178. The many calculations in the text are derived from data in the appendices of this work.

[8] Forsyth, *The Story of a Soldier*, 35; Coffman, *The Old Army*, 219; Utley, *Frontier Regulars*, 18.

noncombat recognition and usually associated with some staff duty far from battlefields). Though the army's brevet system is commonly misunderstood and maligned (and brevets were liberally bestowed at the close of the war), brevets were one of the few means available to the officer corps to recognize aptitude, competence, and actual heroism in combat. A number of Great Sioux War officers also received Medals of Honor for heroic acts during the Civil War, although only Thomas W. Custer received his two medals before 1876; the rest were not awarded until late in individual careers.[9]

Beyond Civil War experience, more than thirty-seven percent of the officers engaged in the Great Sioux War were already veterans of some prior Indian campaign in the West, including over forty-four percent of participating general and field-grade officers. To a certain extent, this is understandable and almost expected, because the post–Civil War assignments of so many regiments, including all cavalry regiments, were in the Trans-Mississippi West. Campaigns there were conducted quite differently from those of the Civil War, occurring on markedly different plains and desert landscapes and employing the unconventional tactics appropriate to Indian warfare. Notably, fifty-nine Great Sioux War officers had specific Indian fighting experience on the northern plains. Several served at Marias River in 1870 and many more along the Yellowstone River in 1871, 1872, or 1873 during the Northern Pacific Railroad surveys, where Sioux resistance to those incursions was pronounced. Nine of these officers were veterans of service along the Bozeman Trail, where battling the Sioux occurred with inordinate frequency and often with dire consequences.

In seeking to explain the army's early failings in the Great Sioux War and especially at Little Big Horn, critics of this officer corps suggest that too many inexperienced or untried officers commanded troops in 1876 and 1877. But that assertion is broadly contradicted by the record, which clearly indicates the breadth of Civil War experience, brevets earned for gallantry in action, and the considerable extent of prior Indian campaign experience. Another critical measure of the combat readiness and aptitude of the Great Sioux War officer corps is apparent in the backgrounds of those officers who actually commanded troops during the war's many and varied deployments (versus those officers who merely supported a colonel or general at a headquarters or a captain or first lieutenant at the

---

[9] Hattaway and Jones, *How the North Won*, 14; Utley, *Frontier Regulars*, 20–21.

company level). Of the thirty-two general or field-grade officers commanding battalions, brigades, or expeditions in the Great Sioux War, twenty-one were West Point graduates (66 percent), all were Civil War veterans, twenty-nine possessed Civil War valor brevets (91 percent), and sixteen had Indian campaign experience prior to 1876 (50 percent). Particularly notable among the senior officers with previous Indian campaign experiences were cavalrymen Eugene A. Carr, George A. Custer, Andrew W. Evans, and Ranald S. Mackenzie; infantry officers Alexander Chambers, Alfred L. Hough, Henry M. Lazelle, and Nelson Miles; and the redoubtable Brigadier General George Crook. Each of these officers had a dominant role in the Great Sioux War.[10]

The breadth of education and experience among officers at the company grades is equally illustrative, whether they commanded battalions or companies and whether they participated in large movements like those led by Crook and Terry or in the innumerable single-company sorties associated with escort service, road patrol, or engaging local raiders. Of the 202 company-grade officers exercising formal, regular command of a company or battalion at some course during the Great Sioux War, 40 were West Point graduates (20 percent), 143 were Civil War veterans (71 percent), 88 possessed Civil War valor brevets (44), and, remarkably, 94 had some form of prior Indian campaign experience (47 percent). In all, the record plainly shows an officer corps at all grades that was not novice, incapable, undereducated, or inexperienced, but distinctly the opposite. When Sioux War battles were lost (infrequently as that actually occurred), explanations more rightly point to the individual and collective fearlessness, prowess, and audacity of the warriors of Old Bear, Crazy Horse, and Gall than to the inexperience or incapability of the officers engaged, with one notable exception.

❧ ❧ ❧

Various congressional acts in the years following the Civil War had eroded the size of the Regular Army by 1876 to some 25,000 enlisted men and 2,000 officers, distributed across the staff bureaus and ten regiments of cavalry, five regiments of artillery, and twenty-five regiments of

[10] Popular indictments of the army and its lack of appropriate training and Indian fighting experience include Taunton, *Army Failures against the Sioux in 1876*, 13–15 (and Kevin Galvin, "Editorial Introduction," 3); Abrams, "The Green Factor at the Little Bighorn"; and Donovan, *A Terrible Glory*, 121–22, 124–25.

infantry. The sizes of the various line regiments were disproportionate. Cavalry regiments had twelve companies with a field-grade staff including a colonel, a lieutenant colonel, and three majors, whereas infantry regiments had ten companies and a field-grade staff including a colonel, a lieutenant colonel, and one major. Though the authorized strength of a cavalry company was seventy men and an infantry company from forty to fifty-four men, companies and regiments were rarely at or near full strength. Companies were always matriculating new recruits to replace men whose enlistments had expired or who had deserted. Although new soldiers usually passed through one of several recruit depots after enlisting, these depots were mere way stations where men were uniformed and introduced to semblances of army discipline and routine but were not formally trained in any meaningful soldier capacity. Training occurred when recruits reached their final assignments, usually under the careful tutelage of company sergeants, who were all proven, skilled leaders.[11]

The persistent impression that an inordinate number of untrained recruits filled the ranks of the army of 1876 does not stand inspection. In the close examination of all matters related to the Little Big Horn battle, the composition of the Seventh Cavalry has been carefully analyzed. Of 577 enlisted men present for duty on the eve of the regiment's fateful campaign, only 11 troopers had been in the army for less than four months (1.9 percent), a length of time acknowledged as probably inadequate for any meaningful exposure to horsemanship, weaponry, and the art of war. Another 101 of those 577 men had been in the army from four months to one year (17.5 percent). Certainly increasing months of service allowed for the refinement of the broad array of necessary soldier skills. Of those same 577 men, 42 had experienced the army for one to two years (7.3 percent), 70 had served from two to three years (12.1 percent), and 353 had experiences extending beyond three years (61.2 percent). If the Seventh Cavalry reflected the army of 1876 as a whole, the notion of a substantial body of steady, capable soldiers led by veteran noncommissioned officers gains deserved credence, even though recruit drafts were continually received, often directly in the field, during the long course of the Great Sioux War.[12]

The backgrounds of the enlisted men filling the ranks of these line regiments also demonstrate the breadth and capability of the force, again despite lurid and oft-repeated statements to the contrary. Although about

---

[11] *Report of the Secretary of War, 1875*, 49; Utley, *Frontier Regulars*, 15; Coffman, *The Old Army*, 336.

[12] MacNeil, "Raw Recruits and Veterans."

half of the men in the post–Civil War Regular Army were native born, the nation's immigrant legacy was also plainly evident. Even in a single company, Italians stood shoulder to shoulder with Scandinavians, Irishmen bunked with Germans, Englishmen marched with Russians. Some men came to the army to escape the rigors of farm life or the privation of the slums, and some harbored false notions about army life, but most enlisted for five years simply because they wanted to be soldiers. And they came from all stations of society: clerks, farmers, laborers, miners, tailors, hostlers, bakers, and carpenters. In turn, the noncommissioned cadre of every company typically promoted from the ranks and usually from the same company. These corporals and sergeants formed the unit's backbone. They were typically older, steady, and thoroughly experienced soldiers, often Civil War veterans, and as a group invariably reflected their company's and regiment's reputation and esprit de corps and instilled it in the ranks.[13]

As with their officers, a noteworthy number of the enlisted men of 1876 were veterans of the Civil War, where their steadiness and valor as soldiers had long been recognized and respected. But that warfare had also taken a fearsome toll on the Regular regiments. In the Eastern Theater (including battles at Second Manassas, Fredericksburg, and Chancellorsville, among many others), Regular units suffered casualty rates that often exceeded fifty percent. Replacements were scarce in the lopsided recruitment chronicles of these troops, Regular units unfairly competing with the financial inducements offered by the volunteer regiments. The toll at Gettysburg in July 1863 was especially devastating, but the Regulars earned timeless honors amid the death and destruction of that battle. Regular infantry regiments filled two brigades of the Second Division of Major General George Sykes's Fifth Army Corps, including the Fourth, Sixth, Seventh, Eleventh, Fourteenth, and Seventeenth, and five others, all commanded by Brigadier General Romeyn B. Ayres. Sykes's Regular Division fought especially valiantly on Gettysburg's second day, prompting an admiring volunteer to recall: "The two small brigades of United States Regulars of Ayres' division had advanced beyond the position of the One Hundred and Fifty-fifth [Pennsylvania] on Little Round Top,

[13] For some particularly colorful examples of this impugning of the enlisted men of the Indian fighting army, see Donovan, *A Terrible Glory*, 36–37, 122–23. The case for a much more stable army is made by Rickey, *Forty Miles a Day on Beans and Hay*, 18–22; Forsyth, *The Story of a Soldier*, 91–93; and Paul L. Hedren, "An Infantry Company in the Sioux Campaign, 1876," in Hedren, ed., *The Great Sioux War 1876–77*, 195–99.

toward the Wheatfield, this movement being made . . . to support General Sickles. The Regulars fought with determined skill and bravery for nearly an hour, and then reluctantly fell back as if on drill, but sharply and bravely contesting every foot of ground. These things I saw, and I am glad, as a volunteer, to bear tribute to the United States Regulars." Thirteen years later, these same regiments and many surviving officers figured prominently in the course of the Great Sioux War.[14]

The 430 companies tallied in the army's line regiments were distributed to some 240 posts, camps, cantonments, depots, and way stations throughout America. Before the onset of the Great Sioux War, the army's five artillery regiments were deployed to the typically substantial masonry fortifications dotting the Atlantic, Gulf, and Pacific coastlines, with two companies of the Fourth Artillery serving in Alaska. No artillery company served inland before this Sioux War; but during the war artillery companies functioning as infantry served throughout the Division of the Missouri, backfilling behind cavalry and infantry regiments transferred to the northern plains as the conflict escalated. Companies of the First, Second, and Third Artillery regiments, for instance, were redeployed from assignments on the Atlantic and Gulf coasts to posts in the Indian Territory during the temporary absence of Ranald Mackenzie's Fourth Cavalry. Similarly, other companies of the Second and Third Artillery were redeployed to posts in Kansas, temporarily succeeding Nelson Miles's Fifth Infantry. And a four-company battalion of the Fourth Artillery was reassigned from the Pacific coast to actual field service in the war, serving first at Camp Robinson, Nebraska, and in the Black Hills and then on Crook's Powder River Expedition in Wyoming.[15]

At the onset of the Great Sioux War, the army's infantry regiments occupied military posts dotting virtually every state and territory in the Union, including the twenty-one designated installations in Terry's Department of Dakota and the nineteen in Crook's Department of the Platte. At these and all posts, infantry utility typically centered on managing the internal affairs of the installation and also protecting the security of lives and property at Indian agencies on or near reservation lands—a matter of resounding importance in the Dakota and Platte departments.

[14] Rickey, *Forty Miles a Day on Beans and Hay*, 20; Reese, *Regulars!* 200–201, 208, 263; Corporal Henry F. Weaver, Company B, 155th Pennsylvania Infantry, "At Gettysburg—Under Front and Rear Fire," in *Under the Maltese Cross*, 552 (quotation).

[15] Prucha, *Guide to the Military Posts of the United States*, 161; *Report of the Secretary of War, 1875*, 38–39; *Report of the Secretary of War, 1876*, 61–62.

In the early field movements of the Great Sioux War, the role of participating infantry companies was limited to protecting a column's vulnerable components, including its wagons and animals. The worth of infantry as a combat force was also demonstrated significantly at the Battle of the Rosebud and foremost in the wintertime deployments on the Yellowstone River under the adept leadership of Colonel Miles and Lieutenant Colonel Elwell S. Otis, commanding the Fifth and Twenty-second regiments, respectively. Curiously, the northern Indians were leery of infantry. None other than Crazy Horse was dismayed at learning of Gibbon's advance up the Little Big Horn River in the wake of the Custer fight. As an informant later told it, "They saw infantry, and they don't seem to like them—they bury themselves in the ground like badgers and it's too slow fighting."[16] John Howard, a mixed-blood scout for Miles in the winter of 1876–77, captured a similar sentiment from later in the war. The Sioux complained bitterly of Miles, Howard wrote. "No sooner would they be comfortably in camp, than their scouts would come in and report the General close again, and they would have to leave. They seem to fear infantry, but not cavalry."[17]

As war with the Sioux exploded across the northern plains, the army's cavalry regiments occupied posts throughout the American West, the single exception being three companies of Seventh Cavalry still deployed on Reconstruction duty, in Louisiana. Owing to the distinct mobility of cavalry, the army generally regarded its mounted troops as its premier combat arm, as reflected in regimental deployments throughout the Great Plains and Southwest near agencies and reservations where Indian warfare was recurrent. Elements of the Second and Third Cavalry served in Crook's Department of the Platte, with most of those companies deployed in close proximity to the Nebraska Sioux agencies. Conversely, infantry troops, not the Montana Battalion of Second Cavalry or Seventh Cavalry, safeguarded agency affairs in Terry's Department of Dakota. Ironically, in its combat role, the army's cavalry doctrine prescribed that mounted troops should ride to the scene of action and then usually dismount and fight as skirmishers on foot, precisely as occurred during Major Marcus A. Reno's initial attack in the Little Big Horn Valley. The cavalry regiments employed in the Great Sioux War fought both mounted and afoot.

---

[16] Bray, *Crazy Horse*, 234, citing John Colhoff to Helen Blish, April 7, 1929, in Bad Heart Bull and Blish, *A Pictographic History of the Oglala Sioux*, 36.

[17] "John Howard Report," June 19, 1877, Nelson A. Miles Papers.

By the early 1870s the American Army had at last largely consumed the excessive stocks of uniforms and accoutrements surviving from the Civil War, when hundreds of thousands of soldiers were uniformed and equipped. The obsolete material was derided by the postwar Regulars for its ill fit, shoddy fabrication, and lack of utility and fashion, but new items gradually replaced the old ones. Although the army "continually w[ore] the blues," as a line in a barrack and stage ditty went, the uniforms issued in the mid-1870s featured newly styled and better-fitting dark-blue woolen fatigue blouses with brass eagle buttons and branch-colored worsted cord trim; sky-blue kersey trousers, reinforced in the breech for cavalry; dark blue woolen forage caps trimmed with brass branch insignias, regimental numbers, and company letters; black felt campaign hats of several varieties; and updated patterns of infantry brogans and cavalry boots. Equipments were newly styled, as well, featuring black leather waist belts with rectangular brass U.S. plates for foot troops and eagle plates for the mounted branches; cartridge boxes of several new patterns; newly styled linen-canvas haversacks for carrying utensils, a tin meat can, and rations; a new tin cup and remodeled canteen; and for the cavalry new pattern holsters, saber hangers, and cartridge loops and pouches. One notable exception in this array of new productions was that the cavalry's ubiquitous carbine slings were retained from the Civil War era. The troops welcomed these changes, which, in all, meant a uniform of superior quality, better fit and durability, and updated styles and accoutrements suitably fashioned for the rigorous demands of the West.[18]

Equally significant improvements occurred in the realm of the army's firearms, which underwent a thorough study and transformation in the early 1870s that resulted in the adoption of one of the finest weapons systems of the day. A weapons board convened in September 1872 (directed by Brigadier General Terry and including Major Reno of the Seventh Cavalry among its members) exhaustively tested nearly one hundred domestic-made and foreign shoulder arms, including single-shot and

[18] This overview is broadly drawn from McChristian, *The U.S. Army in the West,* chapters 2, 3, 5, 6. McChristian is definitive on the subject. Also useful though limited in focus to cavalry is Hutchins, *Boots & Saddles at the Little Bighorn.* The barrack ditty referred to is the iconic song "The Regular Army O!" It was written by New York vaudevillian Edward Harrigan in 1874 and is known with many added soldier-composed verses, including some directly pertaining to the Great Sioux War. See Rickey, *Forty Miles a Day on Beans and Hay,* 189–90; Harrigan, *The Regular Army O!;* and Hedren, "Eben Swift's Army Service on the Plains," 146.

repeating weapons, and concluded that single-shot, breech-loading rifles and carbines produced at the army's Springfield, Massachusetts, Armory best suited its needs. These weapons (a rifle weighing 8.25 pounds and measuring 51⅞ inches long for infantry troops and a carbine weighing 7.9 pounds and measuring 41¼ inches long for cavalry) were of simple design, exceedingly rugged, easily repaired, and effortlessly used. A separate board studied calibers, bullet weights, and powder charges and commended .45 caliber bores, a round-nosed 405-grain lead-tin bullet, a 70-grain powder charge for infantry, and a 55-grain cavalry charge. With a newly styled .45 caliber Colt revolver for the cavalry, the army had an array of weapons that were extremely reliable, powerful, accurate, and lethal at extreme ranges. Despite a continuing penuriousness in some quarters, soldiers in the main were reasonably adept at using these weapons, even though the army's passion for marksmanship was still some years away.[19]

[19] McChristian, *The U.S. Army in the West,* chapter 4; McChristian, *An Army of Marksmen.* Also useful is Frasca and Hill, *The .45-70 Springfield,* chapters 1–2.

On Strategy and Tactics

The awkward paradox facing the American Army in the years following the Civil War and at the very time it was so often overwhelmingly engaged in Indian warfare was its failure to evolve a purposeful, formal Indian fighting doctrine or strategy. The term "strategy" has many meanings and applications. Military dictionaries of the day defined it foremost as the art and science of employing armed forces to secure the objectives of national policy. But in nineteenth-century America no single Indian policy ever endured. The so-called Peace Policy embraced by President Grant during his administration from 1868 through 1876 presumed treaty-making with the Plains tribes, successful adherence to those treaties by Indians and whites alike, and the progressive assimilation of Indians into white society. If the treaties were faithfully implemented and adhered to, warfare with the tribes presumably would cease. But Grant's Peace Policy met abject failure. Treaties were not adhered to, bureaucratic infighting between the Interior and War departments over Indian affairs ensued, assimilation flagged, and warfare with the tribes continued virtually unabated throughout Grant's two terms.[20]

The term "strategy" could also mean the general science of broadly maneuvering an army in the presence of an enemy. Here the army's voices were muddled. Aside from the Mexican War and Civil War, Indian warfare had shaped the army's organization, composition, command and staff, and tactics throughout most of the nineteenth century. But the army devoted no staff to strategic planning, and its few strategic thinkers and congressional overseers seemingly agreed that organization and tactics should be directed toward possible wars with conventional, European-

[20] Wilhelm, *A Military Dictionary and Gazetteer,* 557; "Peace Policy," in Lamar, ed., *The New Encyclopedia of the American West,* 845–47; Utley, "The Contribution of the Frontier to the American Military Tradition," 528–29; Utley, *Frontier Regulars,* 188–92.

style military powers and not toward Indian fighting, which would soon be a thing of the past anyway—or so it was commonly thought. Even Major General Winfield Scott Hancock, hero of Gettysburg, late-1860s campaigner on the southern plains against Cheyennes, Arapahos, Kiowas, and Comanches, and Sheridan's counterpart commanding the Military Division of the Atlantic in the 1870s, advised a congressional committee in 1876 that the army's Indian service was "entitled to no weight" whatsoever in determining the strength, composition, and organization of the service. Meanwhile, West Point devoted precious few classroom hours to the formal study of military strategy, although cadets were introduced to Napoleon Bonaparte's war-making tactics and encouraged to read widely in military history. From 1863 onward the army devoured the *Army and Navy Journal*, a widely distributed weekly newspaper brimming with military news, reviews, exchanges of opinion, and discussions of military theory. But professional journals such as the *Journal of the Military Service Institution* and *Cavalry Journal* promoting the study of military history and theory did not appear until the late 1870s and thereafter.[21]

Despite the army's evident disinterest in evolving a purposeful strategy for Indian warfare (unconventional as it was and fleeting as it was presumed to be), some officers, including Sherman and Sheridan, acknowledged that the army needed new ideas for fighting future battles and particularly needed tactics of its own, independent of European influence and tailored to the American landscape. The widely used Civil War tactics manuals produced by William J. Hardee and Silas Casey broadly embraced European methodologies, but postwar officers too well remembered that frontal assaults in close-ordered lines against defenders armed with rifles and protected by entrenchments invariably ended in disaster. The foremost postwar advocate of a new system of tactics was Emory Upton, an 1861 West Point graduate, Civil War brigadier general of volunteers, and Regular Army lieutenant colonel from 1866 through the 1870s. Endorsed by Grant while he was commanding general of the army, Upton's *Infantry Tactics, Double and Single Rank, Adapted to American Topography and Improved Fire-Arms* was adopted by the War Department in August 1867 as the army's official tactics. By 1874 Upton's tactics had been "assimilated" for each of the combat branches, meaning that commands and formations were made compatible across the infantry,

[21] Wilhelm, *A Military Dictionary and Gazetteer;* Farrow, *Farrow's Military Encyclopedia*, 1:256; Utley, *Frontier Regulars*, 44, 45 (quotation), 114; Jamieson, *Crossing the Deadly Ground*, 36–37; Hattaway and Jones, *How the North Won*, 12–13.

artillery, and cavalry, though each branch still had its own specific manual (each variant also an Upton intellectual product).[22]

By 1875 Upton's manuals were in the hands of almost every officer in the army, and troops trained in "Upton" formations and maneuvers almost daily; infantry troops had utilized the manual since the late 1860s. Upton's system stressed flexibility. Groups of four men ("fours") became the basic functional unit in all manners of marching and movement before or during contact with an enemy. Upton also introduced single-rank tactics, formations that respected the devastating firepower of breech-loading and repeating weapons, and he conceived instructions for skirmishers, which taught men to "economize their strengths, preserve their presence of mind, husband their ammunition, and profit by all the advantages which the ground may offer for cover." Probably unwittingly, Upton had developed tactics quite well suited to Indian warfare.[23]

Beyond Upton's assimilated tactics, which served to govern the army's structured maneuvering on the parade field and plains, freethinking, combat-savvy commanders in the years following the Civil War embraced an array of war-making stratagems directly applicable to the Indian campaigns being waged. Unlike Upton's ideas, these field-evolved tactics were never formally codified or published in any way before the Great Sioux War, aside from one known instance in which "procedures for dealing with Indians" appeared in a limited distribution district-level general order (discussed below). Yet the overarching lessons learned in Indian combat from the 1850s onward were being repeated, including specific tactics such as converging columns, winter war, surprise attacks at dawn, the use of Indian trackers, and total war. These successful war-making tenets were employed by Sheridan and his senior commanders throughout the long course of the Great Sioux War.

The concept of converging columns (meaning multiple forces converging from different directions into the same region in an effort to engage or entrap an enemy) was loosely employed twice against the Sioux in the mid-1860s. In 1863 brigadier generals Alfred Sully and Henry Hastings Sibley conducted retaliatory campaigns in Dakota Territory following the Santee Sioux Uprising in Minnesota the year before. These orchestrations were largely overseen by Major General John Pope, commander

[22] Jamieson, *Crossing the Deadly Ground,* 2–9; Upton, *Infantry Tactics, Double and Single Rank.*

[23] Jamieson, *Crossing the Deadly Ground,* 9; Upton, *Infantry Tactics, Double and Single Rank,* 117 (quotation).

of the newly created Department of the Northwest, headquartered in St. Paul. Sully and Sibley engaged Indians but did little cooperatively.

In the summer of 1865 three semi-independent columns took the field in Wyoming bound for the Powder River country and a fourth column, commanded by Sully, traveled the Missouri River into northern Dakota Territory. Each sought opportunities to retaliate for the widespread hostilities bloodying the plains after Colorado volunteer troops perpetrated the Sand Creek Massacre in late November 1864. The Powder River Expedition that included the Wyoming columns was under the general leadership of Brigadier General Patrick E. Connor, a veteran but controversial officer who had led volunteers in the massacre of more than 250 Shoshoni Indians at Bear River, Idaho, in January 1863. Connor's columns floundered, beset with communications and supply problems and eventually the onset of winter; although they closed with Sioux, Cheyennes, and Arapahos on several occasions, the engagements were of no lasting consequence. The campaigns in 1863 and 1865 engaged volunteer troops, including ex-Confederates or "Galvanized Yankees," but these men and their officers played no role in the campaigns to come. And yet the lessons of those campaigns engrained in men like Pope and Sully were not forgotten.[24]

Converging columns and winter war (campaigns occurring in the season of cold, snow, and ice, when Indians' mobility was disadvantaged and severe weather pinned them in their villages) played to greater effect on the southern plains in an expansive campaign orchestrated by Sheridan in 1868–69 against Southern Cheyennes, Arapahos, and Kiowas. This war featured columns originating in New Mexico, Colorado, and Kansas, converging on the Canadian and Red River drainages in northern Texas and western Indian Territory and led by notable commanders like Sully, now lieutenant colonel of the Third Infantry; Major Andrew W. Evans, Third Cavalry; Major William B. Royall and Major Eugene A. Carr, Fifth Cavalry; and Lieutenant Colonel George A. Custer of the Seventh Cavalry. The most notable engagement among several in this arduous campaign was Custer's gripping break-of-day attack on Black Kettle's Cheyenne village on the Washita River, Indian Territory, in November 1868.[25]

Converging columns and dawn attacks were repeated even more

[24] Jamieson, *Crossing the Deadly Ground,* 38; Utley, *Frontiersmen in Blue,* 270–79, 307–10, 315–36. The standard reference to the campaigning on the northern plains in 1865 is McDermott, *Circle of Fire;* but see also Wagner, *Powder River Odyssey;* and Wagner, *Patrick Connor's War.*

[25] Jamieson, *Crossing the Deadly Ground,* 37–38; Wooster, *The Military and United States Indian Policy,* 132–33; Utley, *Frontier Regulars,* 147–51. The definitive account of this campaign is Greene, *Washita.*

consequentially in the so-called Red River or Buffalo War of 1874–75, aimed at driving resisting Kiowas, Comanches, and Cheyennes from the plains to their agencies once and for all. Sheridan again broadly orchestrated the operation but delegated most organizational matters to his department commanders: General Pope, now commanding the Department of the Missouri based at Fort Leavenworth, Kansas, and Brigadier General Christopher C. Augur, commanding the Department of Texas headquartered in San Antonio. Pope and Augur directed the fielding of five columns, including a mixed force of infantry and cavalry from Kansas commanded by Colonel Nelson A. Miles, Fifth Infantry; a small cavalry column from New Mexico; and three columns from Indian Territory and Texas, including eight companies of the Fourth Cavalry led by Colonel Ranald S. Mackenzie, a force of Eleventh Infantry commanded by Lieutenant Colonel George P. Buell, and another cavalry column from Fort Sill. These columns harassed the Indians throughout the fall of 1874, destroying hastily abandoned villages, routing Comanches in the Battle of Palo Duro Canyon (where more than a thousand captured ponies were slaughtered), liberating several captive white children, and ultimately effecting the complete surrender of the tribesmen and removal and distant incarceration of a number of their chiefs.[26]

Sheridan's blueprint for executing the Great Sioux War lay in the broad strategy and specific field tactics of the Red River War, with converging columns, relentless pursuit, dawn attacks on villages, destruction of personal possessions (including ponies), absolute surrender, and the subsequent incarceration of prominent chiefs. These aggressive tactics amounted to total war, a politically and morally charged strategy, since invariably women and children were victimized by army bullets or were cast out from their villages, often in winter and without food or shelter. The concept of total war was an old one in America, having been directed at Indian and white populations elsewhere, including during the Civil War. Practitioners were always excoriated by eastern humanitarians because of the consequences inflicted on noncombatants. The record on the western frontier suggests that some officers fully comprehended and openly embraced indiscriminate killing while others went to extremes to distinguish combatants from noncombatants. Ruthless and blunt, Sheridan applauded the efficiency and effectiveness of total war and called the

[26] Utley, *Frontier Regulars,* 219–33; Hutton, *Phil Sheridan and His Army,* 245–53; Wooster, *The Military and United States Indian Policy,* 152–59. Though somewhat dated, the single best book-length history of the Red River War is Haley, *The Buffalo War.*

Red River War in particular the "most successful of any Indian campaign in this country since its settlement by the whites."[27]

This array of tactics evolved in Indian campaigning included one additional variable that proved through time to be of extraordinary consequence: the use of savvy plainsmen and Indians as trackers in the field. Without such help, officers commonly groused at their inability to trail opponents. Sherman called it "worse than looking for a needle in a hay stack, rather like looking for a flea in a large clover field."[28] Others saw the same dilemma but suggested answers. In an interesting entry dated September 4, 1867, in his unique introspective journal, Colonel Philippe Régis de Trobriand (Thirteenth Infantry, then stationed at Fort Stevenson, Dakota Territory) urged enrolling frontiersmen who knew Indians and could fight them in their own way as well as Indians themselves, particularly those allied with the United States and at war with the "hostile tribes." De Trobriand applauded General Christopher Augur's recent experiments with recruiting Pawnee Indians as army auxiliaries in the Department of the Platte and was confident that such Indians would provide important services to the army. Pawnee scouts figured significantly in the 1865 Powder River Expedition, as did white and mixed-blood plainsmen, including the old trapper and trailer Jim Bridger.[29]

No campaigner before the Great Sioux War demonstrated the usefulness of Indian auxiliaries better than George Crook, who had successfully employed Indians against Indians in Oregon in the late 1860s and again in Arizona in the early 1870s. Indian trackers invariably knew the land, habits, ideas, and languages of the tribes being pursued. And if pressed into combat, Indian auxiliaries offered a compounding effect. "Nothing will demoralize the hostiles so much as to know that their own people are fighting in the opposite ranks," Crook asserted in 1871—a point manifested in Arizona and played to demonstrable effect in the Great Sioux War.[30]

This array of tactics used so skillfully and consequentially in Sheridan's winter war in 1868–69 and the Red River War of 1874–75 amounted to offensive warfare and represented a lesson learned in the Civil War. Offensive war was more difficult to undertake than defensive combat: defenders invariably chose their ground, enjoyed less stringent command

[27] Utley, *Frontier Regulars,* 51; Jamieson, *Crossing the Deadly Ground,* 48–49; Wooster, *The Military and United States Indian Policy,* 141–42; Hutton, *Phil Sheridan and His Army,* 260–61 (quotation on 261).

[28] Quoted in Jamieson, *Crossing the Deadly Ground,* 38, citing the Sherman Papers, Library of Congress.

[29] Kane, *Military Life in Dakota,* 64–65; McDermott, *Circle of Fire,* 100.

[30] Jamieson, *Crossing the Deadly Ground,* 39, 40 (quotation); Utley, *Frontier Regulars,* 53–54; Wooster, *The Military and United States Indian Policy,* 148–49; Dunlay, *Wolves for the Blue Soldiers,* 133–45.

and control requirements, usually knew the terrain better, and could retreat. But Sheridan and his leading Indian fighters, all of whom were veterans of the closing year of the Civil War when the North took strategic offensive in all its theaters and relentlessly pressed it to the end, were now witnessing comparable results in the American West. Offensive war would be put to an even greater challenge on the northern plains against the Sioux and Northern Cheyennes, but the results would prove just as conclusive in the long run.[31]

The Plains Indian wars of the 1860s and early 1870s served as a training ground for many officers who would play critical roles in the Great Sioux War. During those early campaigns, officers implemented war-making strategies passed largely by word of mouth in sessions with Sheridan, Terry, Crook, Pope, Custer, Mackenzie, and Miles, among junior officers at countless army posts, and probably even around campfires on the campaign trails. To date, no published textbook or professional journal told of these tactics, for this was a manner of warfare that historians, not contemporaries, labeled unconventional. De Trobriand's journal contained prescient thought on Indian warfare and matters such as the worth of frontiersmen and Indian scouts, but he was as yet only writing for himself. Alfred Sully composed a general field order in September 1868 for the benefit of his command, though probably no one else. In that order Sully offered interesting prescriptions for combating warriors, reading Indian trails, and reacting to Indian tactics, but again the circulation of that document was limited. And while all of this occurred before the general outpouring of narrative accounts of Indian warfare penned by participating officers and eyewitnesses, George Custer's widely read autobiography (*My Life on the Plains,* published in 1874) reflected considerably on the tribulations of the southern plains campaigns. Although they were not described in print before the commencement of the Great Sioux War, the precepts of converging columns, winter war, native trackers, relentless pursuit, dawn attacks, offensive war, and total war were understood and well exercised by Sheridan's army (and especially by campaign-hardened officers such as Evans, Royall, Carr, Custer, Mackenzie, and particularly Miles). Seasoned regiments including the Second, Third, Fourth, Fifth, and Seventh Cavalry and Fifth and Eleventh Infantry would soon ply these tenets to great effect against Sioux and Northern Cheyenne Indians on the northern plains.[32]

---

[31] Jamieson, *Crossing the Deadly Ground,* 52–53; Wooster, *The Military and United States Indian Policy,* 134–35; Hattaway and Jones, *How the North Won,* 705.

[32] General Field Orders No. 3, Headquarters District of the Upper Arkansas [in the Field], Fort Dodge, Kansas, September 26, 1868, in Greene, *Washita,* 67; Custer, *My Life on the Plains.*

The Great Sioux War Begins

The Great Sioux War was officially announced on February 8, 1876, when Sheridan forwarded written instructions to Terry and Crook to commence military operations against those Indians who had spurned the Department of the Interior's directive to remove themselves from the unceded territory in Wyoming and Montana and report to their agencies on the Great Sioux Reservation. This order was the culmination of a winter of political maneuvering involving President Grant, secretary of war William Belknap, secretary of the interior Zachariah Chandler, commissioner of Indian affairs Edward P. Smith, and Sherman, Sheridan, Terry, and Crook over the legalities of opening and settling the Black Hills and ending Sioux obstructionism to settlement throughout the vast northern plains region forever.

Sheridan's directions for mounting this campaign were exceedingly simple. Terry was to dispatch troops from his Department of Dakota into the Little Missouri River countryside or westward, targeting Sitting Bull's followers (perhaps seventy warriors). Crook was to dispatch a column from his Department of the Platte into the headwaters of the Big Horn, Rosebud, Tongue, and Powder rivers where Crazy Horse's allies (perhaps two hundred warriors) were thought to reside. These illogically small warrior estimates were based upon midwinter reports received from the commissioner of Indian affairs. The simple objective at the onset was to compel these northerners to abandon their timeless haunts and move to the Great Sioux Reservation. The orders called for disregard of department lines, operations without concert, and communications between the field commands (seemingly encouraged though not demanded or expected) to be forwarded via Sheridan's Division Headquarters in Chicago. The tenets of converging columns, winter war, Indian trackers, and other such practices were not mentioned in Sheridan's orders but were plainly evident in the orchestrations and doubtless primed in face-to-face conversations throughout the winter. The army's unwritten orthodoxy for Indian warfare would be embraced however necessary, mirroring at least partly the tactics used so successfully in the Red River War.[33]

❦ ❦ ❦

Despite Sheridan's initial presumption that Terry and Crook would field expeditions relatively concurrently and in a hastened manner, only Crook hurried troops to the field within weeks of receiving the order to do so, despite troublesome weather and logistical issues in Wyoming Territory. At the onset of the Great Sioux War, Crook commanded in his Department of the Platte eight companies of the Second Cavalry Regiment (with Terry controlling the so-called Montana Battalion), plus the Third Cavalry and four infantry regiments: the Fourth, Ninth, Fourteenth, and Twenty-third. As the Sioux War progressed, Crook rotated nearly every company of every regiment in his command to the conflict. The few exceptions amounted to scattered companies at the extremes of the department at places like Fort Hartsuff, Nebraska, Fort Cameron, Utah Territory, and Fort Hall, Idaho Territory. Troop deployments were quite different in Terry's department, as will be seen.

Critical anomalies in the Department of the Platte included the Union Pacific Railroad, which linked Omaha, Nebraska, and Ogden, Utah, and continued westward from Ogden to Sacramento, California, via the Central Pacific Railroad. The Union Pacific provided easy, year-round transportation across the department and featured seven military posts along its route, including Fort McPherson, North Platte Station, and Sidney Barracks in Nebraska and Forts D. A. Russell, Sanders, Fred Steele, and Bridger in Wyoming. By 1876 the critical importance of most of these railroad posts, which had been built in the 1860s to safeguard railroad construction, had waned, but each still quartered troops that were drawn to the war in due course. In the northern extremes of Wyoming, Crook squarely faced the nettlesome unceded territory in the Powder River Basin, just as Terry did in the lower Yellowstone River Basin in adjacent Montana. This vast, uninhabited, buffalo-rich landscape was contested throughout the war and was Sheridan's target for converging columns. Interestingly, some officers in Crook's varied Sioux War deployments were familiar with the old Bozeman Trail, which bisected the Powder

[33] "Report of Lieut. Gen. P. H. Sheridan," in *Report of the Secretary of War, 1876*, 440–41; Utley, *Frontier Regulars*, 246–49; Hedren, *Fort Laramie in 1876*, 52.

River Basin from Fort Fetterman north-northwestward, having served at posts along its course in the 1860s. Though it was barely used any longer and its protectorate forts were in ruin, this old road had a well-scored track that Crook's troops would renew repeatedly during the war.

Crook's twenty Second Cavalry and Third Cavalry companies were scattered to posts surrounding the Powder River Basin and southern Black Hills, with single companies at Forts Fred Steele and Fetterman and Camps Brown and Stambaugh, Wyoming, and Camp Sheridan, Nebraska; two companies each at Forts Sanders and Laramie, Wyoming; three companies at Fort McPherson and Sidney Barracks, Nebraska; and five companies at Fort D. A. Russell, near Cheyenne, on the Union Pacific. Fort D. A. Russell was the department's largest cavalry post before the war. Wherever stationed, these cavalry companies all were relatively easily deployed (whether to the Nebraska agencies, the Black Hills, or the war), and peacekeeping and treaty enforcement had already been added to their duties in recent years.

Crook's forty infantry companies, meanwhile, were dispersed widely, with the Fourth Regiment scattered to Forts Fetterman, Fred Steele, Sanders, and Bridger and Camp Brown, Wyoming; the Ninth garrisoning Fort Laramie, Wyoming, and Camps Robinson and Sheridan, Nebraska; and the Twenty-third scattered to Omaha Barracks, Fort Hartsuff, and North Platte, Nebraska, and Fort D. A. Russell and Camp at Cheyenne Depot, Wyoming (the department's westernmost quartermaster station on the railroad). The Fourteenth Infantry was deployed to the westernmost reaches of the department, occupying Fort Cameron and Camp Douglas, Utah, and Fort Hall, Idaho.

The Department of the Platte's initial Great Sioux War deployment in March drew all five Third Cavalry companies from Fort D. A. Russell; Second Cavalry companies from Forts Fetterman, Laramie, and Fred Steele; and two of Fort Fetterman's three Fourth Infantry companies. Crook steadfastly embraced the mobility and striking capability of mounted troops (an army orthodoxy) and built this expedition and two subsequent ones around battalions of cavalry. Infantry troops accompanied this and his other columns but invariably served defensive purposes. The new column was formally named the Big Horn Expedition (Deployment No. 2). Crook did not personally command the expedition but accompanied it, ostensibly as an observer. The organization and command of the column fell to Colonel Joseph J. Reynolds, Third Cavalry, who divided the units into two-company battalions, five of cavalry and one of infantry.

Reynolds's headquarters section included an adjutant (who tended the preparation and dissemination of communications and orders between the colonel and the various components), one officer performing quartermaster and commissary duties, a chief of scouts, and a surgeon. Several of these officers were drawn from the Third Cavalry. Reynolds's senior medical officer, assistant surgeon Curtis E. Munn, who immediately prior to this had served as post surgeon at Camp Robinson, was supported by two assistants, and Crook was supported by an aide-de-camp.

Crook and Reynolds were the lone field-grade officers marching north in this opening deployment in the Department of the Platte (Major Thaddeus Stanton of the Paymaster Department also accompanied but did not command troops). At age forty-seven, Crook was one of the most seasoned and respected Indian fighters in the American Army, though none of his experiences involved Plains tribes. An 1852 West Point graduate, Civil War major general of volunteers and recipient of numerous valor brevets, and commander of the Department of Arizona from June 1871 to March 1875 and Department of the Platte since April 1875, Crook was a plainspoken, innovative campaigner who issued few orders, trusted his officers implicitly, and embraced independent thinking.[34] Affable fifty-four-year-old Reynolds was also a West Pointer (class of 1843 with Grant), distinguished Civil War major general of volunteers with valor brevets, and commander in his volunteer rank of the Department of Texas from April 1870 to January 1872, where, unfortunately, his reputation was tarnished by contractor scandals. The opportunity to command the Big Horn Expedition was a chance for Reynolds, who was kindly viewed by Crook, to redeem his reputation.[35]

The line officers and men of the Big Horn Expedition were generally skilled campaigners. The participating Second Cavalry companies were often in the field in Wyoming and Nebraska in the late 1860s and early 1870s, but their engagements were mostly small. The Third Cavalry companies had spent the same period in New Mexico and Arizona, where they were often deployed against Apache Indians, before transferring to the Department of the Platte in 1872. Among the twenty line officers leading troops, seven were West Point graduates, sixteen were Civil

[34] Jerome A. Greene, "George Crook," in Hutton, ed., *Soldiers West,* 115–21; Thain, *Notes Illustrating the Military Geography of the United States,* 52. The standard biography of Crook is Robinson, *General Crook and the Western Frontier.*

[35] Vaughn, *The Reynolds Campaign on Powder River,* 25; Thain, *Notes Illustrating the Military Geography of the United States,* 99–100; Bourke, *On the Border with Crook,* 270.

War veterans, half had previous experience in Indian combat, and two (Henry E. Noyes and Thomas B. Dewees, both of the Second Cavalry) had served on the Bozeman Trail in the late 1860s.[36]

Reynolds and three of his cavalry battalions struck an Indian village of perhaps 105 lodges on the Powder River in Montana at dawn, March 17 (Deployment No. 3). After they had driven off the occupants and captured their ponies, the tide turned against the soldiers. They unceremoniously withdrew from the camp before fully destroying it, abandoned their fatalities in the hasty movement, and later lost the ponies before they slaughtered them. Crook was furious at the evident mismanagement of the fight and brought court-martial charges against Reynolds and two company captains, Noyes and Alexander Moore. Confounded by the setback and continuing severe weather, Crook returned to Fort Fetterman and ended the Big Horn Expedition after one month in the field. Sheridan's soldiers had located Indians—not Crazy Horse's people as first presumed but instead a band of Northern Cheyennes led by Old Bear. The Northern Cheyennes, already steadfast allies of the Sioux, were brought into the war by this encounter. In Sheridan's view, the first visible movement of the Great Sioux War had ended in failure, and he could already foresee that the prospects of a winter war were fading rapidly.

❧ ❧ ❧

As Crook and Reynolds wended their way northward in Wyoming, Terry planned two deployments in the Department of Dakota. At the commencement of the Great Sioux War, he had at his disposal four companies of the Second Cavalry, concentrated at Fort Ellis in western Montana Territory, plus the Seventh Infantry, garrisoning Forts Shaw, Ellis, and Benton and Camp Baker, all in western Montana. Occupying posts and agencies in Dakota Territory were nine companies of the Seventh Cavalry, scattered at Forts Totten, Abraham Lincoln, and Rice; the First Infantry, deployed along the middle Missouri River at Forts Randall and Sully and Lower Brule Agency; the Sixth Infantry, occupying Forts Buford, Abraham Lincoln, and Stevenson and the Standing Rock Agency, also along the Upper Missouri; and the Seventeenth Infantry, scattered across Forts Abercrombie, Abraham Lincoln, Wadsworth, and Rice, plus Cheyenne River Agency and Camp Hancock (a one-company quartermaster depot

---

[36] Rodenbough and Haskins, *The Army of the United States*, 182–83, 203–205.

on the Northern Pacific Railroad at Bismarck). Terry also had available the Twentieth Infantry, occupying Forts Snelling and Ripley in Minnesota and Pembina, Totten, and Seward in northeastern Dakota.[37]

The scattering of troops in the Department of Dakota was evidence that geography was no ally to Terry in the normal administrative affairs of his department or in this looming Sioux war, with fourteen companies located in far western Montana, forty-five companies positioned in Dakota along and east of the Missouri River, and four companies in Minnesota. Most striking in the department was the vast outback reaching from the Missouri River in Dakota westward to the Rocky Mountains in Montana, which amounted to fully one-third of the landed width of the jurisdiction and possessed no military posts, no cities, and no avenues of interior travel aside from the Yellowstone and Missouri rivers. In all, this outback was a locale where whites had never yet fared well, most recently at the besieged Fort Pease.

Terry's deployments initially and throughout the Great Sioux War suggest an unstated intent to achieve minimal disruption of the garrison status quo in his department. Moving infantry companies from eastern Dakota or Minnesota would have skeletonized many of those posts (though Crook unhesitatingly did so in his department) and incurred unwelcome expenses on the Northern Pacific Railroad. Drawing troops from Missouri River stations below Fort Rice would have incurred similar transportation expenses on river steamers and, more importantly, would have disrupted ordinary and desired stability at the Sioux agencies. Accordingly, neither the First nor Twentieth Infantry regiments played any substantial role in the opening phases of the Great Sioux War, aside from the participation of one small provisional Twentieth Infantry detachment manning Gatling guns with Terry's Column. Similarly, the Seventeenth Infantry tended garrison duties foremost and had no substantial role in this war. Meanwhile, Terry's cavalry, the Montana Battalion of the Second at Fort Ellis, and the Seventh (drawn to full twelve-company strength in April upon the transfer of three companies from Reconstruction service in Louisiana) bore the war's full brunt. Terry also fully utilized the Sixth and Seventh Infantry regiments, apart from scattered companies retained on garrison duty. With few exceptions, the Second and Seventh Cavalry and Sixth Infantry were deployed to the war from start to finish.[38]

---

[37] "Report of General Terry," in *Report of the Secretary of War, 1876*, 455.
[38] Ibid.

Winter weather stymied Terry's initial organizational movements in Dakota, where snow and extreme cold routinely impeded traffic on the Northern Pacific Railroad and made cross-country travel exceedingly hazardous. Terry also belatedly elected to await the arrival of Companies B, G, and K, Seventh Cavalry, from Louisiana before embarking for the field. Irrespective of these delays in the east, on February 27 Terry directed Colonel John Gibbon to field all the troops that could be spared in western Montana. In a very short while, six companies of the Seventh Infantry and the Montana Battalion of Second Cavalry marched for the Yellowstone River, though Gibbon necessarily awaited the return of Major James S. Brisbin's cavalry force that had ridden to the relief of Fort Pease, a small besieged trader's outpost located near the mouth of the Big Horn River (Deployment No. 1). Throughout the 1876 campaign, Gibbon's force was most commonly known simply as Gibbon's Column, which historians later dubbed the Montana Column. It was never formally named.

Gibbon and Brisbin were the lone field-grade officers participating from Montana; although both were distinguished soldiers, neither was an experienced Indian fighter. Forty-eight-year-old Gibbon was an 1847 West Point graduate, a veteran of the Mexican War, and a major general of volunteers during the Civil War, where he was repeatedly wounded, including receiving a crippling pelvic injury at Gettysburg. As colonel of the Thirty-sixth and then Seventh Infantry regiments after the war, Gibbon served on the plains and in the mountain West but never campaigned against its tribes.[39] Stocky, thirty-eight-year-old Brisbin was commissioned from the enlisted ranks early in the Civil War and held the grade of brigadier general of volunteers by its end. He too was repeatedly wounded and held several valor brevets. Brisbin arrived at Fort Ellis in the fall of 1870 and subsequently commanded the distinctive Montana Battalion, renowned in regimental annals because of its fifteen-year isolated service in the Department of Dakota. Brisbin took a unique interest in the agricultural worth of Montana and was given the nickname "Grasshopper Jim" by his soldiers. He suffered from crippling rheumatism, a condition exacerbated by endless hours in the saddle and Montana's severe winters. Alone among field-grade officers, Brisbin earned the unheralded distinction of campaigning the longest in the Great Sioux War, from participation in the February 1876 Fort

[39] Carroll and Price, *Roll Call on the Little Big Horn*, 59–60; Robinson, *A Good Year to Die*, 94.

Pease sortie through the Little Missouri Expedition that closed the war in September 1877.[40]

Gibbon's ten-company command was the smallest initially fielded in the Great Sioux War (Deployment No. 4). His headquarters component included an adjutant, one officer with both quartermaster and commissary duties, one chief of scouts—all drawn from his command—and one lone doctor. Gibbon had limited cavalry from a single regiment and limited infantry from another, so each branch functioned as a battalion. His force also included a small artillery component. Of the two battalions, Gibbon's cavalry was slightly better seasoned to Indian campaigning, having participated in the 1870 fight on the Marias River and escorted Northern Pacific Railroad surveyors in 1872. Five of his line officers were West Pointers, fourteen had Civil War experience, and ten had some form of Indian combat experience gained on the Bozeman Trail, at Marias River, or on the Yellowstone.

Terry finally took the field on May 17 at the head of a fifteen-company expedition known in contemporary accounts simply as Terry's Column and by historians later as the Dakota Column (Deployment No. 7). Terry's headquarters detachment was markedly larger than Gibbon's, though the structure was nearly the same. Terry's staff included an adjutant, quartermaster (responsible in the field for transportation, clothing, and forage), commissary officer (responsible for subsistence matters), chief of scouts, chief medical officer, ordnance officer, and engineer. Several of these officers enjoyed support staff, including five additional doctors reporting to assistant surgeon John W. Williams. Terry relied on key department staff from St. Paul joining him in the field. His column's adjutant, ordnance officer, engineer, and medical officer were chiefs of those sections in the Department of Dakota. Terry also drew administrative support from the field. The column's quartermaster, First Lieutenant Henry J. Nowlan, was regimental quartermaster of the Seventh Cavalry. Among the line units in Terry's column, only the Seventh Cavalry structured itself: Custer divided it into equally sized wings and battalions. Terry's infantry companies and Gatling battery functioned relatively independently.

Of the two field-grade officers accompanying Terry to the field, only George Custer was a veteran Indian campaigner, experienced in campaigns on the southern plains in 1867 and 1868–69 and also on the

[40] Rodenbough, *From Everglade to Cañon with the Second Dragoons*, 447–48; Hanson, *The Conquest of the Missouri*, 249; Utley, *Frontier Regulars*, 252.

northern plains in 1873, when he led troops in several clashes with Sioux warriors. Now age thirty-six, Custer was an 1861 West Point graduate who rose rapidly through the volunteer ranks during the Civil War and reached the rank of major general of volunteers by war's end, having participated in many of its most famous engagements. He was wounded several times and repeatedly brevetted. Custer was charismatic and fearless, qualities that endeared him to Sheridan and made him an exceptional cavalry officer. But he was also blindly ambitious and outspoken and had incurred Grant's displeasure for criticizing the administration as war with the Sioux loomed in 1876. Grant initially forbade Custer's participation in the coming campaign but relented after Terry's and Sheridan's intercession and Custer's personal pleading.[41]

Custer's chief subordinate on the campaign and no particular friend was Major Marcus Reno. An 1857 West Point graduate, Reno had considerable Civil War experience but little on the plains. He had participated in Terry's weapons board examinations in 1872 and most recently commanded the escort accompanying the Northern Boundary Survey Commission engaged in 1873 and 1874 in marking the international border from Minnesota westward.[42]

Terry, meanwhile, was an unlikely campaigner but capable administrator and commanded the Dakota column in 1876 because Grant would not permit Custer to do so. A Yale-trained lawyer, fond of the arts, fluent in French and German, and a student of military science, Terry served with distinction during the Civil War, attaining the rank of major general of volunteers by its end and receiving the formal Thanks of Congress for capturing Fort Fisher (a critical Confederate post protecting the port of Wilmington, North Carolina) in January 1865. Terry commanded the Department of Dakota from September 1866 to May 1869 and from January 1873 onward and was among those who negotiated the Fort Laramie Treaty of 1868, ending Red Cloud's Bozeman Trail War but also presaging this current conflict. Terry was Crook's senior in grade by eight years and was the senior ranking officer to take the field in the Great Sioux War.[43]

---

[41] Carroll and Price, *Roll Call on the Little Big Horn*, 49–50; Hutton, *Phil Sheridan and His Army*, 310–11. Custer biographies are rife. Recommended are Barnett, *Touched by Fire;* and Utley, *Cavalier in Buckskin.*

[42] Nichols, *In Custer's Shadow*, 116–20, 127–28, 130–36.

[43] Bailey, *Pacifying the Plains*, 4–5; Hutton, *Phil Sheridan and His Army*, 130–31; Thain, *Notes Illustrating the Military Geography of the United States*, 58.

Of the troops marching west with Terry in May and all the cavalry regiments in Sheridan's Military Division of the Missouri, none exhibited the same breadth and depth of Indian campaign experience as the Seventh Cavalry. Largely commanded since its founding in 1866 by its lieutenant colonel, Custer, in the routine absence of its colonels (initially Andrew J. Smith and since May 1869 Samuel D. Sturgis), the Seventh had campaigned with distinction in Kansas and Indian Territory in the late 1860s and in Montana in 1873 during the third year of the Northern Pacific Railroad surveys. Although it was more a field movement with scientific objectives than an Indian campaign, Custer and most of the Seventh also explored the Black Hills in the summer of 1874, announcing gold and helping set in motion the confrontation with the Sioux now unfolding.

The high level of preparedness and breadth of combat experience among the company-grade officers in Terry's Column (not including those in the headquarters contingent) is evident in the record. It was easily the most noteworthy of any of the columns assembled for the Great Sioux War. Of thirty-five company-grade officers commanding troops at one time or another with Terry, eleven were West Point graduates, twenty had been under fire during the Civil War, twelve possessed brevets for valor in the Civil War, and Captain Thomas W. Custer, George's brother, held two Medals of Honor for acts of Civil War heroism. Twenty of these officers also had experience in Indian warfare. In the Seventh Cavalry alone, eighteen of its twenty-four participating company-grade officers had combat experience in some Indian campaign, including sixteen who had engaged on the Yellowstone River in 1873 against Sioux Indians.

❧ ❧ ❧

Twelve days after Terry's departure from Fort Abraham Lincoln, Crook led a second column north from Fort Fetterman. Of fifteen cavalry companies ordered to this new movement, nine had participated in the Big Horn Expedition in March, with the fresh cavalry companies drawn from Fort McPherson and Sidney Barracks, Nebraska, and Fort Fred Steele, Wyoming, all along the Union Pacific. None of the five infantry companies on this expedition had participated in the March campaign. These infantry companies originated at Forts Fred Steele, Laramie, and Fetterman, all reasonably near at hand. This time Crook personally commanded the column, which was formally dubbed the Big Horn and Yellowstone

Expedition (Deployment No. 8). The headquarters contingent for this expedition had expanded somewhat from that supporting the March movement and now included an adjutant, quartermaster, commissary of subsistence, engineer, chief of scouts, medical director, and, uniquely, chiefs of a pack train and wagon train. The troops marching north with Crook were divided into battalions, two cavalry and one infantry, and the two mounted battalions formed a cavalry brigade commanded by Lieutenant Colonel William B. Royall, Third Cavalry, a veteran of Sheridan's winter campaign of 1868.

Royall was one of three field-grade officers joining Crook and commanding troops on this movement, and each was an experienced, long-serving soldier. Fifty-one-year-old Royall was a Mexican War veteran who later fought Comanches in New Mexico. Six saber cuts received at Old Church, Virginia, in 1862 incapacitated him for the remainder of the Civil War, but in the postwar years he actively campaigned with the Fifth Cavalry against Cheyenne Indians on the central plains, participating in the engagements at Prairie Dog Creek, Kansas, and Summit Springs, Colorado. Royall promoted to the Third Cavalry in December 1875.[44]

Major Andrew W. Evans commanded the Battalion of Third Cavalry in Royall's Cavalry Brigade. A melancholy, bookish forty-six-year-old, Evans was an 1852 West Point graduate and classmate of Crook and a veteran of Civil War service in New Mexico and with the Army of the Potomac and had commanded a mixed column of cavalry and infantry from New Mexico during Sheridan's winter war on the southern plains in 1868–69.[45] Major Alexander Chambers, Fourth Infantry, commanded the expedition's Infantry Battalion, composed of two companies from the Fourth Regiment and three from the Ninth. Chambers, a methodical forty-three-year-old, was an 1853 West Point graduate. During the Civil War he had been wounded twice (at Shiloh, Tennessee, and again at Iuka, Mississippi), had participated in the siege of Vicksburg, and had received numerous valor brevets. He was assigned to the Fourth Infantry in 1870 and commanded Fort Fetterman and Camp Sheridan before the Great Sioux War.[46]

Although nine cavalry companies on this movement also had participated in the Big Horn Expedition, only nine company-grade officers out

[44] Altshuler, *Cavalry Yellow & Infantry Blue*, 288–89; *Records of Living Officers of the United States Army*, 118–20.

[45] Altshuler, *Cavalry Yellow & Infantry Blue*, 123; Greene, *Washita*, 176–77.

[46] *Records of Living Officers of the United States Army*, 329–30; Hedren, *We Trailed the Sioux*, 13.

of twenty from that campaign were now with Crook. Of thirty company officers experiencing this war for the first time, nine were West Point graduates, twenty-three were Civil War veterans (with fourteen receiving valor brevets), and thirteen were veterans of some prior Indian campaign or engagement. Infantry captains Thomas B. Burrowes and Andrew S. Burt both had experienced service along the Bozeman Trail in the late 1860s. The Big Horn and Yellowstone Expedition featured cavalry mobility, again as Crook desired it, plus an exceptional level of combat experience among the field-grade officers and a notable depth of experience in the company grades. By these measures, as in the case of Terry's Column, this was a well-rounded, fully capable command: indeed, one of the several best assembled during the Great Sioux War.

Before Crook's Big Horn and Yellowstone Expedition could find the Sioux, they found him. On June 9, as the command settled into camp along the Tongue River in northern Wyoming, hundreds of Sioux and Cheyenne warriors appeared on the high bluffs across the river and audaciously fired into the scattered troops and camp. Although the demonstration inflicted no particular harm, Crook was obliged to dispatch four Third Cavalry companies across the river to drive the Indians off. The display was stunning, however, and cast a pall of caution on the column and its commander as they continued northward into Montana.[47]

On June 17, having crossed from the Tongue valley onto the headlands of Rosebud Creek, Crook's expedition was jumped by upward of a thousand warriors, who attacked the column and commenced a spirited fight that lasted through much of the day. With perhaps two thousand combatants on the field, the Battle of the Rosebud was the largest engagement of the Great Sioux War and had pivotal consequences. Crook took high ground and commanded his troops as a general should, countering a succession of Indian attacks across the field while also probing offensively. In all, his officers and soldiers conducted themselves well in sequences of advances, flanking movements, escapes, and bold maneuvers. After hours of fighting, a serendipitous attack on the Indians' rear caused the Sioux to withdraw, leaving the field in Crook's hands.

Crook's column suffered nine killed and twenty-one wounded. He rightly proclaimed the Rosebud Creek fight a victory, but his actions immediately thereafter negated any success and demonstrated that this aggressive attack by the enemy, particularly in light of the actions at the

---

[47] Bourke, *On the Border with Crook*, 296–97.

Tongue River a week earlier and Powder River in March, actually delivered a rather critical blow to the army. Instead of returning his wounded to Fort Fetterman under a suitable guard and then proceeding on, Crook abandoned the front and back-trailed to Goose Creek, Wyoming, in the lee of the Big Horn Mountains. This retirement fatefully altered the dynamic of the war and made the disaster soon to come inevitable. Faithful to his original orders from Sheridan, Crook hurried reports of the battle to Chicago, the awkward hinge in any communication with Terry, who was beyond direct contact but presumably somewhere north in Montana.[48]

By June 17, while Crook engaged hundreds of astonishingly aggressive Sioux and Northern Cheyenne warriors in the headlands of Rosebud Creek, Terry's Column, having been joined by Gibbon's, was cautiously ascending the Yellowstone River. Scouting forays had discovered evidence of growing numbers of northern Indians south of the Yellowstone, particularly on the middle reaches of Rosebud Creek (Deployment No. 9). Eager to close with those Indians, Terry turned Custer and the Seventh Cavalry onto the Rosebud. He offered Custer Brisbin's Montana Battalion and the column's Gatling guns, but the self-assured cavalier marched his regiment alone. Terry also made it clear that he intended to advance the remaining troops up the Yellowstone to the mouth of the Big Horn River and up the Big Horn and even Little Big Horn and that a concerted action by all forces could be possible by June 26.

Custer cut from the Yellowstone on June 22 and soon came onto an increasingly broad Indian trail running up Rosebud Creek and then turning west into the valley of the Little Big Horn River (Deployment No. 11). Fearing that these tribesmen would flee if his column was discovered and in fact believing that he had been discovered, Custer struck an unreconnoitered, massive Sioux village on the afternoon of June 25. By most accounts, Custer deployed his troops rationally, and at the onset his officers and soldiers performed commendably. But virtually every element of the Battle of the Little Big Horn soon went against the Seventh Cavalry. Reno's three-company battalion, having struck the southern end of the vast encampment, was quickly repulsed and soon engulfed, and pandemonium reigned as survivors scurried in retreat to the high bluffs east of the river. Meanwhile, Custer and five companies, oblivious to the brutal counterattack and collapse of Reno's troops, deployed east of the river near the

48 Ibid., 311–16.

village's center but were destroyed in detail. Captain Frederick Benteen's three-company battalion, separated initially to block any Indian flight up the river, subsequently joined Reno. Gunfire could be heard north on Custer's trail, but neither senior officer advanced to that clarion.

Custer had attacked a village numbering some five thousand Indians, with perhaps fifteen hundred warriors, representing every Lakota council fire plus allied Northern Cheyennes, Arapahos, and Santee Sioux. He had compromised the potential gains from a dawn attack and a converging attack with Terry's force. He had no precise sense of the enormity of the village, though the size of the Indian trail and forewarning from his scouts suggested as much. As the sun set on June 25, Custer and 260 Seventh Cavalrymen lay dead along the Little Big Horn in the worst catastrophe that ever befell the U.S. Army in the American West and certainly the worst calamity of the Great Sioux War. That view, of course, was the army's. Clouded momentarily by their great victory, unfathomable catastrophes also awaited the Indians in this war.

❧ ❧ ❧

Crook's retirement to Wyoming after the Rosebud battle and Custer's stunning defeat at the Little Big Horn changed everything. Sheridan's vision of a quick wintertime war against a few hundred northern Indians using troops easily deployed from the Departments of Dakota and the Platte lay in shambles. It was now midsummer. The army's ablest cavalry regiment had been destroyed. The army's most astute Indian fighting general wanted more troops and quietly confessed to Sheridan that he did not know what to do. Terry and Gibbon nursed wounds on the Yellowstone in an unshakable melancholy. And in many ways the Great Sioux War had only just begun.

The Black Hills Front

In the spring of 1876, while Crook and Terry organized respective field movements at Forts Fetterman and Abraham Lincoln and bound ultimately for the Indians' unceded buffalo-hunting territory in northern Wyoming and eastern Montana, Sheridan dispersed other troops in response to increasingly troublesome Indian raiding south of the Black Hills (Deployment No. 5). Attacks attributed largely to warriors from the White River agencies were occurring against Black Hillers, freighters, and a newly operating stage and express company, jeopardizing unfettered access to the beckoning and economically vital gold country. The boldest moves of Sheridan, who was intent on securing this commerce, involved stationing infantry companies on the Black Hills Road in the proximity of much of this turmoil, which had proven heaviest along a thirty-mile-long intersection with an east-west Indian trail linking the Red Cloud and Spotted Tail agencies with the buffalo country in northern Wyoming. These companies, drawn respectively from Omaha Barracks and Fort Bridger, established and garrisoned Camp on Sage Creek (located midway between Fort Laramie and the Black Hills) and Camp Mouth of Red Cañon (located at the road's southwestern entry into the Black Hills) and quickly brought measured calm to the road.[49]

More than focusing on the troubles occurring along the Black Hills Road, Sheridan rightly viewed the Indians' Powder River Trail as an unpoliced avenue between the Nebraska agencies and the northern Indian camps that was rife with the movement of warriors and war-making matériel and sought to shut the trail down with cavalry put in constant motion. With no uncommitted mounted units remaining in the Department of the Platte, Sheridan arranged the transfer of eight companies of Fifth Cavalry from General Pope's Department of the Missouri.

---

[49] Hedren, *Fort Laramie in 1876*, 76–78, 83–86, 103–104, 107–108; Hedren, "Garrisoning the Black Hills Road."

By mid-June these units were en route to Fort Laramie, the regiment's point of rendezvous and base for the coming operation (Deployment No. 10). The Fifth Cavalry was another of Sheridan's well-seasoned Indian-fighting regiments, having engaged Plains warriors in Nebraska, Kansas, and Colorado in the 1868–69 war (most notably at Summit Springs, Colorado, in July 1869) and thereafter fighting Apache warriors in Arizona in the early 1870s while Crook commanded the Department of Arizona.

Commanded in the field at the outset by its lieutenant colonel, Eugene A. Carr, and after July 1 by its newly promoted colonel, Wesley Merritt, the Fifth Cavalry initially functioned as an independent column on an independent mission: stemming Indian traffic on the Powder River Trail. Carr accordingly organized the regiment for this autonomous service, creating a small but appropriate headquarters section detailed from the regiment and adding a doctor drawn from one of its Kansas posts and a civilian chief of scouts, William F. "Buffalo Bill" Cody. Cody was a regimental favorite from earlier days together in Nebraska and Kansas and also a friend of Sheridan. After Merritt joined, the headquarters complement was expanded slightly by engaging two aides-de-camp.

Of the regiment's field-grade staff participating in this unique deployment on the southern margins of the Great Sioux War, Merritt, Carr, and Major John J. Upham were all West Point graduates (1860, 1850, and 1859, respectively) and all exceptionally experienced Civil War veterans. Merritt served as a major general of volunteers and Carr as a brigadier general of volunteers, and both received brevets for valorous service. Of the three, however, only Carr had distinguished service on the Indian frontier, notably leading troops in many movements associated with Sheridan's winter war of 1868–69 and its continuation into the summer of 1869. He commanded troops in engagements with Cheyennes at Beaver Creek, Kansas, Spring Creek, Nebraska, and Rock Creek and Summit Springs, Colorado, earning the congratulations of Augur, Sheridan, and Sherman and thanks from the legislatures of Nebraska and Colorado.[50]

From the start, the Fifth uniquely campaigned in the Great Sioux War with all of its company captains present for duty (eight initially and ten by late July). It boasted that this circumstance was unique in the war, which it was, and exceptional for the army at any time. It was altogether common then for officers at almost any grade to be engaged at one time

[50] Price, *Across the Continent with the Fifth Cavalry*, 263, 305–306. The standard biographies of Merritt and Carr are Alberts, *Brandy Station to Manila Bay;* and King, *War Eagle.*

or another in some manner of detached service, whether recruiting for the army, on an equipment review board, as a member of a court-martial board, as a staff assistant to a general officer at some headquarters, or on a myriad of similar assignments. In the absences of seniors, junior officers filled in—and sometimes for years. The Fifth's colonel, William H. Emory, detached from the regiment in 1871 to command the Department of the Gulf and never returned. One of the Seventh Cavalry's original captains, Michael V. Sheridan, detached from that regiment in August 1870 to serve on his brother's staff in Chicago, an association lasting well into the 1880s. Beyond the mere presence of all its captains, the Fifth Cavalry's company-grade officers in Wyoming were a uniquely distinguished lot. Among the fourteen officers attached to companies at the onset of this service, four were West Point graduates, ten were Civil War veterans (including seven with valor brevets), and, notably, every officer had some form of prior Indian combat experience. The Fifth Cavalry, like the Seventh, was one of the most skilled and experienced Indian fighting regiments in the American Army.[51]

For all its initial promise, the Fifth's service on the Powder River Trail and in the Cheyenne River countryside of eastern Wyoming was tedious and profitless. The presence of troops was known at the agencies and Indian camps. Almost every resident at Red Cloud and Spotted Tail wishing to join Crazy Horse probably had done so weeks or months earlier in time for the Rosebud and Little Big Horn battles, with one notable exception. Merritt's troops learned the dismaying news of Custer's death on July 6 while paused at the infantry camp on Sage Creek and on the eleventh were ordered to resupply at Fort Laramie and join Crook's column, a move eagerly anticipated by the Fifth's officers. But while en route to Fort Laramie, Merritt received a dramatic dispatch announcing that some eight hundred Northern Cheyenne Indians were set to bolt from Red Cloud Agency and head for the northern coalition. These tribesmen would most certainly travel the Powder River Trail. Merritt confirmed the report with Camp Robinson's commanding officer and then commenced a forced march, first north and then east, to place himself directly in front of the oncoming Cheyennes. He engaged and turned back the Cheyennes in a surprise encounter on the morning of July 17 at Warbonnet Creek, Nebraska, where Cody collected a much-celebrated

---

[51] King, *Campaigning with Crook and Stories of Army Life*, x; Price, *Across the Continent with the Fifth Cavalry*, 223.

"first scalp for Custer." The small clash became big news in the wake of Custer's defeat, a victory of sorts, small as it was, after three consecutive reversals. Merritt's Warbonnet detour consumed more than a week, but by July 23 his troops were en route from Fort Laramie to Crook's camp on Goose Creek.[52]

Continuing episodes of horse stealing, attacks on small parties of citizens, and unrest at the agencies led Sheridan to renew his request to the Interior Department to cede control of the agencies to his officers, thereby enabling him to carry out a policy of arresting, disarming, and dismounting the northern Indians when they appeared. The Department of the Interior had ignored a similar request in May but could hardly ignore it now and on July 22 authorized the army to assume control of all the agencies in Sioux Country. At that moment Sheridan was not well prepared to serve his wishes, but continuing troop deployments from outside of the Platte and Dakota departments and other actions in coming months led to results that markedly shaped the outcome of the Great Sioux War.[53]

---

[52] Hedren, *First Scalp for Custer*, 23–40.

[53] "Report of Lieut. Gen. P. H. Sheridan," in *Report of the Secretary of War, 1876*, 445.

Reinforcements and Starting Over

Despite the despondency in Crook's and Terry's camps, Sheridan squandered no time in reenergizing their campaigns. Crook had already ordered forth five additional infantry companies from his department and had learned of Merritt's deployment on the Black Hills front and requested those troops as well; Sheridan obliged. Not wanting to vacate the precarious southern Black Hills, in the Fifth's stead Sheridan maneuvered the transfer of Colonel Ranald S. Mackenzie and six companies of the Fourth Cavalry from Texas, plus four companies of Fourth Artillery from the San Francisco Bay area. These battalions were directed to Camp Robinson, the tumultuous post adjacent to Red Cloud Agency.[54]

Sheridan sent infantry troops both to enable the resumption of Terry's summer campaign and eventually to succeed him on the Yellowstone. Other new infantry troops also augmented the garrisons at several of the Sioux agencies within the Department of Dakota, much as Mackenzie's Fourth Cavalry and the Fourth Artillery battalion served in Nebraska. Recognizing the limitations imposed by the vast expanses of the Dakota Department (with existing military posts in the east and west but none in the middle) plus the still-unknown qualities of that interior and the short river navigation season in Dakota and Montana, Sheridan and Sherman had importuned Congress for military posts in the Yellowstone Country for years, only to be ignored until calamity struck. Now two new posts in Sioux Country would be realized, with the first to be constructed by the Fifth Infantry commanded by Colonel Nelson A. Miles, ordered to the Yellowstone from Kansas, and six Twenty-second Infantry companies commanded by Lieutenant Colonel Elwell S. Otis, already en route from Michigan. Otis and Miles reported to Terry in early August and devoted their attention partly to reenergizing Terry's listless campaign but also to

[54] "Report of General Pope," in *Report of the Secretary of War, 1876*, 451.

establishing themselves on the Yellowstone permanently. Meanwhile, in September the entire Eleventh Infantry commanded in the field by its lieutenant colonel, George P. Buell, was dispatched from Texas to the Standing Rock and Cheyenne River agencies, substantially bolstering the existing small infantry garrisons at each and poised when the time was right to garrison the second new Yellowstone River fort.[55]

Having too long ignored one of the great axioms applicable to multiple columns operating on the same front—the need for current, direct communications between commanders—in mid-July Terry dispatched three couriers overland to Crook. Sheridan's original orders commencing operations in 1876 placed no particular importance on the coordination of movements, the concentration of forces, or direct communication and simply urged communications via his headquarters in Chicago. But that lengthy and untimely routing completely disregarded the current precariousness of these commands and the supposed continuing audacity and numerical superiority of the Indians. The successful ride of three Seventh Infantry volunteers from the Yellowstone River to Goose Creek, Wyoming, was widely heralded. More importantly, the dispatches that these doughboys carried then and on their return confirmed the locations of Terry's and Crook's forces, their mutual desire to coordinate movements, and timing predictions for renewed active campaigning.[56]

Crook's substantially bolstered Big Horn and Yellowstone Expedition marched north from Goose Creek on August 4, bound for the Rosebud and his counterpart, General Terry (Deployment No. 12). His column had nearly doubled in size, growing from twenty companies to thirty-five, including twenty-five of cavalry. The headquarters section remained much as before, although personnel changes occurred and the number of physicians serving the column grew from three to six. The number of field-grade officers commanding troops grew too, from three to seven, counting Merritt, Royall, Evans, Carr, Upham, Chambers, and Major Julius W. Mason (recently promoted to the Third Cavalry from the Fifth Cavalry but electing to serve with his former regiment until the close of the current campaign). Like the others in this group, forty-one-year-old Mason was a respected, combat-savvy officer with deep experience in the Civil War and on the Indian frontier.[57]

---

[55] "Report of Lieut. Gen. P. H. Sheridan," 442; and "Report of General Terry," in *Report of the Secretary of War, 1876*, 455–56; Robert M. Utley, "War Houses in the Sioux Country," in Hedren, ed., *The Great Sioux War 1876–77*, 252–63.

[56] Hedren, "'Three Cool, Determined Men.'"

[57] Price, *Across the Continent with the Fifth Cavalry*, 370–74.

The essential framework of Crook's column remained as it had been in June, but with several branches added to accommodate the newly joined units. Colonel Merritt assumed command of the Cavalry Brigade in lieu of Lieutenant Colonel Royall, and Royall assumed command of the Second and Third Cavalry battalions, while Lieutenant Colonel Carr assumed command of the Fifth Cavalry, itself divided into two battalions. Major Alexander Chambers remained in command of the Infantry Battalion, which doubled in size but again divided into respective regimental components: the Fourth, Ninth, and Fourteenth infantries. Crook parked his substantial wagon train at Goose Creek under the command of Captain John V. Furey, Quartermaster Department, who oversaw hundreds of civilian wagonmasters, teamsters, and herders, plus several officers who were leaving the column and two contract doctors. This quartermaster train would not rejoin the column until late in September, when the expedition ambled in the Black Hills.

Terry, having been reinforced by twelve infantry companies led by Miles and Otis, resumed active campaigning on the Yellowstone on August 8, marching up Rosebud Creek (Deployment No. 13). Terry's headquarters component did not change markedly, though, like Crook, he was now supported by several additional physicians who arrived with the Fifth and Twenty-second regiments. Three field-grade officers were new to the command, joining Gibbon, Brisbin, and Reno. Major Orlando H. Moore, Sixth Infantry from Fort Buford, had already served on the Yellowstone since May, commanding an ever-changing configuration of Sixth and Seventeenth Infantry companies guarding supply caches and steamboat traffic on the river in support of Terry's and Gibbon's movements (Deployment No. 6). Terry elected now to divert Moore and his three Sixth Infantry companies to direct combat service, leaving Seventeenth Infantry companies and dismounted Seventh Cavalry troopers to tend Yellowstone River supply and security matters. At age forty-nine, Moore was a twenty-year veteran officer, experienced on the frontier before and after the Civil War, repeatedly brevetted for Civil War valor, and most recently in command of troops that had successfully engaged Sioux warriors at the freshly abandoned Powder River Depot one week before Terry commenced this current movement. Uniquely, all of Moore's Regular Army service was with the Sixth Infantry, where he had been promoted from second lieutenant to major.[58]

[58] *Records of Living Officers of the United States Army,* 312–13; Carroll and Price, *Roll Call on the Little Big Horn,* 146.

Now thirty-seven years old, Nelson A. Miles had earned many laurels in the Civil War, rising to the grade of brigadier general of volunteers during the conflict and major general of volunteers before the release of the volunteer forces and many times brevetted for valorous service. Assigned to command the Fifth Infantry in March 1869, Miles led a column in the Red River War, where he fought in a succession of engagements and notably rescued the German sisters held captive by Cheyennes.[59] Elwell S. Otis was also a Civil War veteran with several valor brevets. Assigned to the Twenty-second Infantry as its lieutenant colonel in July 1866, Otis had no particular experience on the frontier before this deployment, although his regiment was periodically stationed in the West, including in the Department of Dakota.[60]

Terry's cavalry marched relatively independently, Brisbin again commanding the small Montana Battalion of the Second and Reno commanding eight companies of the Seventh functioning in two battalions. The Seventh Cavalry still remained a shadow of itself, having suffered shattered companies and a great loss of horses at Little Big Horn. Its unhorsed survivors remained on the Yellowstone, guarding supplies. Gibbon and Miles were both appointed colonels in the Regular Army on July 28, 1866, but Terry assigned command of the Infantry Brigade to Gibbon, a West Pointer. Gibbon was the longer-serving officer by nearly twenty years and the longer-serving major general of volunteers during the Civil War, yet this matter of command quietly rankled Miles, who possessed great leadership drive and skill but also an equally substantial and easily bruised ego.

Crook's and Terry's burgeoning columns met on August 10 on the middle Rosebud and ambled along together for a week. They then spent a second week on the Yellowstone, tending to logistical matters and pondering the campaign; steamboats and a robust sutler trade were peculiar curiosities to the Wyoming troops. By then no fresh Indian trail beckoned, and both generals realized that the Great Sioux War could not be won with a concentrated force of such substantial size, especially when its enormity strained quartermaster and commissary lines. Crook had proved that already. Moreover, these columns represented a curious mix

[59] Greene, *Yellowstone Command*, 18–19; Altshuler, *Cavalry Yellow & Infantry Blue*, 229. Recommended biographies of Miles include Wooster, *Nelson A. Miles and the Twilight of the Frontier Army;* and DeMontravel, *A Hero to His Fighting Men.*

[60] *Records of Living Officers of the United States Army*, 325; Rodenbough and Haskins, *The Army of the United States*, 680–85.

of campaign-weary soldiers, battle-stunned men, relatively new arrivals, and new arrivals with a very specific mission of hutting themselves on the Yellowstone before Montana's winter set in. By month's end Crook's Big Horn and Yellowstone Expedition departed the Yellowstone, following a faint Indian trail eastward into Dakota, while Miles and Otis concentrated their energies at the mouth of the Tongue River, establishing the first of Sheridan's cantonments. Meanwhile, Terry maneuvered his troops with the quiet purpose of disbanding his column. In early September Gibbon marched west along the Yellowstone toward home, while Terry marched downriver to Fort Buford and also then home.

If Terry's expedition ended with nary a whimper, Crook's ended with an agonized yelp. After crossing the Little Missouri River in northwestern Dakota, he turned his column south toward the Black Hills, despite extreme shortages of rations. Having advanced ahead of the column bound for Deadwood to procure foodstuffs, 150 of his cavalry struck a small Sioux village of 37 tipis and 260 people on September 9 in the Slim Buttes in western Dakota. The cavalrymen attacked at dawn, driving the inhabitants onto the buttes and capturing 400 ponies. Crook came later in the day and remained on-site overnight, suffering initially desultory fire that escalated into a protracted engagement as warriors from other nearby camps joined the fray. Instead of aggressively attacking those warriors and their distant but evident villages, Crook mounted a purposeful defense and then continued his plodding march to the Black Hills, necessarily deploying troops to cover his withdrawal from the field. The Battle of Slim Buttes was hailed as a victory, but again Crook's decision after the fight tarnished its value. His failure to move on any other camp and the thoroughly exhausted condition of his command brought the Big Horn and Yellowstone Expedition to a pathetic end. After being supplied from the mining camps and spending nearly a month in the Black Hills, largely in reenergizing the horse stock, Crook's Expedition (commanded in the end by Merritt) pushed on and disbanded at Camp Robinson in late October.

Neither Crook nor Terry had much of a showing thus far in the Great Sioux War. After the Big Horn and Yellowstone Expedition's commendable deportment at Rosebud Creek, Crook might have pressed an advantage that could have changed the entire course of the war, but instead he withdrew. This emboldened his foes, who met and defeated Custer on the Little Big Horn eight days later. Terry and Gibbon, meanwhile, demonstrated no offensive zeal whatsoever before or after Little Big Horn, when, as history tells, the great Sioux coalition had either not yet formed or no longer existed. Both columns quietly retired with few of their soldiers other than the Seventh Cavalry having even once fired weapons. But the Great Sioux War had already exhibited defining moments. The Battle of the Little Big Horn touched the nation and over time came to represent the price that America paid for Manifest Destiny, its conviction that it was entitled to the lands of the frontier irrespective of any other claim or cost. And Little Big Horn immortalized Custer and his mythic "last stand," sparking an intrigue that endures to this day. Crook's column had a defining moment too, not at Rosebud Creek or Slim Buttes, but in its "Starvation March" in September. The command wasted hideously for want of salt pork, hardcrackers, coffee, and tobacco, grubbed for scarce prairie berries, and ate horse and mule flesh, often nearly raw due to the dearth of fire on the sodden sage prairie. Crook's soldiers never forgave him for the extreme pain and suffering inflicted in Dakota. It was "the worst campaign I ever experienced," one veteran Fourteenth infantryman said bitterly, as if speaking for all.[61]

❧ ❧ ❧

The situation across the northern plains in early October 1876 seemingly held faint promise for a satisfactory conclusion to the Great Sioux War, but in fact the keys to victory were in place and about to be revealed. Although at that moment no major campaign was scouring the countryside for Indians, several scattered, tenuous garrisons now occupied Sioux Country. The largest assembled at the burgeoning Tongue River Cantonment, where Miles had concentrated his entire Fifth Infantry and portions of the Twenty-second (Deployment No. 14). Downriver opposite the mouth of Glendive Creek, Elwell Otis, soon succeeded by Major Alfred L. Hough, and companies of the Twenty-second Infantry established and occupied Glendive Cantonment on the receding Yellowstone to receive and transfer supplies, munitions, and construction materials destined for the Tongue River post. And in Wyoming's Powder River Basin infantry troops occupied the new Cantonment Reno, established near the Bozeman Trail's old Fort Reno as a supply base for Crook's announced third major campaign of 1876 (Deployment No. 16). This troop presence in

[61] Hedren, "'The Worst Campaign I Ever Experienced,'" 12 (quotation). On the notion of defining moments of the Great Sioux War, see Hedren, *We Trailed the Sioux,* 17, 56, 68.

Sioux Country was part of Sheridan's vision of permanent army garrisons where only yesterday Indians had hunted buffalo and evaded calls to the agencies and now were warring over the right to remain free. Although two of these three garrisons would be relocated in 1877, the situation at the time was satisfying, even if conditions throughout the countryside remained in flux. Some of the so-called summer roamers had reappeared at the agencies, but mass surrenders were not yet occurring. The "Rule of 1876" (meaning the disarming and unhorsing of the northern Indians whenever they appeared) was not yet widely imposed. Notably, Crook was assembling the elements of a third campaign at Camp Robinson, and Miles also envisioned active campaigning in the Yellowstone country as fall gave way to winter.[62]

While the Rule of 1876 had not yet been forced on the Indians of the north, in October Sheridan ordered its implementation at the Sioux agencies as a measure of ensuring that residents would be less able to aid those residing in the Powder and Yellowstone basins. Substantial orchestrations against the camps near the agencies on the Missouri River and in the Pine Ridge country occurred simultaneously. Colonel Samuel D. Sturgis and Major Reno of the Seventh Cavalry carried out disarmings and unhorsings at the Standing Rock and Cheyenne River agencies, and Colonel Ranald S. Mackenzie led a similar deployment at the Red Cloud Agency (Deployment No. 18). In the main, these actions affected Indians who had taken little or no part in the Great Sioux War, yet they served to set clear and unbending expectations when other surrenders finally did occur.

❧ ❧ ❧

On the war front, Miles struck the next blows. When a train of supplies and construction matériel from Glendive Cantonment failed to reach the Tongue River in mid-October as expected, Miles mustered the entire Fifth Infantry and marched down the Yellowstone to its relief. Troops guarding the train from Glendive led by Otis had come under siege from Sitting Bull's warriors (Deployment No. 15), but Miles's column successfully relieved the wagons and then turned north and followed the Sioux trail to the divide between the Yellowstone and Missouri drainages. There Miles actually parleyed twice with Sitting Bull and other Sioux headmen

---

[62] The term "Rule of 1876" is noted in correspondence from Alfred H. Terry to the Adjutant General, Military Division of the Missouri, March 24, 1881, in "Sioux Campaign" (National Archives).

before striking and destroying the chief's village nestled in the headlands of Cedar Creek (Deployment No. 17). This was the first instance in the Great Sioux War where protagonists met and discussed ending the fighting, though the parleys came to no resolve. Miles deployed his troops with perfect determination and precisely as prescribed in Upton's tactics manual: fanning skirmishers across a broad front, protecting his flanks, maintaining a reserve, and skillfully utilizing two artillery pieces. For the first time in the war the Sioux bore the full sting of Miles's unflinching resolve and the deadly accuracy of disciplined infantry troops shouldering long-range .45-70 Springfield rifles.[63]

This was the second time an Indian village was struck after Little Big Horn, though the first for Miles. As at Slim Buttes, this was a smaller camp, estimated in the monthly Tongue River post return to number 500 to 600 people. This tally was probably inflated but was clear evidence that the Little Big Horn coalition no longer existed. The Little Big Horn numbers were staggering in comparison, with some 1,000 to 1,200 tipis and 5,000 to 7,000 men, women, and children, including perhaps 1,200 to 1,500 warriors. But that phenomenal concentration began scattering almost immediately after the battle. It was increasingly evident that the Sitting Bull faction, all northerners, sought to elude troops in the trackless Big Open country north of the Yellowstone and separate from Crazy Horse. The Crazy Horse faction, meanwhile, all southerners, sought haven well south and east of the river and often closer to the Black Hills. Army strategists took heed. With the coalition dead, this had become a different war.[64]

After briefly returning to the Tongue River to resupply, on November 6 Miles sent his regiment back to the field, this time bound north to the Fort Peck Agency on the Missouri River. Sitting Bull had been spotted there, but a sortie attempting to capture him led by Colonel William B. Hazen and four Sixth Infantry companies from Fort Buford traveling by steamboat may instead have hastened his departure (Deployment No. 19). Sitting Bull's trace was cold when Miles arrived, but he determined to scour the countryside south of the river for these elusive Sioux. At Fort

[63] "Report of the General of the Army," in *Report of the Secretary of War, 1876,* 37; "Report of General Nelson A. Miles," in *Report of the Secretary of War, 1876,* 483.

[64] Fort Keogh Post Return, October 1876 (National Archives). Little Big Horn village numbers have varied over the years; the ranges of tipis and inhabitants presented here reflect the prevailing thinking of the battle's most recent scholars. See Harry H. Anderson, foreword, in Buecker and Paul, eds., *The Crazy Horse Surrender Ledger,* xii–xiii; Sklenar, *To Hell with Honor,* 163; Liddic, *Vanishing Victory,* 82–84; Donovan, *A Terrible Glory,* 231; and Greene, *Stricken Field,* 13.

Peck Miles divided his command into three independent battalions that fanned southward (Deployment No. 20). Only companies G, H, and I led by First Lieutenant Frank D. Baldwin succeeded in locating Hunkpapas, skirmishing with them on the Missouri east of Fort Peck and then successfully attacking their village on Ash Creek, near the Yellowstone divide, on December 18. Sitting Bull's camp, consisting of 122 lodges, was destroyed, along with 60 horses and mules. Again Sitting Bull's people were exposed to the ravages of the northern plains winter and suffered greatly. In due course, Sitting Bull and his followers fled to Canada and no longer presented a wartime target.

❧ ❧ ❧

While Miles scoured the Big Open in Montana, Crook mounted a third formal campaign in Wyoming, largely organizing at Camp Robinson and departing from Fort Fetterman on November 14. Crook named this movement the Powder River Expedition (Deployment No. 21). The column featured eleven companies of cavalry drawn from the Second, Third, Fourth, and Fifth regiments; four companies of Fourth Artillery serving as infantry; and eleven companies of infantry, drawn from the Ninth, Fourteenth, and Twenty-third regiments. These units had not yet participated in a previous large-scale expedition against the Sioux, but most companies were already veterans of lesser-scale Great Sioux War service, particularly on the Black Hills Front, where patrolling roads, escort duties, and the imposition of the Rule of 1876 at the Red Cloud Agency had dominated activities in recent months. A notable exception was the participation of Company K, Second Cavalry, commanded by Captain James Egan. This unit participated in Crook's Big Horn Expedition and fought at Powder River on March 17. Thereafter it was almost continuously deployed on the Black Hills Road, including escorting Crook to Fort Laramie in mid-September to confer with Sheridan and engaging Sioux warriors on Richard Creek south of Fort Laramie as recently as October 14, when an enlisted man had been killed. Crook and Egan were longtime friends, and on this campaign Company K served solely as Headquarters Provost Guard.[65]

Crook's headquarters detail featured the standard assignments and many of the same officers who had participated with him on the earlier

[65] Hedren, *Fort Laramie in 1876*, 183.

Sioux War campaigns. First Lieutenant John G. Bourke was now acting assistant adjutant general; Captain John V. Furey, quartermaster and ordnance officer; First Lieutenant Walter S. Schuyler, aide-de-camp; and Captain George M. Randall, chief of scouts. On this expedition chief medical officer Joseph R. Gibson oversaw five other doctors, all new to a major campaign but not necessarily to the Great Sioux War. And the expedition featured four field-grade officers: Colonel Ranald S. Mackenzie and Major George A. Gordon commanding cavalry, and Lieutenant Colonel Richard I. Dodge and Major Edwin F. Townsend commanding infantry and dismounted artillery.

Ranald Mackenzie, like Custer and Merritt, was another of Sheridan's trusted and seasoned cavalry officers and very well versed in the general's Indian fighting precepts. First in his class at West Point (graduating in 1862), Mackenzie amassed a stellar Civil War record, participating in most of the great battles in the East, including Fredericksburg, Gettysburg, Petersburg, and Cedar Creek. He was wounded six times in the war and lost two fingers and was brevetted repeatedly. Mackenzie was promoted to colonel in the Regular Army in 1867 and in 1870 transferred to the Fourth Cavalry, where he led six companies in the daring cross-border action at Remolina, Mexico, in 1873 and commanded troops in the Red River War, including at Palo Duro Canyon, Texas. On the Powder River Expedition, thirty-six-year-old Mackenzie commanded the cavalry battalion consisting of two five-company squadrons that was to form Crook's attack force.[66] Major George Gordon, Fifth Cavalry, led one of Mackenzie's cavalry squadrons on the expedition. The forty-three-year-old West Pointer (class of 1854) served in the West with the Second Dragoons and had participated in the Utah Expedition before the Civil War. Gordon fought at Antietam, Gettysburg, and elsewhere and received several valor brevets. Though he was assigned to the Fourth Cavalry in 1867 and Fifth Cavalry in 1873, Gordon's postwar service was largely marked by administrative assignments and did not include any notable Indian campaign experience.[67]

Forty-nine-year-old Lieutenant Colonel Richard Dodge of the Twenty-third Infantry was a well-seasoned plains officer. A West Point graduate (class of 1848), Dodge spent most of his pre–Civil War years in Texas and his early postwar years along the lengthening course of the

---

[66] J'Nell L. Pate, "Ranald S. Mackenzie," in Hutton, ed., *Soldiers West*, 177–78; Robinson, *Bad Hand*, 7–17.

[67] Price, *Across the Continent with the Fifth Cavalry*, 302–304.

Union Pacific Railroad, commanding troops that were protecting its construction. His Civil War service was mostly administrative. Fascinated by Indian cultures and the plains environment, Dodge was an intellectual driven to write books. One published title predated the Great Sioux War: a geological and environmental history of the Black Hills drawn from his time commanding the military escort there with the Newton-Jenney Expedition of 1875. On the Powder River Expedition, Dodge commanded the Artillery and Infantry battalions.[68] His senior subordinate, Major Edwin F. Townsend of the Ninth Infantry, had most recently commanded Fort Laramie, where he was well immersed in the Sioux War matters of the Southern Front. An 1854 West Point graduate with Major Gordon, fifty-two-year-old Townsend was a brevetted Civil War veteran but had no particular field experience against Indians.[69]

Crook's route northward again followed the well-scored Bozeman Trail. His objective at the onset was Crazy Horse and his followers, believed to be wintering on the Rosebud or Tongue. After pausing briefly at Cantonment Reno (the small four-company outpost established on the Powder River a month earlier largely as a forward supply base for operations like this), Crook learned from an Indian scout of a winter camp of Northern Cheyennes nestled in a deep canyon in the southern Big Horn Mountains. Crook immediately dispatched Mackenzie and the cavalry, plus several hundred Indian auxiliaries, to strike the village (Deployment No. 22). Mackenzie's column numbered some eleven hundred combatants. After threading their way up the Powder River and the pinched valley of the Red Fork, including a night march in bitter moonlit cold, they struck the camp at dawn on November 25. The village, numbering some two hundred tipis and twelve hundred inhabitants, was surprised and thoroughly routed. The fighting was vigorous for several hours and casualties were heavy on both sides, including one officer killed. Cheyenne women and children, exposed to the ravages of winter, were especially victimized that night.

Mackenzie destroyed the lodges and all they held and most of the seven hundred captured ponies. The village was home to nearly every member of the Northern Cheyenne tribe. This Battle of the Red Fork of the Powder River (also known as the Dull Knife fight or Morning Star battle for the Cheyenne leader whose village it was) was a turning point

---

[68] *Records of Living Officers of the United States Army*, 281–82; Kime, *Colonel Richard Irving Dodge*, xiii, 16, 100; Dodge, *The Black Hills*.

[69] *Records of Living Officers of the United States Army*, 282; Hedren, *Fort Laramie in 1876*, 29–30.

in the Great Sioux War for these people in particular, but ultimately for all the northern Indians. For the fourth time since Little Big Horn, an Indian village was routed and destroyed. This time the devastation befell the Northern Cheyennes, steadfast allies of the Sioux, who ironically had suffered the war's first aggression at Powder River in March and had been turned at Warbonnet Creek in July. They had also fought valiantly with the Sioux at Tongue River Heights, Rosebud Creek, and Little Big Horn during the heady preeminence of the northerners. But now these tribesmen were destitute and were a weighty burden on Crazy Horse's people, with whom they took refuge. Moreover, a larger message was emerging. With Crook and Miles in the field in the middle of winter and army camps like Tongue River and Reno established in the midst of the buffalo country, attacks like this and Slim Buttes and Cedar Creek could occur again and again. The only plausible alternative, many Indians were coming to believe, was surrender at an agency. In fact some northerners were already quietly making their way southeastward, though dramatic surrenders were not yet occurring.

This devastation on the Red Fork of the Powder had another meaning to the Northern Cheyennes. Almost all of the old Northern Cheyenne material beauty—elaborately decorated lodges, exquisitely quilled and beaded clothing, sacred shields, scalp shirts, war bonnets, sacred bundles, and the like—died in the flames of that camp. In the words of the tribe's preeminent historian, "Never again would Northern Cheyenne material culture reach the heights of richness and splendor that the people knew before that bitter day in the Big Horns."[70]

Crook folded his Powder River Expedition one month later but presumed that he would renew operations again in the spring. Miles, meanwhile, had learned of Crazy Horse's presence on the Tongue in the rugged Wolf Mountains and promptly led seven companies drawn from the Fifth and Twenty-second regiments upriver on December 29. He skirmished with warriors on January 7 some ninety-eight miles south and closed with them the next day in a morning-long battle initiated by Crazy Horse, not the troops (Deployment No. 23). This Wolf Mountains fight was remarkable for its thrusts and counters in a manner strikingly similar to the Rosebud battle, another engagement where Crazy Horse precipitated the action and led prominently. Here Miles's infantry and Crazy Horse's warriors, including refugee Cheyennes, contested

[70] Powell, *Sweet Medicine*, 1:166–67.

towering knolls and ridges in the picturesque pine- and cedar-studded valley, several miles north of the Indian camp. Neither side demonstrated an advantage through most of the engagement. An untimely blizzard ended the fight. Miles held the field and advanced on the abandoned campsite the next day. Although it was not comprehended at the time, the Battle of Wolf Mountains signaled the end of offensive war for Crazy Horse's people, who now even more gravely deliberated surrender.

Miles retired to Tongue River Cantonment to outwait the winter. Crook retired to Cheyenne to participate in the January courts-martial of Colonel Joseph Reynolds and Captain Alexander Moore of the Third Cavalry for their failings at Powder River in the opening action of the war. And the scattered northerners received Indian emissaries from the Spotted Tail and Red Cloud agencies urging their surrender and bearing assurances that no harm would come to them. Massive surrenders at Tongue River Cantonment and the Standing Rock, Cheyenne River, Red Cloud, and Spotted Tail agencies, particularly in April and May and including Crazy Horse's surrender on May 6 at Camp Robinson, rather quietly ended the active phase of the Great Sioux War for most people.[71]

Despite these outward appearances, however, Sheridan assumed that many Indians would leave the agencies for the buffalo country just as quickly as the grass greened in the spring. And notable holdouts remained in the Yellowstone country, including Lame Deer and several hundred Miniconjou Sioux followers. Lame Deer had vowed never to surrender, and Sheridan viewed him as a figure capable of rallying warriors who wished to prolong the war. To secure his gains, Sheridan directed Terry and Crook to field fresh columns as quickly as possible in the spring, while Miles, on his own volition, focused on Lame Deer.

Miles's opportunity to move against the Miniconjous came in late April. Mustering six companies of infantry and the Montana Battalion of Second Cavalry, recently transferred from Fort Ellis to his command at Tongue River Cantonment, he intercepted a fresh trail south of the cantonment. He followed it to the place where it crossed from the Tongue River Valley into the Rosebud Valley then followed it up the Rosebud and a small tributary known as Muddy Creek and today as Lame Deer Creek (Deployment No. 24). Miles found Lame Deer's village of some sixty lodges a few miles up Muddy Creek and attacked at

[71] The story of the wintertime efforts to induce surrenders is well told in Anderson, "Indian Peace Talkers and the Conclusion of the Sioux War of 1876"; Knight, "War or Peace"; Robinson, *A Good Year to Die*, 325–32; and Buecker and Paul, *The Crazy Horse Surrender Ledger*, 1–19.

dawn on May 7. The villagers largely scattered into the adjacent hillsides, but Lame Deer was killed and the village and pony herd were destroyed. Miles subsequently retired to Tongue River Cantonment, assuming that he would take the field again as necessary. Emissaries reported that the Sioux had all but disappeared from the landscape except for survivors from Lame Deer's camp, who became the objects of pursuit throughout the summer.

As directed by Sheridan, two other columns took the field in May. Colonel Samuel D. Sturgis led eleven companies of reorganized Seventh Cavalry west from Fort Abraham Lincoln on May 1, marching via Fort Buford and bound for the lower Yellowstone River (Deployment No. 25). Captain John M. Hamilton led five companies of the Fifth Cavalry north from Fort D. A. Russell, Wyoming, on May 29, bound for the countryside north of Cantonment Reno (Deployment No. 26). Major Verling K. Hart succeeded Hamilton in late June. Accompanying Sturgis were Lieutenant Colonel Elmer Otis, Custer's direct successor, and Major Lewis Merrill, one of Reno's counterparts. Sturgis had participated in the disarming and unhorsing actions at the Missouri River agencies the previous October, but Hart, Otis, and Merrill had not yet taken the field in the Great Sioux War. Both commands scoured Sioux haunts continuously throughout the summer, occasionally diverting companies to duties such as retrieving officer casualties from the Little Big Horn Battlefield and reburying those who died on that field, but never once encountered northern Indians.

Miles also directed Major Henry M. Lazelle of the First Infantry and nine companies of First Infantry and Twenty-second Infantry, plus one Seventh Cavalry company detached from Sturgis's camp, into southeastern Montana and western Dakota to pursue Lame Deer's skittish followers (Deployment No. 27). Lazelle was a West Point graduate (class of 1855) and very experienced on the frontier and in the Civil War. He had been seriously wounded in an Apache fight before the Civil War and commanded troops on the 1871 and 1872 Northern Pacific Railroad surveys in the Yellowstone Valley.[72] Lazelle and these First Infantry companies had recently been detailed to the Yellowstone from Standing Rock Agency and Fort Sully. This movement, dubbed the Little Missouri Expedition by historians, represented the last formal combat orchestration of the Great Sioux War. It featured the war's final exchange of gunshots, on

[72] *Records of Living Officers of the United States Army*, 339.

July 3 along the Little Missouri River, when Lazelle's infantry closed with a handful of Sioux warriors. As Lazelle followed the Indian trail leading to that July 3 encounter, he requested additional support. Miles promptly dispatched the Montana Battalion of cavalry, led initially by Captain Edward Ball and then by Major Brisbin, and additional companies of Seventh Cavalry from Sturgis's camp. It was ironic that Ball and Brisbin should again take the field. Both had participated in the opening movement of the Great Sioux War, the relief of Fort Pease in February 1876, and eighteen months later were once again fielded in the war's final movement. Lazelle's and Brisbin's troops returned to Tongue River Cantonment on September 1, with very little to show for two and a half months of arduous maneuvering.

After nearly nineteenth months of continuous engagement, the final orchestration of the Great Sioux War occurred in early July 1877, when Lieutenant Colonel George P. Buell consolidated six companies of Eleventh Infantry on the high bluff overlooking the confluence of the Big Horn and Little Big Horn rivers and established Big Horn Post. This was the second of the so-called Yellowstone River forts authorized by Congress after Custer's defeat in 1876 (Deployment No. 28). Buell, a valor-brevetted Civil War veteran, had commanded a column with distinction in the Red River War against southern plains tribes and most recently had led his regiment north from Texas to augment the garrisons at several of the Missouri River Sioux agencies. Buell's troops fired no shots in the Great Sioux War but came to Sioux Country before its end. Their crowning duty at this post, soon called Fort Custer, was bearing witness to the army's enduring legacy of this war, evident just fifteen miles upriver in the already fascinating debris-strewn Indian village at Little Big Horn and the shallow graves of Custer's dead scattered across the river's eastern highlands. Buell's ancillary responsibility was maintaining this "holy ground," as Crook's aide John Bourke called it.[73]

[73] Heitman, *Historical Register and Dictionary of the United States Army,* 1:260; Hutton, *Phil Sheridan and His Army,* 257; Paul L. Hedren, "'Holy Ground': The United States Army Embraces Custer's Battlefield," in Rankin, ed., *Legacy,* 189–206; Robinson, *The Diaries of John Gregory Bourke, Volume Two,* 339.

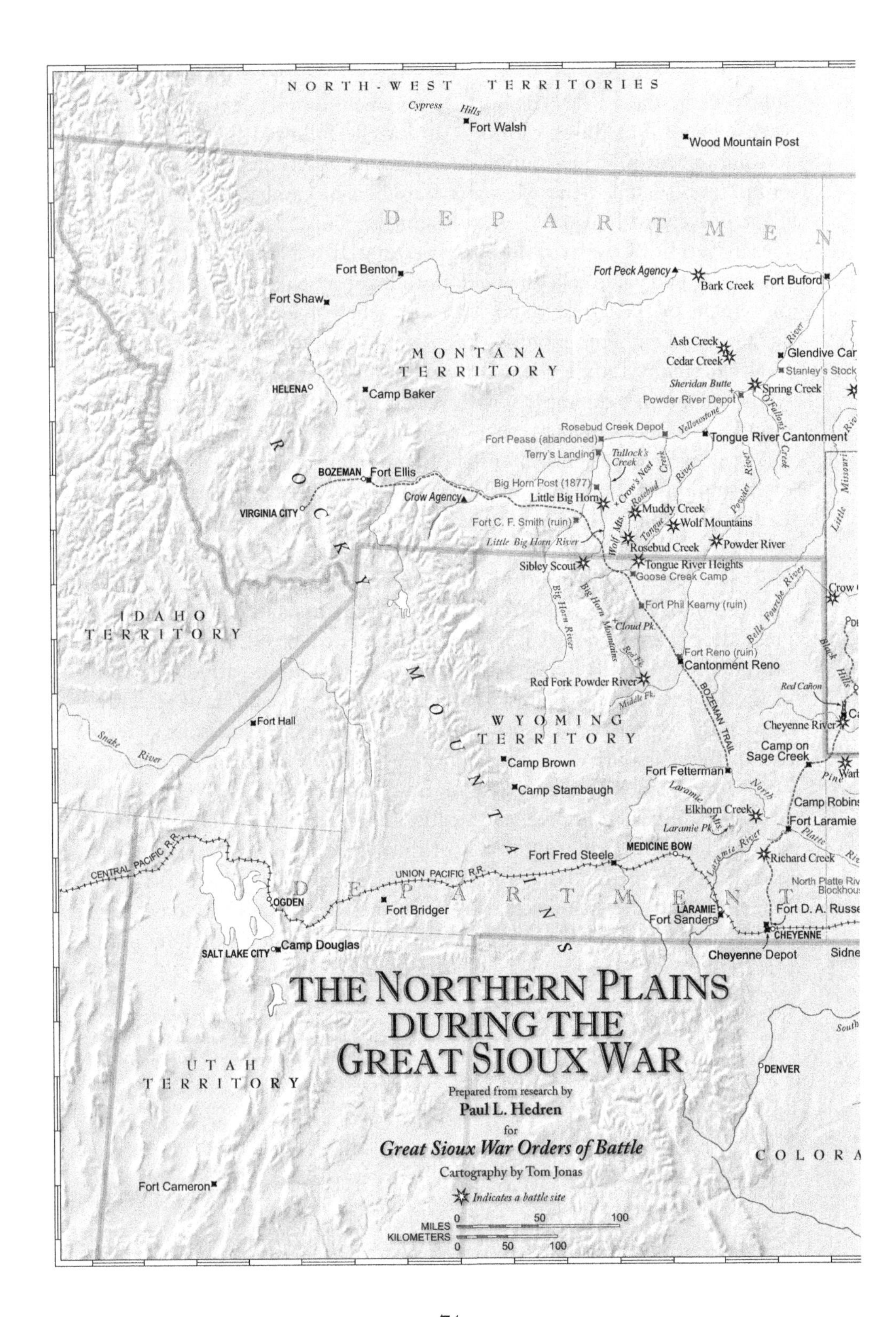

NORTH-WEST TERRITORIES
Cypress Hills
Fort Walsh
Wood Mountain Post
DEPARTMENT
Fort Benton
Fort Shaw
Fort Peck Agency
Bark Creek
Fort Buford
MONTANA TERRITORY
HELENA
Camp Baker
Ash Creek
Cedar Creek
Glendive Car
Stanley's Stock
Sheridan Butte
Spring Creek
Powder River Depot
Rosebud Creek Depot
Fort Pease (abandoned)
Tongue River Cantonment
Terry's Landing
Tullock's Creek
BOZEMAN
Fort Ellis
Big Horn Post (1877)
Crow Agency
Little Big Horn
VIRGINIA CITY
Muddy Creek
Wolf Mountains
Fort C. F. Smith (ruin)
Little Big Horn River
Rosebud Creek
Powder River
Sibley Scout
Tongue River Heights
Goose Creek Camp
ROCKY MOUNTAINS
IDAHO TERRITORY
Fort Phil Kearny (ruin)
Cloud Pk.
Fort Reno (ruin)
Cantonment Reno
Red Fork Powder River
Red Cañon
Fort Hall
WYOMING TERRITORY
Cheyenne River
Snake River
Camp on Sage Creek
Camp Brown
Fort Fetterman
Camp Stambaugh
Camp Robins
Elkhorn Creek
Fort Laramie
Laramie Pk.
MEDICINE BOW
Fort Fred Steele
Richard Creek
CENTRAL PACIFIC R.R.
UNION PACIFIC R.R.
North Platte Riv Blockhous
OGDEN
Fort Bridger
LARAMIE
Fort Sanders
Fort D. A. Russe
CHEYENNE
SALT LAKE CITY
Camp Douglas
Cheyenne Depot
Sidne
BOZEMAN TRAIL
THE NORTHERN PLAINS DURING THE GREAT SIOUX WAR
Prepared from research by
Paul L. Hedren
for
Great Sioux War Orders of Battle
Cartography by Tom Jonas
Indicates a battle site
UTAH TERRITORY
DENVER
COLORA
Fort Cameron
MILES 0 50 100
KILOMETERS 0 50 100

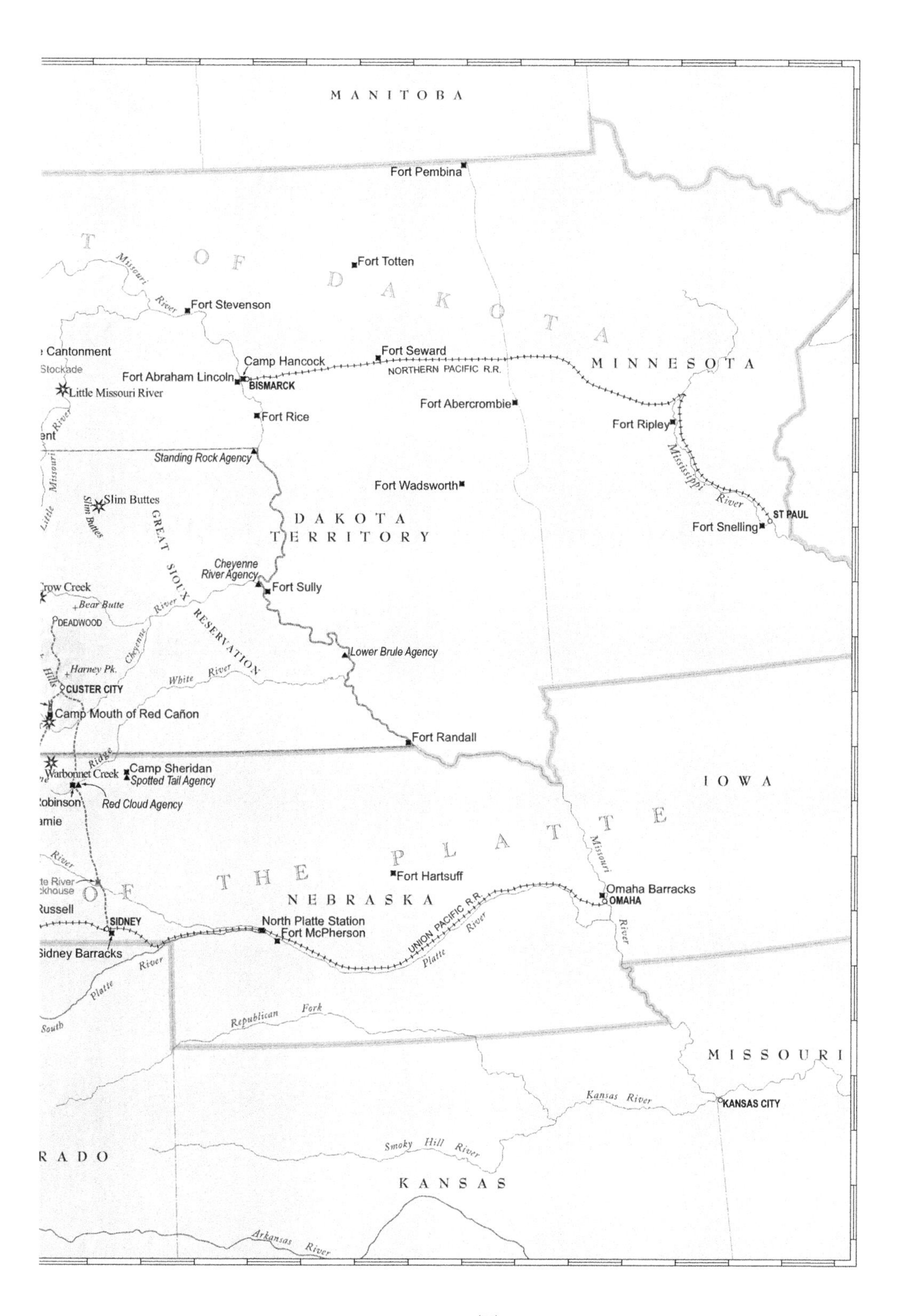
MANITOBA
Fort Pembina
Fort Totten
Missouri River
Fort Stevenson
DAKOTA
Cantonment
Stockade
Camp Hancock
Fort Seward
NORTHERN PACIFIC R.R.
MINNESOTA
Fort Abraham Lincoln
BISMARCK
Little Missouri River
Fort Abercrombie
Fort Rice
Fort Ripley
Standing Rock Agency
Mississippi River
Fort Wadsworth
Slim Buttes
GREAT SIOUX RESERVATION
DAKOTA TERRITORY
ST PAUL
Fort Snelling
Cheyenne River Agency
Fort Sully
Crow Creek
Bear Butte
DEADWOOD
Cheyenne River
Lower Brule Agency
Harney Pk.
White River
CUSTER CITY
Camp Mouth of Red Cañon
Fort Randall
Warbonnet Creek
Camp Sheridan
Spotted Tail Agency
IOWA
Red Cloud Agency
THE PLATTE
Missouri River
Fort Hartsuff
Omaha Barracks
OMAHA
NEBRASKA
UNION PACIFIC R.R.
SIDNEY
North Platte Station
Fort McPherson
Sidney Barracks
Platte River
South Platte River
Republican Fork
MISSOURI
Kansas River
KANSAS CITY
Smoky Hill River
KANSAS
Arkansas River

Part II

Deployments of the Great Sioux War

DEPLOYMENT NO. 1.

Fort Pease Relief

Montana, February 22–March 17, 1876

The small trader's and wolfer's stockade known as Fort Pease, established in June 1875 on the north bank of the Yellowstone River just below and opposite the mouth of the Big Horn River to engage in trade with the Crow Tribe and profit from the land, endured a nearly continual siege by Sioux warriors throughout its ten-month existence. Conditions were so dire by February 1876 that military assistance was sought. Brigadier General Alfred H. Terry, commanding the Department of Dakota, directed Major James S. Brisbin, Second Cavalry, commanding Fort Ellis near Bozeman, to relieve the small outpost. Leading the four Second Cavalry companies at his disposal—the regiment's renowned Montana Battalion—plus a Seventh Infantry detachment tending a 12-pounder Napoleon smooth-bore cannon, Brisbin's rescue party reached Fort Pease on March 4. He ushered nineteen weary survivors to Bozeman (Indians had killed six men and wounded eight during the siege). Ironically, the abandoned fort was not immediately destroyed. An American flag continued to fly aloft for many subsequent months, a curiosity often noted when other campaigners occupied the Yellowstone Valley that summer. Brisbin's movement was the first in Sioux Country in 1876. Although it was only tangentially related to the campaigns ahead, it served to expose these particular soldiers to a highly contested landscape and a foe exhibiting a unique, fearsome resolve in a conflict that came to be known as the Great Sioux War.[1]

---

[1] The primary archival sources for the Fort Pease Relief troop deployment are Second Cavalry Regimental Returns, February–March 1876; and Seventh Infantry Regimental Returns, February–March 1876. Useful secondary sources identifying support personnel and providing a general narrative include Edgar I. Stewart, "Major Brisbin's Relief of Fort Pease: A Prelude to the Bloody Little Big Horn Massacre," in Hedren, ed., *The Great Sioux War 1876–77*, 115–21; and Gray, *Custer's Last Campaign*, 117–19, 125–30.

Officers and Organization
Maj. James S. Brisbin, Second Cavalry, Commanding
2nd Lt. Charles B. Schofield, Second Cavalry, Battalion Adjutant
2nd Lt. Lovell H. Jerome, Second Cavalry, Chief of Scouts
Asst. Surg. and 1st Lt. Holmes O. Paulding

Second Cavalry

Co. F, Capt. George L. Tyler
2nd Lt. Charles F. Roe
Co. G, Capt. James N. Wheelan
1st Lt. Gustavus C. Doane
2nd Lt. Edward J. McClernand
Co. H, Capt. Edward Ball
1st Lt. James G. MacAdams
Co. L, Capt. Lewis Thompson
1st Lt. Samuel T. Hamilton

Seventh Infantry

Co. C (det.), 1st Lt. William Quinton

DEPLOYMENT NO. 2

Big Horn Expedition
Wyoming and Montana, March 1–26, 1876

Brigadier General George Crook of the Department of the Platte was the first of Lieutenant General Philip H. Sheridan's senior commanders to wage a formal campaign against the Sioux in 1876. Staged at Fort Fetterman, his Big Horn Expedition drew ten companies of cavalry, two of infantry, and medical support from posts in the near proximity of Fetterman. Despite the ferocity of the lingering winter, Crook's expedition marched north on March 1 following the well-scored Bozeman Trail, an avenue from another era but never erased. With Crook along as an observer, Colonel Joseph J. Reynolds, Third Cavalry, commanded, having organized the various companies into six battalions, each supported by packers and mules. The column was also supported by eighty-one wagons and four ambulances and was rationed for forty days.

On March 16 the expedition's scouts discovered an Indian village numbering some one hundred lodges nestled along the Powder River barely inside Montana. Drawing three cavalry battalions from the column, some three hundred men, Reynolds attacked the village at daybreak on March 17. Crook, meanwhile, retained the remaining battalions to shield the wagons and supplies from a counterattack that he supposed would occur.

Reynolds's attack on the village of Old Bear's Northern Cheyenne Indians was largely unsuccessful. After routing the camp, under heavy counterfire he unceremoniously withdrew, leaving behind two soldier casualties, inflicting few casualties himself, and losing the Indian horse herd, which he had meant to destroy. Crook was incensed by the poor showing of Reynolds and of captains Alexander Moore and Henry Noyes, who were all subsequently court-martialed. In the face of unrelenting bitter cold and with rations nearly exhausted, Crook returned to Fort Fetterman in failure. The expedition's lack of success was only the first of several army misfortunes to come. The battle brought the Northern Cheyennes, already steady Sioux allies for generations, directly into the Great Sioux War.[2]

Officers and Organization

Col. Joseph J. Reynolds, Third Cavalry, Commanding Expedition
Brig. Gen. George Crook, Department of the Platte
2nd Lt. Charles Morton, Third Cavalry, Expedition Adjutant (det. from Co. A)
Maj. Thaddeus H. Stanton, Pay Department, Chief of Scouts
1st Lt. George A. Drew, Third Cavalry, Regimental Quartermaster, AAQM and ACS
2nd Lt. John G. Bourke, Third Cavalry, ADC (det. from Co. D)
Asst. Surg. and Capt. Curtis E. Munn
AAS John V. Ridgely
AAS Charles R. Stevens
Thomas Moore, Master of Transportation

First Battalion

Co. M, Third Cavalry, Capt. Anson Mills, Commanding Battalion and Co.
1st Lt. Augustus C. Paul
Co. E, Third Cavalry, 1st Lt. John B. Johnson, Regimental Adjutant (det.)

[2] Primary archival sources for Crook's Big Horn Expedition include the Second Cavalry Regimental Return, March 1876; Third Cavalry Regimental Return, March 1876; and Fourth Infantry Regimental Return, March 1876. The standard primary narrative is Bourke, *On the Border with Crook*, chapters 14–16. The standard secondary account is Vaughn, *The Reynolds Campaign on Powder River*. Also useful is Robinson, *A Good Year to Die*, chapters 6–7.

Second Battalion

Co. A, Third Cavalry, Capt. William Hawley, Commanding Battalion and Co.
  1st Lt. Joseph Lawson
Co. D, Third Cavalry, 2nd Lt. William W. Robinson, Jr. (det. from Co. H)

Third Battalion

Co. I, Second Cavalry, Capt. Henry E. Noyes, Commanding Battalion and Co.
  1st Lt. Christopher T. Hall
Co. K, Second Cavalry, Capt. James Egan

Fourth Battalion

Co. A, Second Cavalry, Capt. Thomas B. Dewees, Commanding Battalion and Co.
  1st Lt. Martin E. O'Brien
  2nd Lt. Daniel C. Pearson
Co. B, Second Cavalry, Capt. James T. Peale
  2nd Lt. Frank U. Robinson

Fifth Battalion

Co. F, Third Cavalry, Capt. Alexander Moore, Commanding Battalion and Co.
  2nd Lt. Bainbridge Reynolds
Co. E, Second Cavalry, 1st Lt. William C. Rawolle (det. from Co. B)
  2nd Lt. Frederick W. Sibley

Sixth Battalion

Co. C, Fourth Infantry, Capt. Edwin M. Coates, Commanding Battalion and Co.
Co. I, Fourth Infantry, Capt. Samuel P. Ferris

DEPLOYMENT NO. 3

Powder River

Montana, March 16–18, 1876

Colonel Joseph J. Reynolds's unsuccessful engagement with Northern Cheyenne Indians on March 17 is discussed within the narrative of the encompassing Big Horn Expedition (Deployment No. 2) and more particularly analyzed in part III.

Officers and Organization

Col. Joseph J. Reynolds, Third Cavalry, Commanding
2nd Lt. Charles Morton, Third Cavalry, Expedition Adjutant
1st Lt. George A. Drew, Third Cavalry, Regimental Quartermaster (RQM), AAQM and ACS
Maj. Thaddeus H. Stanton, Pay Department, Chief of Scouts
2nd Lt. John G. Bourke, Third Cavalry, Asst. Chief of Scouts
Asst. Surg. and Capt. Curtis E. Munn

First Battalion

Co. M, Third Cavalry, Capt. Anson Mills, Commanding Battalion and Co.
1st Lt. Augustus C. Paul
Co. E, Third Cavalry, 1st Lt. John B. Johnson, Regimental Adjutant

Third Battalion

Co. I, Second Cavalry, Capt. Henry E. Noyes, Commanding Battalion and Co.
1st Lt. Christopher T. Hall
Co. K, Second Cavalry, Capt. James Egan

Fifth Battalion

Co. F, Third Cavalry, Capt. Alexander Moore, Commanding Battalion and Co.
2nd Lt. Bainbridge Reynolds
Co. E, Second Cavalry, 1st Lt. William C. Rawolle (wounded in action: WIA)
2nd Lt. Frederick W. Sibley

DEPLOYMENT NO. 4

Gibbon's Column

Montana, March 17–October 6, 1876

Five companies of Seventh Infantry initially commanded by a succession of senior company officers marched southeast from Fort Shaw, Montana, on March 17 bound for Fort Ellis. There they were joined by an additional infantry company and the Montana Battalion of Second Cavalry to form Gibbon's Column, also commonly known by historians as the Montana Column. Colonel John Gibbon, Seventh Infantry, assumed command on April 7. Gibbon's Column functioned independently at the onset of the Great Sioux War and was prepared to search for northern Indians, engage them if an opportunity allowed, and also generally contain the tribesmen south of the Yellowstone River.

Gibbon's march down the Yellowstone was initially uneventful. By April 21 he reached and partly reoccupied the abandoned Fort Pease below the mouth of the Big Horn River and from there dispatched troops for a gentle probe of the surroundings to the south. The most notable exploration was commanded by Captain Edward Ball, who on April 24 led companies F and H, Second Cavalry, up the Big Horn Valley to the site of old Fort C. F. Smith then east across the divide into the Little Big Horn River valley, north to near that river's mouth, and then across the eastern divide into the valley of Tullock's Creek. On Ball's eight-day foray, evidence of Indians was common, including a Sun Dance campsite from the previous summer, but as yet they encountered no warriors.

As Gibbon's Column continued east along the Yellowstone in May, the presence of Sioux Indians increased. The column passed campsites with fresh fire pits and even occasionally fended off warriors raiding on the cavalry horse herd or firing on mail couriers and the baggage train.

When the column passed the mouth of Rosebud Creek on May 16, Gibbon dispatched First Lieutenant James Bradley and a handful of soldier volunteers and Crow scouts south, seeking the location of a Sioux village detected by the Crows. Bradley crossed the divide into the Tongue River valley and observed evidence of a village nearby but did not specifically locate it. With this information in hand, Gibbon ordered his column to cross the Yellowstone and advance, but the turbulent river was a formidable obstacle. Chaos ensued in the water, with several horses drowning. Gibbon countermanded the order and regrouped on the north bank. For the next several days Sioux warriors were plainly observed watching the troops from the high bluffs along the south bank of the river, but Gibbon made no other attempt to cross and cautiously continued down the valley.

On June 8 Gibbon's advance came upon the steamboat *Far West* near Buffalo Rapids, the boat chiefly supporting Terry's advancing Dakota Column at that time. Gibbon and Terry met that evening and over the next several days merged their columns. From that time onward, Gibbon's Column functioned as a critical subset of Terry's operation until those two commands separated in early September.

Gibbon's Column returned to Fort Ellis on September 29, and the Seventh Infantry components reached Fort Shaw on October 6. The column once again traversed nearly the entire length of the Yellowstone on its return. Gibbon's men helped bury Custer, marched and countermarched throughout the Yellowstone Valley, but fired few rounds in actual combat. At its close, in the words of Doctor Holmes O. Paulding, "the expedition against hostile Sioux died a natural death."[3]

Officers and Organization

Capt. Charles C. Rawn, Seventh Infantry, Commanding (det., sick, 3-19)
Capt. Henry B. Freeman, Seventh Infantry, Commanding (3-19 to 4-7)
Col. John Gibbon, Seventh Infantry, Commanding (joined 4-7)
1st Lt. Levi F. Burnett, Seventh Infantry, Regimental Adjutant, AAAG (joined 4-7)
1st Lt. Joshua W. Jacobs, Seventh Infantry, RQM, AAQM, ACS (joined 4-7)
1st Lt. James H. Bradley, Seventh Infantry, Chief of Scouts (since 4-10)
2nd Lt. Edward J. McClernand, Second Cavalry, Acting Engineer Officer (since 4-8)
AAS C. H. Hart (det., sick, 3-19)
Asst. Surg. and 1st Lt. Holmes O. Paulding (joined 4-8)

Seventh Infantry Battalion

Co. A, Capt. William Logan
1st Lt. Charles A. Coolidge
2nd Lt. Francis Woodbridge (joined 8-17)
Co. B, Capt. Thaddeus S. Kirtland
1st Lt. James H. Bradley
2nd Lt. Charles A. Booth
Co. E (joined 4-8), Capt. Walter Clifford
1st Lt. William I. Reed (joined 8-17)
2nd Lt. George S. Young
Co. H, Capt. Henry B. Freeman
2nd Lt. Frederick M. H. Kendrick
Co. I, Capt. Charles C. Rawn (det., sick, 3-19)
1st Lt. William L. English (commanding co. since 3-19)
2nd Lt. Alfred B. Johnson
Co. K, Capt. James M. J. Sanno

[3] For the conformation of the Montana Column, see Seventh Infantry Regimental Returns, March–October 1876; and Second Cavalry Regimental Returns, March–October 1876. Other significant primary accounts abound, including notably Gibbon's "Last Summer's Expedition against the Sioux Indians and Its Great Catastrophe" and "Hunting Sitting Bull"; and Bradley's *The March of the Montana Column*. The most useful secondary account is Willert, *To the Edge of Darkness*. The quotation is from Willert, *March of the Columns*, 508.

Second Cavalry Battalion (joined 4-8)

Maj. James S. Brisbin, Commanding (joined 4-7)
2nd Lt. Charles B. Schofield, Battalion Adjutant
Co. F, 2nd Lt. Charles F. Roe
Co. G, Capt. James N. Wheelan
  1st Lt. Gustavus C. Doane
Co. H, Capt. Edward Ball
  1st Lt. James G. MacAdams
Co. L, Capt. Lewis Thompson (suicide, 7-19)
  1st Lt. Samuel T. Hamilton

Artillery Detachment

2nd Lt. Charles A. Woodruff, Seventh Infantry, Infantry Battalion Adjutant

DEPLOYMENT NO. 5

Black Hills Front

Wyoming, Dakota, and Nebraska, May 8, 1876–June 27, 1877

While the principal movements by Gibbon, Terry, and Crook in spring 1876 filled the Powder and Yellowstone River basins with troops seeking agency-averse Sioux and Northern Cheyennes, Sheridan also addressed different but equally explosive matters with the Indians on the southern margins of the Black Hills. Roads tying Sidney, Nebraska, and Cheyenne, Wyoming, with the Black Hills boomtowns and other roads linking Fort Laramie with Fort Fetterman and with Camps Robinson and Sheridan suffered increasing Indian predation and corresponding civilian and military casualties. This brought a substantial and prolonged army response that created, as it evolved, an intense and politically charged Southern or Black Hills Front in the Great Sioux War.

Initially Sheridan believed that the critical roads leading to the Black Hills could be made safe by distributing single cavalry and infantry companies along them. But early deployments from Fort Laramie and Camp Robinson were only marginally successful, especially when the assigned units further weakened campaign-diminished garrisons. A more logical solution was the use of infantry and cavalry from beyond the front-line posts, resulting in the deployment in early June of a Twenty-third Infantry company from Omaha Barracks and a Fourth Infantry company from Fort Bridger, each directed to establish summer camps on the Black Hills Road north of Fort Laramie. At the same time, eight companies of the Fifth Cavalry from posts in Kansas, Colorado, and the Indian Territory in the Department of the Missouri were ordered for duty on the Cheyenne–Black Hills Road at its intersection with the Powder River Trail, a heavily trafficked Indian route linking the Red Cloud and Spotted Tail agencies in Nebraska with the camps of Crazy Horse and Sitting Bull in the Powder and Yellowstone River country (see Deployment No. 10 below).

By mid-June these deployments noticeably curtailed but did not eliminate bloodshed on the Cheyenne–Black Hills Road. At the same time, Third Cavalry companies from Camp Robinson and Sidney Barracks ranged the Sidney–Black Hills Road and elements of a Twenty-third Infantry company from Sidney Barracks erected a two-story blockhouse on the north bank of the North Platte River in Nebraska, where the Sidney Road crossed.

Indian encounters on this Southern Front were never comparable in scale to those occurring in northern Wyoming and southeastern Montana but were notable locally. The Fifth Cavalry's successful interception of Northern Cheyenne Indians at Warbonnet Creek, Nebraska, on July 17, for instance, was heralded as the army's first battlefield success in the Great Sioux War after three consecutive reversals. Clashes with Indians on the Cheyenne River, Dakota, on the late evening of August 1 and on Richard Creek, Wyoming, on October 14 were also noteworthy.

When the Fifth Cavalry departed the Southern Front in late July to join Crook's Expedition, their stead was taken by battalions of Fourth Cavalry, commanded by Colonel Ranald S. Mackenzie, and Fourth Artillery, commanded by Captain Joseph B. Campbell, each staging from outlying encampments near Camp Robinson. While in Nebraska, these units protected roads, escorted military freight, and augmented the small Camp Robinson garrison until redirected to Crook's Powder River Expedition in November.

Scattered stock raiding on the northern margins of the Black Hills generated two army sorties to that locale in 1877, with responses originating from Camp Robinson and Fort Laramie in the Department of the

Platte, although the Black Hills were situated within the bounds of the Department of Dakota. A notable engagement occurred on Crow Creek, near Spearfish, Dakota, on February 23, 1877, when Company C, Third Cavalry, led by Second Lieutenant Joseph F. Cummings, routed the inhabitants of a small Indian camp and recovered stolen domestic stock, including more than 800 sheep. A three-company sortie in the summer of 1877 returned to Fort Laramie, "having seen no Indians" whatsoever. It was evident to all by then that the Great Sioux War was over.[4]

Officers and Organization

Cheyenne–Black Hills Road, Wyoming, May 8–October 31, 1876

Second Cavalry, May 8–October 31

Co. K, Capt. James Egan
2nd Lt. James N. Allison
AAS Charles V. Petteys (det. 5-29)

Ninth Infantry, May 8–29, July 5–31

Co. F, 1st Lt. William W. Rogers

Ninth Infantry, August 8–16

Co. E, Capt. Edwin Pollock
AAS Charles V. Petteys

Camp on White River, Nebraska, June 10–July 20, 1876

Ninth Infantry

Co. D, Capt. Michael J. Fitzgerald

[4] Primary archival sources documenting the varied small troop deployments on the Black Hills Front include Second Cavalry Regimental Returns, May–December 1876; Third Cavalry Regimental Returns, June 1876–August 1877; Fourth Cavalry Regimental Returns, August–November 1876; Fourth Infantry Regimental Returns, June 1876–June 1877; Ninth Infantry Regimental Returns, May–August 1876; Fourteenth Infantry Regimental Returns, December 1876–June 1877; Twenty-third Infantry Regimental Returns, June–December 1876; Fourth Artillery Regimental Returns, August–November 1876; Fort Laramie Post Returns, May–October 1876; and Personal History of Surgeons Serving in the Department of the Platte, 1876–77. A potpourri of primary source matter related to activities occurring during the war in the White River country and southern Black Hills is found in Jensen, *The Indian Interviews of Eli S. Ricker.* Among principal secondary accounts, see Hedren, *Fort Laramie in 1876;* Hedren, *First Scalp for Custer;* Hedren, "Garrisoning the Black Hills Road"; Buecker *Fort Robinson and the American West;* and Buecker, "'Can You Send Us Immediate Relief?'" The quotation is from "Record of Events," Third Cavalry Regimental Return, August 1877.

Camp on Sage Creek (aka Camp Hat Creek), Wyoming, June 12, 1876–June 27, 1877[5]

Twenty-third Infantry, June 12–December 13, 1876

Co. H, Capt. Richard I. Eskridge (joined 12-1)
1st Lt. George McM. Taylor
2nd Lt. Julius H. Pardee, Acting Adjutant and AAQM (det. 7-16)
AAS Abraham P. Frick (joined 7-22, det. 8-23)

Fourteenth Infantry, December 12, 1876–June 27, 1877

Co. I, 1st Lt. Charles A. Johnson (det. from Co. F until 1-77)
1st Lt. Frank Taylor (joined 1-77)
2nd Lt. Richard T. Yeatman

Camp Mouth of Red Cañon, Dakota, June 12, 1876–June 13, 1877

Fourth Infantry

Co. K, Capt. William S. Collier
1st Lt. Rufus P. Brown, Acting Adjutant and Quartermaster
2nd Lt. Lewis Merriam (joined 12-17)
AAS Richard M. Reynolds (contract annulled 1-31-77)
AAS Albert Chenoweth (joined 1-29-77; contract annulled 2-9)
AAS William T. Owsley (joined 3-3-77)

Sidney–Black Hills Road, Nebraska, June 26–September 27, 1876

Third Cavalry

Co. K, Capt. Gerald Russell

Sidney Bridge (North Platte), Nebraska, June 6–October 29, 1876

Third Cavalry

Co. H, Capt. Henry W. Wessells, Jr.
1st Lt. Royal E. Whitman (joined 8-5; det. 9-22)
2nd Lt. Charles L. Hammond (joined 9-27)
AAS Samuel S. Boyer (joined 8-14)

Twenty-third Infantry

Co. I (detachments)

[5] The terminal date given for the Sage Creek camp coincides with the departure of Company I, Fourteenth Infantry. The use of this small camp continued a while longer, but its wartime involvement had ended.

Camp Custer, Nebraska, August 11–November 1, 1876

Fourth Cavalry

Col. Ranald S. Mackenzie
1st Lt. Wentz C. Miller, Regimental Adjutant (resigned position 10-31)
2nd Lt. Joseph H. Dorst, Regimental Adjutant (since 10-31)
1st Lt. Henry W. Lawton, RQM (det. 11-30)
AAS Louis A. La Garde
AAS Albert Chenoweth
Co. B, Capt. Clarence Mauck
 1st Lt. Wentz C. Miller (since 10-31)
 2nd Lt. John W. Martin (det., sick, 11-20)
Co. D, Capt. John Lee
 1st Lt. Charles M. Callahan
 2nd Lt. Stanton A. Mason
Co. E, 1st Lt. David A. Irwin (det., sick, 11-8)
 2nd Lt. Henry H. Bellas
Co. F, Capt. Wirt Davis
 1st Lt. Frank L. Shoemaker
 2nd Lt. J. Wesley Rosenquest (joined 10-7)
 2nd Lt. Augustus C. Tyler (det. from Co. G)
Co. I, Capt. William C. Hemphill
 1st Lt. Otho W. Budd
Co. M, Capt. William O'Connell (det. 10-29)
 1st Lt. John A. McKinney (det. from Co. G)
 2nd Lt. Harrison G. Otis

Camp Canby, Nebraska, August 28–November 1, 1876

Fourth Artillery

Capt. Joseph B. Campbell, Commanding Battalion and Co. F
Asst. Surg. and 1st Lt. Curtis E. Price
Co. C, Capt. Harry C. Cushing
 1st Lt. Sydney W. Taylor
 2nd Lt. James M. Jones
Co. F, Capt. Joseph B. Campbell
 1st Lt. Albert S. Cummins (joined and Battalion Adjutant since 10-9)
 2nd Lt. William Crozier (joined 10-2)
Co. H, Capt. Frank G. Smith
 1st Lt. Harry R. Anderson (Battalion Adjutant since 8-16)
Co. K, 1st Lt. Walter Howe (commanding co. until 9-25)
 1st Lt. George G. Greenough (commanding co. since 9-25)
 2nd Lt. John T. French, Jr. (joined 10-20)
 2nd Lt. James L. Wilson (det. from Co. H since 8-29; det. 9-26)

Deadwood Expedition, Dakota, February 16–April 19, 1877

Third Cavalry

Capt. Peter D. Vroom, Commanding Battalion and Co. L
Co. B, 2nd Lt. James F. Simpson
Co. C, 2nd Lt. Joseph F. Cummings (det. from Co. L.)
Co. L, Capt. Peter D. Vroom
AAS Valentine T. McGillycuddy

Black Hills Expedition, Dakota, July 27–August 25, 1877

Third Cavalry

Co. A, 2nd Lt. George F. Chase
Co. G, Capt. Deane Monahan
Co. H, Capt. Henry W. Wessells, Jr.
2nd Lt. Charles L. Hammond (det. 8-21)

DEPLOYMENT NO. 6

Yellowstone River

Montana, May 14, 1876–September 1, 1877

The Yellowstone River was navigable some 485 river miles from its mouth at Fort Buford, Dakota, to beyond Pompey's Pillar, Montana, and flowed through the very heart of Sioux Country. Availing himself of a logical adjunct to his campaign, General Terry employed steamboats belonging to the Coulson Packet Line to support his 1876 field operation. Throughout the season, the heralded steamers *Far West* and *Josephine* delivered supplies to Yellowstone River staging camps and shuttled matériel and troops to and fro. The *Far West* carried desperately wounded cavalrymen from the Little Big Horn Battlefield to hospital care at Fort Abraham Lincoln. These boats also carried sutler goods relished by Terry's, Gibbon's, and Crook's troops when the columns converged on the river in August.

Before the 1876 navigation season ended, other boats owned or chartered by Coulson joined the campaign, including *Carroll*, *E. H. Durfee*, and *Yellowstone*. They delivered men of the Twenty-second and Fifth

Infantry regiments to reinforce Terry and also immense quantities of construction matériel, supplies, and forage destined for the envisioned Tongue River Cantonment, the sizable infantry outpost established in August at the mouth of the Tongue River.

The succession of small Yellowstone River supply depots established, abandoned, and occasionally reoccupied in 1876 reflected the changing needs of the campaign and the ever-shifting locations of troops. Depot garrisons also largely reflected the exigencies of the moment. The principal depot force engaged during the summer of 1876 was commanded by Major Orlando H. Moore, Sixth Infantry, from Fort Buford. Moore initially led three Sixth Infantry companies from Buford but also gained infantry companies and the Seventh Cavalry Band from Terry's Column after their arrival. The depot guard was an amorphous lot: companies, wholly or in part, were often detached to serve as boat guards, particularly when the *Far West* and *Josephine* navigated the Yellowstone above the mouth of the Powder in what was thought to be an exceedingly dangerous reach of river. Other infantry companies from Fort Buford also served as boat guards. No steamboat operating anywhere on the Yellowstone in 1876 and 1877 traveled without a military escort commanded by a commissioned officer.

A force led by Moore also engaged Sioux Indians at the then-abandoned Powder River Depot on August 2. This command was ferried downriver from the Rosebud Depot to collect seventy-five tons of oats stockpiled at the lower site. Moore found oat sacks opened and their contents strewn as well as the exhumed body of Private William George, a Little Big Horn casualty buried there in July when the *Far West* paused during the evacuation of the Seventh Cavalry's wounded. He also observed warriors on the bluffs south of the depot and scattered them with several well-placed shots from a twelve-pounder Napoleon. Before the oats could be rebagged and loaded, however, several of Moore's civilian scouts skirmished with those same warriors. One scout was killed. Artillery fire again dispersed the Indians.

River travel posed its own unique peril during the Great Sioux War. Indians fired on the steamer *Key West* on August 14 as it navigated the Missouri River four miles below Fort Buford, without casualty. Perhaps the same warriors exchanged fire on August 23 with the Sixth Infantry detachment led by First Lieutenant Nelson Bronson aboard the steamer *Yellowstone* on the Yellowstone River about midway between Fort Buford and Glendive Creek. In this instance, the warriors were well concealed in timber and dense undergrowth. One private was killed before the attackers withdrew and the steamer continued on its way.

As the 1876 Yellowstone navigation season drew to a close and waters receded, supplies destined for the new Tongue River Cantonment (eventually called Fort Keogh) traveled by boat, usually only as far as the mouth of Glendive Creek and later only to Fort Buford. Whether delivered by boat directly or by wagon from Fort Buford, these stores were stockpiled on the left bank at Glendive, well guarded by troops, and ushered to Tongue River Cantonment by wagon. As in the case of boat protection largely provided by Sixth Infantry companies and squads from Fort Buford, wagon protection between Buford and Glendive was provided in the same manner by troops from that garrison.

The Glendive Cantonment, amounting to a cluster of log huts, an earthen parapet, and mountainous tarpaulined barrels and crates, was garrisoned in mid-September by companies from the Seventeenth Infantry and Twenty-second Infantry. Portions of this command skirmished vigorously with Sioux Indians on several occasions in October 1876 (as noted in Deployment No. 15 below).

In July 1877 Terry helped locate a small freight transfer station on the Yellowstone several miles above the mouth of the Big Horn River to receive construction matériel, quartermaster and commissary goods, and other supplies bound for the new Big Horn Post, soon called Fort Custer. In the waning days of the Great Sioux War, Terry's Landing was garrisoned by a company of Eleventh Infantry drawn from Big Horn Post.[6]

---

[6] The deployment of Yellowstone River depot and steamboat guards is detailed in Sixth Infantry Regimental Returns, May 1876–September 1877; Eleventh Infantry Regimental Returns, July–September 1877; Seventeenth Infantry Regimental Returns, June–December 1876; Twenty-second Infantry Regimental Returns, September 1876–May 1877; and Seventh Cavalry Regimental Returns, June–September 1876. Moore's report on the Powder River Depot sortie appears in *Report of the Secretary of War, 1876*, 480–81. An important primary narrative documenting the Glendive Cantonment (largely the reminiscence of Major Alfred L. Hough, Twenty-second Infantry) is Athearn, "A Winter Campaign against the Sioux." The coming and going of the various river commands is best documented in several significant secondary sources, including Heski, "Soldiers, Surveyors, Steamboats & Stanley's Stockade"; Brown, "The Yellowstone Supply Depot"; Heski, "Camp Powell"; and Greene, *Yellowstone Command.* The story of steamboat support for the army during the Great Sioux War is well told by William E. Lass, "Steamboats on the Yellowstone," in Hedren, ed., *The Great Sioux War 1876–77*, 206–29. Grant Marsh's personal story and the boatmen's perspective on the Great Sioux War is developed in Hanson's timeless book *The Conquest of the Missouri.*

Officers and Organization

Stanley's Stockade, May 15–June 13, 1876

Sixth Infantry

Maj. Orlando H. Moore
Asst. Surg. and 1st Lt. George E. Lord
Co. C (until 6-10), Capt. James W. Powell
    2nd Lt. Bernard A. Byrne, AAQM and ACS
Co. D, Capt. Daniel H. Murdock
    1st Lt. Frederick W. Thibaut, Battalion Adjutant
Co. I (until 6-5), 2nd Lt. George B. Walker

Steamboat Escort Service, Far West, Josephine, E. H. Durfee, Yellowstone, Carroll, John M. Chambers, Benton, Silver Lake, *May 14–October 20, 1876*

Sixth Infantry

Co. B (*Far West*, 6-15 to 7-26), Capt. Stephen Baker
    1st Lt. John Carland
Co. D, 1st Lt. Frederick W. Thibaut
Co. E, Capt. Thomas Britton
    2nd Lt. Richard T. Jacob, Jr.
Co. G, 1st Lt. Nelson Bronson
    2nd Lt. Arthur L. Wagner
AAS J. A. McKinney (Fort Buford)

Seventeenth Infantry

Co. C (8-1 to 8-24) Capt. Malcolm McArthur
    1st Lt. Frank D. Garretty
    2nd Lt. James D. Nickerson
Co. G (7-1 to 7-20), Capt. Louis H. Sanger
    1st Lt. Josiah Chance
    2nd Lt. Henry P. Walker

Powder River Depot, June 6–July 21, 1876

Sixth Infantry

Major Orlando H. Moore (since 6-13)
Asst. Surg. and 1st Lt. George E. Lord (since 6-13, det. 6-15)
AAS Elbert J. Clark (since 6-13)
AAS Isaiah H. Ashton (since 6-13)

Co. C (since 6-11), Capt. James W. Powell
2nd Lt. Bernard A. Byrne, ACS
Co. D (since 6-13), Capt. Daniel H. Murdock
1st Lt. Frederick W. Thibaut
Co. I, 2nd Lt. George B. Walker

Seventeenth Infantry (since 6-11)

Co. C, Capt. Malcolm McArthur
1st Lt. Frank D. Garretty
2nd Lt. James D. Nickerson
Co. G (det. 7-1 to 7-20), Capt. Louis H. Sanger
1st Lt. Josiah Chance, Depot QM (since 6-14)
2nd Lt. Henry P. Walker

Seventh Cavalry (since 6-14)

Band

Rosebud Creek Depot, July 27–August 22, 1876

Major Orlando H. Moore, Sixth Infantry (until 8-5)
AAS Elbert J. Clark
AAS Isaiah H. Ashton

Sixth Infantry (until 8-5)

Co. B, Capt. Stephen Baker
1st Lt. John Carland
Co. C, Capt. James W. Powell
2nd Lt. Bernard A. Byrne
Co. D, Capt. Daniel H. Murdock
1st Lt. Frederick W. Thibaut
Co. I, 2nd Lt. George B. Walker

Seventeenth Infantry

Co. C (until 8-1), Capt. Malcolm McArthur
1st Lt. Frank D. Garretty
2nd Lt. James D. Nickerson
Co. G, Capt. Louis H. Sanger, Commanding Depot since 8-5
1st Lt. Josiah Chance
2nd Lt. Henry P. Walker (det. 8-3)

Seventh Cavalry (since 8-8)

Band
Co. E, 1st Lt. Charles C. De Rudio
Co. F, 1st Lt. Edwin P. Eckerson (det. from Co. D)
Co. I, 1st Lt. Luther R. Hare
Co. L

Powder River Depot Sortie, July 31–August 4, 1876

Maj. Orlando H. Moore, Sixth Infantry
AAS Henry R. Porter

Sixth Infantry

Co. D, Capt. Daniel H. Murdock
1st Lt. Frederick W. Thibaut
Co. I, 2nd Lt. George B. Walker

Seventeenth Infantry

Co. C, Capt. Malcolm McArthur
1st Lt. Frank D. Garretty
2nd Lt. James D. Nickerson

Artillery Detachment

2nd Lt. Charles A. Woodruff, Seventh Infantry

Powder River Depot, August 23–September 5, 1876

Seventeenth Infantry

Co. C, Capt. Malcolm McArthur
1st Lt. Frank D. Garretty, Depot Adjutant (since 8-28)
2nd Lt. James D. Nickerson
Co. G, Capt. Louis H. Sanger, Commanding Depot and Co.
1st Lt. Josiah Chance, Depot QM

Glendive Cantonment, September 5, 1876–May 25, 1877

Lt. Col. Elwell S. Otis, Twenty-second Infantry (det. 10-28)
Maj. Alfred L. Hough, Twenty-second Infantry (joined 9-24)
1st Lt. Oskaloosa M. Smith, Twenty-second Infantry, Battalion Adjutant (rejoined Co. H, 3-4-77)

1st Lt. William J. Campbell, Twenty-second Infantry, AAQM and ACS (det. from Co. K)
Asst. Surg. and 1st Lt. Paul R. Brown
AAS Charles T. Gibson

Seventeenth Infantry (until 12-5)
Co. C, Capt. Malcolm McArthur
1st Lt. Frank D. Garretty
2nd Lt. James D. Nickerson
Co. G, Capt. Louis H. Sanger
1st Lt. Josiah Chance

Twenty-second Infantry
Co. E (det. 9-11), Capt. Charles J. Dickey
Co. F (det. 9-11), 1st Lt. Cornelius C. Cusick
2nd Lt. Edward W. Casey
Co. G (det. 3-6-77), Capt. Charles W. Miner
1st Lt. Benjamin C. Lockwood
2nd Lt. William N. Dykman (resigned 10-1)
Co. H (det. 3-6-77), Capt. De Witt C. Poole
2nd Lt. Alfred C. Sharpe (joined 10-1)
Co. I, Capt. Francis Clarke
1st Lt. William Conway
2nd Lt. James E. Macklin (dismissed 10-18)
Co. K, Capt. Mott Hooton
2nd Lt. William H. Kell

Custer Creek Camp, September 18–October 1, 1876

Twenty-second Infantry
Co. E, Capt. Charles J. Dickey
Co. F, 1st Lt. Cornelius C. Cusick
2nd Lt. Edward W. Casey

Fort Buford–Glendive Cantonment Freight Escort Service, October 4, 1876–January 28, 1877

Sixth Infantry
Col. William B. Hazen (10-15 to 10-21, 12-18 to 12-29-76)
AAS J. A. McKinney (10-15 to 10-21, 12-18 to 12-29-76)
Co. C, 2nd Lt. Bernard A. Byrne

Co. D, Capt. Daniel H. Murdock
Co. E, Capt. Thomas Britton
2nd Lt. Richard T. Jacob, Jr.
Co. F, Capt. William W. Sanders
Co. G, 1st. Lt. Nelson Bronson
2nd Lt. Arthur L. Wagner
Co. I, 2nd Lt. George B. Walker

Steamboat Escort Service, Tidal Wave, Key West, Peninah, Fanchon, John M. Chambers, Rosebud, *May 30–September 1, 1877*[7]

Sixth Infantry
1st Lt. Charles G. Penney, RQM
Co. E, Capt. Thomas Britton
2nd Lt. Richard T. Jacob, Jr.
Co. G, 1st Lt. Nelson Bronson
2nd Lt. Arthur L. Wagner
Co. H, Capt. Jeremiah P. Schindel
2nd Lt. Charles L. Gurley

Terry's Landing, July 25–September 1, 1877[8]

Eleventh Infantry
Co. H, Capt. Erasmus C. Gilbreath
1st Lt. Ogden B. Read

DEPLOYMENT NO. 7

Terry's Column

Dakota and Montana, May 17–June 22, 1876

Brigadier General Alfred H. Terry led a column of cavalry and infantry westward from Fort Abraham Lincoln, Dakota, on May 17. Consisting

[7] The terminal date provided here is arbitrary and reflects the general cessation of hostilities associated with the Great Sioux War. Escort services continued.

[8] The use of this landing supporting Fort Custer continued beyond the span of the Great Sioux War.

of all twelve companies of the Seventh Cavalry drawn from posts across northern Dakota Territory and several laggardly companies withdrawn from Reconstruction duty in the South plus three infantry companies and three Gatling guns serviced by a small provisional infantry detachment, Terry's Column, also later known by historians as the Dakota Column, numbered 925 officers and men. Provisions for the command trailed in 150 wagons. Additional supplies were forwarded on the Missouri and Yellowstone rivers aboard the steamers *Far West* and *Josephine,* captained respectively by veteran boatmen Grant Marsh and Martin Coulson.

Often fighting weather on their westerly march, Terry's Column passed the rugged Little Missouri River badlands at month's end and in early June reached the Powder River, where they briefly encamped. Eager to locate Gibbon, Terry and two Seventh Cavalry companies advanced downriver, reaching the *Far West* at the mouth of the Powder on June 8. From there Terry steamed upriver to confer with his Montana column commander. Still oblivious to Crook's advance into northern Wyoming and the audacious Indian harassment encountered on Tongue River, Terry determined to advance his supply base from near Glendive Creek to the mouth of the Powder, where he would park his wagons, infantry, and Seventh Cavalry Band, and thereafter consolidate his column and Gibbon's column at the mouth of Rosebud Creek. En route, Terry intended to probe the Powder River upstream of his column's present camp and also the lower Tongue River to the Yellowstone. Command of this exploration was given to Major Marcus A. Reno, Seventh Cavalry, who subsequently confirmed news of an Indian trail leading up Rosebud Creek (this movement is detailed in Deployment No. 9 below).

Lieutenant Colonel George A. Custer, commanding the Seventh Cavalry that season, was given the opportunity to lead his regiment against the northern Indians supposed by Reno and others to be located west of Rosebud Creek. Terry expressed his intent to position Gibbon's force on the Big Horn or lower Little Big Horn River on or about June 26 and encouraged coordination while not firmly obliging Custer to act in concert. Custer demurred when offered Gibbon's four Second Cavalry companies and also declined the Gatling detachment.

Custer's departure on the afternoon of June 22 reduced the remaining operative force under Terry's command to his headquarters detachment, Gibbon's four cavalry and six infantry companies, and the Gatling guns. With the demise of Custer and the Seventh Cavalry in the Battle of the

Little Big Horn and the scattering of the column's small infantry component to the shifting supply camps on the Yellowstone, Terry's Column would not soon again be an effective combat force.[9]

Officers and Organization

Brig. Gen. Alfred H. Terry, Department of Dakota, Commanding
Capt. Edward W. Smith, Eighteenth Infantry, AAAG (det. 7-3)
Capt. Otho E. Michaelis, Ordnance Department, Chief Ordnance Officer
Capt. Robert P. Hughes, Third Infantry, ADC
1st Lt. Eugene B. Gibbs, Sixth Infantry, ADC
1st Lt. Henry J. Nowlan, Seventh Cavalry, RQM, AAQM
1st Lt. Edward Maguire, Corps of Engineers, Chief Engineer
2nd Lt. Richard E. Thompson, Sixth Infantry, ACS
2nd Lt. Charles A. Varnum, Seventh Cavalry, Commanding Indian Scouts
Asst. Surg. and Capt. John W. Williams, Chief Medical Officer
Asst. Surg. and 1st Lt. George E. Lord (joined 6-15)
AAS Elbert J. Clark, Cavalry, Left Wing (det. 6-15)
AAS James M. DeWolf, Cavalry, Right Wing
AAS Isaiah H. Ashton, Infantry (det. 6-15)
AAS Henry R. Porter, Headquarters and Battery

Seventh Cavalry

Lt. Col. George A. Custer
1st Lt. William W. Cooke, Regimental Adjutant, Commanding Non-Commissioned Staff and Band
Vet. Surg. Carl A. Stein
Band

Right Wing, Maj. Marcus A. Reno, Commanding

First Battalion, Capt. Myles W. Keogh, Commanding Battalion and Co. I

[9] Primary archival sources for Terry's Column include the Seventh Cavalry Regimental Returns, May–June 1876; Sixth Infantry Regimental Returns, May–June 1876; Seventeenth Infantry Regimental Returns, May–June 1876; and Twentieth Infantry Regimental Returns, May–June 1876. Most of the abundant diaries, reports, and other primary accounts of this movement are referenced in four useful secondary sources: Stewart, *Custer's Luck*; Willert, *Little Big Horn Diary*; Willert, *To the Edge of Darkness;* and Donovan, *A Terrible Glory*. The definitive history of Terry's Gatling gun detachment, with particulars on the provisional company assembled from the Twentieth Infantry, is Noyes, *The Guns "Long Hair" Left Behind.*

Co. B, Capt. Thomas M. McDougall
2nd Lt. Benjamin H. Hodgson, Wing Adjutant
Co. C, Capt. Thomas W. Custer
2nd Lt. Henry M. Harrington
Co. I, Capt. Myles W. Keogh
1st Lt. James E. Porter

Second Battalion, Capt. George W. Yates, Commanding Battalion and Co. F

Co. E, 1st Lt. Algernon E. Smith (det. from Co. A)
2nd Lt. James G. Sturgis (det. from Co. M)
Co. F, Capt. George W. Yates
2nd Lt. William Van W. Reily
Co. L, 1st Lt. James Calhoun (det. from Co. C)
2nd Lt. John J. Crittenden, Twentieth Infantry (det. from Co. G)

Left Wing, Capt. Frederick W. Benteen, Commanding Left Wing and Co. H

Third Battalion, Capt. Thomas B. Weir, Commanding Battalion and Co. D

Co. A, Capt. Myles Moylan
1st Lt. Charles C. De Rudio, Wing Adjutant (det. from Co. E)
Co. D, Capt. Thomas B. Weir
2nd Lt. Winfield S. Edgerly
Co. H, Capt. Frederick W. Benteen
1st Lt. Francis M. Gibson

Fourth Battalion, Capt. Thomas H. French, Commanding Battalion and Co. M

Co. G, 1st Lt. Donald McIntosh
2nd Lt. George D. Wallace
Co. K, 1st Lt. Edward S. Godfrey
2nd Lt. Luther R. Hare
Co. M, Capt. Thomas H. French
1st Lt. Edward G. Mathey

Infantry Battalion

Capt. Louis H. Sanger, Seventeenth Infantry, Commanding Battalion and Co. G

Sixth Infantry (det. 6-14)
Co. B, Capt. Stephen Baker
1st Lt. John Carland

Seventeenth Infantry (det. 6-14)
Co. C, Capt. Malcolm McArthur
1st Lt. Frank D. Garretty
2nd Lt. James D. Nickerson
Co. G, Capt. Louis H. Sanger
1st Lt. Josiah Chance, Infantry Battalion Adjutant
2nd Lt. Henry P. Walker

Gatling Gun Battery
Twentieth Infantry
Provisional Company, 2nd Lt. William H. Low, Jr., Co. C, Commanding
2nd Lt. Frank X. Kinzie, Co. F

DEPLOYMENT NO. 8

Big Horn and Yellowstone Expedition I
Wyoming and Montana, May 29–July 12, 1876

Crook's second movement into Sioux Country, formally christened the Big Horn and Yellowstone Expedition, brought to the field troops from throughout the vast Department of the Platte and also returned cavalry that had participated in the Big Horn Expedition in March. Again organized at Fort Fetterman, the column tallied fifteen cavalry and five infantry companies totaling nearly eleven hundred men, parceled into sizable battalions and a cavalry brigade, and supported by 120 wagons and 1,000 pack mules.

After establishing a base camp on Goose Creek, Wyoming, a small tributary of the Tongue River in northern Wyoming, Crook's force continued northward, reaching the Tongue on June 7. Two days later hundreds of Indians appeared there on the river bluffs opposite the mouth of Prairie Dog Creek and overlooking Crook's camp and rained annoying but not particularly lethal fire on the soldiers. The Indians' appearance was daring, however, and required the deployment of four cavalry companies to disperse.

The expedition continued its northerly course, crossing Tongue River and advancing onto the headlands of Rosebud Creek, Montana. As the command prepared morning coffee there on June 17, more than 750 Sioux Indians led by Crazy Horse attacked suddenly and with astonishing determination. The Battle of the Rosebud lasted six hours, with parries and thrusts occurring on an undulating prairie and timber-speckled battlefield several miles wide and long. Crook quickly took high ground on the field and masterfully commanded his troops, deflecting repeated Indian attacks from all quarters. Convinced that an Indian village was downstream, in the midst of the engagement he ordered a cavalry battalion led by Captain Anson Mills to advance northward. He believed that the warriors would withdraw when noncombatants were threatened and intended to support this movement immediately thereafter.

The Sioux could not be turned, however, and Crook recalled Mills, who returned to the battlefield from a different direction, opportunely behind the attacking warriors. When pressed from the rear, the Indians summarily withdrew and the battle ended. Crook held the field and claimed a victory. But his casualties numbered nine killed and twenty-one wounded, including an officer, and his command had expended some 25,000 rounds of ammunition by one account. Owing to the needs of the wounded and depleted carbine and rifle ammunition and general provisions, Crook abandoned his advance and returned to Goose Creek. From there he ushered the wounded to medical care at Fort Fetterman, escorted by companies C and F, Ninth Infantry, commanded by Major Alexander Chambers.

On July 6 Crook dispatched Second Lieutenant Frederick W. Sibley and thirty scouts to the Crow Indian Agency to enlist additional Indian allies for the column. Two days into their advance up the Bozeman Trail, Sibley's small force chanced onto Sioux and Northern Cheyennes encamped in the northern Big Horn Mountains following the Little Big Horn Battle. This triggered a running fight into the Big Horns as Sibley's force scrambled to evade a vigorous pursuit. Sibley's circuitous escape took him high into the mountains. He returned to Crook's Goose Creek camp on July 9, safe but not having reached Crow Agency.

At Goose Creek, Crook fretted over his predicament and the astounding aggressiveness of these northern Indians, who had now boldly parried with his troops three times. He immediately called for five additional companies of infantry. After learning that Sheridan had deployed eight companies of Fifth Cavalry to secure the Black Hills Road, he requested those troops as well. Crook's lament in a private letter to Sheridan in late July captured his malaise. "I am at a loss what to do," he confessed.[10]

Officers and Organization

Brig. Gen. George Crook, Department of the Platte, Commanding
Capt. Azor H. Nickerson, Twenty-third Infantry, ADC and AAAG (det. 6- 21)
Capt. William S. Stanton, Corps of Engineers, Chief Engineer
Capt. John V. Furey, Quartermaster Department, Chief Quartermaster
1st Lt. John W. Bubb, Fourth Infantry, Chief Commissary of Subsistence
Capt. George M. Randall, Twenty-third Infantry, Chief of Scouts
1st Lt. John G. Bourke, Third Cavalry, ADC and AAAG (since 6-21)
2nd Lt. Walter S. Schuyler, Fifth Cavalry, ADC (joined 6-23)
Maj. William Arthur, Pay Department (joined 7-13)
Asst. Surg. and Capt. Albert Hartsuff, Medical Director (Surg. and Maj., 6-26)
Asst. Surg. and Capt. Julius H. Patzki
AAS Charles R. Stevens
Thomas Moore, Chief of Pack Train
Charles Russell, Chief of Wagon Train

Cavalry Brigade

Lt. Col. William B. Royall, Third Cavalry, Commanding
2nd Lt. Henry R. Lemly, Third Cavalry, Cavalry Battalion Adjutant
2nd Lt. Charles Morton, Third Cavalry, Battalion AAQM and Acting Regimental Adjutant

Second Cavalry Battalion

Capt. Henry E. Noyes, Commanding Battalion and Co. I

[10] Primary archival sources for the composition of the first iteration of George Crook's Big Horn and Yellowstone Expedition include Second Cavalry Regimental Returns, May–August 1876; Third Cavalry Regimental Returns, May–August 1876; Fourth Infantry Regimental Returns, May–August 1876; and Ninth Infantry Regimental Returns, May–August 1876. Of the rich array of diaries, narratives, and other primary materials documenting this expedition (recognized in the recommended secondary literature noted below), John Bourke's diaries are indispensable. See Robinson, *The Diaries of John Gregory Bourke, Volume One.* A primary narrative detailing the Sibley Scout is Baptiste Pourier, "Sibley's Ordeal in the Big Horns, July 6–9, 1876," in Greene, ed., *Battles and Skirmishes of the Great Sioux War,* 63–78. Among secondary accounts detailing the organization and initial movement of this expedition, three books stand out: Vaughn, *With Crook at the Rosebud;* Mangum, *Battle of the Rosebud;* and Hedren, *Fort Laramie in 1876.* A useful secondary account of the Sibley Scout is Willert, "The Sibley Scout." Crook's quotation is from King, "General Crook at Camp Cloud Peak," 126.

Co. A, Capt. Thomas B. Dewees
1st Lt. Martin E. O'Brien (joined 7-12)
2nd Lt. Daniel C. Pearson
Co. B, 1st Lt. William C. Rawolle
Co. D, 1st Lt. Samuel M. Swigert
2nd Lt. Henry D. Huntington
Co. E, Capt. Elijah R. Wells
2nd Lt. Frederick W. Sibley
Co. I, Capt. Henry E. Noyes
2nd Lt. Frederick W. Kingsbury

Third Cavalry Battalion

Maj. Andrew W. Evans, Commanding
Co. A, 1st Lt. Joseph Lawson
Co. B, Capt. Charles Meinhold
2nd Lt. James F. Simpson (det. 6-19)
Co. C, Capt. Frederick Van Vliet
1st Lt. Adolphus H. Von Luettwitz (det. 6-12)
Co. D, Capt. Guy V. Henry (WIA, 6-17; det. 6-21)
2nd Lt. James F. Simpson (det. from Co. B since 6-19)
Co. E, Capt. Alexander Sutorius (relinquished command 7-20)
1st Lt. Adolphus H. Von Luettwitz (det. from Co. C since 6-12)
Co. F, 2nd Lt. Bainbridge Reynolds
Co. G, 1st Lt. Emmet Crawford
Co. I, Capt. William H. Andrews
1st Lt. Albert D. King (joined 7-14)
2nd Lt. James E. H. Foster
Co. L, Capt. Peter D. Vroom
2nd Lt. George F. Chase
Co. M, Capt. Anson Mills
1st Lt. Augustus C. Paul
2nd Lt. Frederick Schwatka

Infantry Battalion

Maj. Alexander Chambers, Fourth Infantry, Commanding
1st Lt. Henry Seton, Fourth Infantry, Battalion Adjutant (det. 6-21)
1st Lt. Thaddeus H. Capron, Ninth Infantry, Battalion Adjutant (since 7-4)

Fourth Infantry

Co. D, Capt. Avery B. Cain
Co. F, Capt. Gerhard L. Luhn

Ninth Infantry

Co. C, Capt. Samuel Munson
1st Lt. Thaddeus H. Capron (det. 7-4)
2nd Lt. Hayden De Lany (joined 6-28)
Co. G, Capt. Thomas B. Burrowes
1st Lt. William L. Carpenter
Co. H, Capt. Andrew S. Burt
2nd Lt. Edgar B. Robertson

Medicine Bow Freight Escort, Wyoming, June 25–July 13, 1876

Fourth Infantry

Co. G, Capt. William H. Powell
2nd Lt. Albert B. Crittenden

DEPLOYMENT NO. 9

Reno Scout

Montana, June 10–18, 1876

Major Marcus Reno led six companies of the Seventh Cavalry on an exploration of the Powder and Tongue rivers, departing Terry's camp on June 10. Finding a fresh Indian trail leading westward across the divide from the Tongue into the valley of Rosebud Creek, Reno followed despite instruction from Terry to explore the lower Tongue carefully. The trail led to freshly abandoned Indian camps in the Rosebud Valley. On June 17, while General Crook fought Sioux warriors on the Rosebud barely forty miles upstream, Reno turned for the Yellowstone. His report of fresh camps and a significant trail heading up Rosebud Creek was not altogether news to Terry or Gibbon, Gibbon's own scouts also having observed such signs. But this put into motion a general plan for entrapping the Indians, perhaps on Rosebud Creek or more likely in the next drainage west, that of the Little Big Horn River.[11]

[11] Willert's *Little Big Horn Diary* and *To the Edge of Darkness* carefully chronicle the Reno Scout. Also useful are Hardorff, "The Reno Scout"; and Willert, "Another Look at the Reno Scout."

OFFICERS AND ORGANIZATION

Seventh Cavalry

Maj. Marcus A. Reno, Commanding
2nd Lt. Benjamin H. Hodgson, Battalion Adjutant
AAS Henry R. Porter
AAS James M. DeWolf
Co. B, Capt. Thomas M. McDougall
Co. C, 2nd Lt. Henry M. Harrington
Co. E, 1st Lt. Algernon E. Smith
2nd Lt. James G. Sturgis
Co. F, Capt. George W. Yates
2nd Lt. William Van W. Reily
Co. I, Capt. Myles W. Keogh
1st Lt. James E. Porter
Co. L, 1st Lt. James Calhoun
2nd Lt. John J. Crittenden, Twentieth Infantry

Gatling Gun, 2nd Lt. Frank X. Kinzie, Twentieth Infantry

DEPLOYMENT NO. 10

Powder River Trail
Wyoming and Nebraska, June 22–July 23, 1876

Sheridan's reassignment of the Fifth Cavalry in mid-June from posts in the Department of the Missouri to field service north of Fort Laramie acknowledged recurring bloodletting on the Black Hills Road. Attacks were especially common where it intersected with the well-worn Powder River Trail linking the Sioux agencies in Nebraska with the buffalo country of the Powder River Basin in Wyoming and Montana and, in 1876, the welcoming camps of Crazy Horse and Sitting Bull.

For the most part, the Fifth's month-long service in eastern Wyoming was uneventful, while news from the north of Indian battles at Rosebud Creek and Little Big Horn River made clear the Sioux War's growing intensity elsewhere. In mid-July Merritt was ordered to join Crook in northern Wyoming. While en route to Fort Laramie to resupply, he learned of the flight of some eight hundred Northern Cheyenne Indians from the Red Cloud Agency, supposedly intent on joining Crazy Horse. Determined to intercept these Indians, Merritt backtracked his column to the infantry camp in the Hat Creek Breaks, where he turned east and followed the Powder River Trail to Warbonnet Creek in northwestern Nebraska. There at daybreak on July 17 his troops clashed with scouts from the Indian camp. The Fifth's scout and accomplished showman William F. "Buffalo Bill" Cody killed one of those Indians, Yellow Hair, and scalped him, proclaiming it the "first scalp for Custer." The other scouts and villagers scurried back to Red Cloud Agency, pushed all the while by the cavalry. Merritt gained for Sheridan's Army a first, if modest, battlefield accomplishment at Warbonnet Creek in this still unfolding, dismal war.[12]

Officers and Organization

Fifth Cavalry

Col. Wesley Merritt (joined 7-1)
Lt. Col. Eugene A. Carr
Maj. John J. Upham
1st Lt. William C. Forbush, Regimental Adjutant and AAAG District of the Black Hills
Maj. Thaddeus H. Stanton, Pay Department
1st Lt. William P. Hall, AAQM
2nd Lt. Robert H. Young, Fourth Infantry, ADC (joined 7-10)
2nd Lt. Julius H. Pardee, Twenty-third Infantry, ADC (joined 7-16)
AAS Junius L. Powell
Co. A, Capt. Robert P. Wilson (det. 7-15)
  2nd Lt. Robert London (det. from Co. I, 7-15 to 25)
Co. B, Capt. Robert H. Montgomery
Co. C, Capt. Emil Adam (joined 7-7)
  2nd Lt. Edward L. Keyes
Co. D, Capt. Samuel S. Sumner
Co. G, Capt. Edward M. Hayes
  2nd Lt. Hoel S. Bishop
Co. I, Capt. Sanford C. Kellogg
  1st Lt. Bernard Reilly, Jr.
  2nd Lt. Robert London

[12] This deployment is accounted for in Fifth Cavalry Regimental Returns, June–July 1876. A primary narrative of considerable importance is Charles King, *Campaigning with Crook*. The principal secondary account of the Warbonnet action is Hedren, *First Scalp for Custer*.

Co. K, Capt. Julius W. Mason (Maj., Third Cavalry, 7-1)
1st Lt. Charles King
Co. M, Capt. Edward H. Leib
2nd Lt. Charles H. Watts (det. 7-7)

DEPLOYMENT NO. 11

Little Big Horn River

Montana, June 25–26, 1876

Custer's departure from Terry's and Gibbon's Yellowstone River camp on the afternoon of June 22 stripped from that consolidated command its principal combat arm, the Seventh Cavalry. The segmenting of the Seventh into wings and battalions that had characterized its organization from Fort Abraham Lincoln westward to the Yellowstone was abandoned, and the unit initially functioned as twelve independent companies under Custer's direct command. The Seventh was provisioned for fifteen days, with grain, ammunition, and rations carried by mules.

Custer attempted a steady pace up Rosebud Creek, but the width of the valley constricted almost immediately and the creek wound exasperatingly across its floor, impeding speed. Soon the enormity of the successive abandoned Indian camps along the creek aroused both curiosity and suspicion and duly impressed on the men of the Seventh Cavalry that this valley belonged to the Sioux.

By June 24 Custer had advanced more than fifty miles up the Rosebud, all the while passing abandoned Indian village sites, including a vast and recent Sun Dance camp. The Indians' lodge pole and pony trail continued to swell and was fresh. Near sunset, Custer's scouts reported that the broad trail veered westward across the divide into the Little Big Horn Valley. The column paused briefly at sunset, but Custer returned his scouts to the trail, hoping to locate the village ahead. Assuming that he was closing on the tribesmen, after a brief pause Custer led a night march that brought his command nearer to the divide separating the Rosebud and Little Big Horn.

Just after daybreak on June 25 a courier from the scouts returned to the column, bearing news that an Indian village had indeed been located in the Little Big Horn Valley. Custer joined his scouts on the divide at a location known as the Crow's Nest, but his view of alleged campfire smoke and an immense horse herd some fifteen miles ahead was obscured by morning haze. Intending to rest the column that day and attack on the following morning, Custer heard disquieting reports that his force had been discovered by opposing scouts and by warriors on the Seventh's back trail, who were seen rummaging through provisions lost during the night march.

Fearing that the element of surprise was now compromised and that the villagers would flee, Custer determined to attack the camp immediately. After crossing the divide and gaining a tributary of the Little Big Horn, and again plainly following a broad trail of lodge pole and pony tracks, Custer commenced deploying his troops for battle. Captain Frederick Benteen and Companies D, H, and K were diverted obliquely to the left, ostensibly to intercept any Indians attempting to escape or flee southward. Custer ordered Major Reno and Companies A, G, and M to cross the Little Big Horn and attack the upper end of the encampment. Custer, meanwhile, led Companies C, E, F, I, and L to a presumed attack on the village at its flank or lower end, while Captain Thomas McDougall and Company B escorted the mule train and followed all of the battalions.

The battle opened as planned. The village was surprised and had not been forewarned, but its immense size proved immediately overwhelming. Warriors easily halted Reno's attack and quickly deflected his companies, first to a dense copse of cottonwoods along the river and then to the high bluffs on the east side. Custer observed Reno's attack before its initial repulse and advanced northward into a drainage known as Medicine Tail Coulee, where he began deploying his five companies, sending several into the coulee and toward the river while retaining the others on high ground. By now Reno's force was in the timber, and this second threat to the village brought almost all Indian combatants northward to meet Custer, who was quickly put on the defensive and defeated in detail in a chaotic struggle that may have lasted an hour.

By late afternoon Benteen's and McDougall's still-unengaged companies joined Reno on the bluffs about five miles south of where Custer engaged. Pandemonium reigned. Some heard firing from Custer's sector and attempted a movement northward, only to be repulsed by aggressive warriors who swarmed south after finishing Custer. Soon the survivors entrenched and fought desperately in the closing daylight of June 25 and through most of the twenty-sixth, until the abrupt and unexplained disengagement of the tribesmen late that afternoon. The Indians knew of Terry's and Gibbon's approach from down valley on June 26 as planned, though Reno and Benteen as yet did not.

On June 27 the Seventh's survivors learned of Custer's death and the next day joined the relief force in burying some 260 casualties where they had fallen and then rather unceremoniously abandoned the field. The demoralized column ushered forty-one wounded troopers to the *Far West*, which, at Terry's urging, had pushed up the Big Horn River to the mouth of the Little Big Horn. From there the wounded were carried downriver to medical care at Fort Abraham Lincoln, below Bismarck. Couriers, meanwhile, hurried the news of the Battle of the Little Big Horn to the nearest telegraph, in Bozeman. From there the horrific news of Custer's defeat reached the nation as its citizens enjoyed the Centennial celebration.

Terry's devastated and thoroughly demoralized command remained on the Yellowstone in the proximity of Fort Pease through nearly all of July. The Battle of the Little Big Horn was the greatest army disaster in the Great Sioux War. After setbacks at Powder River, Rosebud Creek, and now Little Big Horn, Sheridan could only regroup and forge on.[13]

Officers and Organization

Seventh Cavalry

Lt. Col. George A. Custer, Seventh Cavalry, Commanding Regiment and Battalion
1st Lt. William W. Cooke, Regimental Adjutant

Benteen Battalion, Capt. Frederick W. Benteen, Commanding Battalion and Co. H.

Co. D, Capt. Thomas B. Weir
2nd Lt. Winfield S. Edgerly

[13] The basic deployment of the Seventh Cavalry at the Little Big Horn is provided in the Seventh Cavalry Regimental Return, June 1876. The two-day engagement was exceedingly complex, with nuanced movements and conflicting participant understandings and interpretations of what occurred. Much is known and as much unknown. An extraordinary body of primary source material exists, not the least being transcripts from Reno's Court of Inquiry in 1879: see Nichols, *Reno Court of Inquiry*. Four secondary accounts utilizing these primary sources exceptionally well are Stewart, *Custer's Luck;* Sklenar, *To Hell with Honor;* Liddic, *Vanishing Victory;* and Donovan, *A Terrible Glory*. A unique account of the Little Big Horn battle developed from Indian sources is Michno, *Lakota Noon*.

Co. H, Capt. Frederick W. Benteen (WIA)
1st Lt. Francis M. Gibson
Co. K, 1st Lt. Edward S. Godfrey

Reno Battalion, Maj. Marcus A. Reno

2nd Lt. Benjamin H. Hodgson, Battalion Adjutant (killed in action: KIA)
AAS James M. DeWolf (KIA)
AAS Henry R. Porter
Co. A, Capt. Myles Moylan
1st Lt. Charles C. De Rudio
Co. G, 1st Lt. Donald McIntosh (KIA)
2nd Lt. George D. Wallace
Co. M, Capt. Thomas H. French
Indian Scouts, 2nd Lt. Charles A. Varnum (WIA)
2nd Lt. Luther R. Hare

Custer Battalion, Lt. Col. George A. Custer (KIA)

1st Lt. William W. Cooke, Regimental Adjutant (KIA)
Asst. Surg. and 1st Lt. George E. Lord, Chief Medical Officer (KIA)
Co. C, Capt. Thomas W. Custer (KIA)
2nd Lt. Henry M. Harrington (KIA)
Co. E, 1st Lt. Algernon E. Smith (KIA)
2nd Lt. James G. Sturgis (KIA)
Co. F, Capt. George W. Yates (KIA)
2nd Lt. William Van W. Reily (KIA)
Co. I, Capt. Myles W. Keogh (KIA)
1st Lt. James E. Porter (KIA)
Co. L, 1st Lt. James Calhoun (KIA)
2nd Lt. John J. Crittenden, Twentieth Infantry (KIA)

Pack Train, 1st Lt. Edward G. Mathey
Co. B, Capt. Thomas M. McDougall

DEPLOYMENT NO. 12

Big Horn and Yellowstone Expedition II

Wyoming, Montana, Dakota, and Nebraska, August 5–October 24, 1876

While the name "Big Horn and Yellowstone Expedition" survived, the expedition barely resembled its former self when General Crook finally marched north from Camp Cloud Peak, Wyoming, on August 5. Several key staff officers had departed the command, several others remained behind at the wagon corral, and the medical staff was bolstered substantially. Most critically, the column was reinforced with the arrival of five companies of infantry, drawn largely from the Fourteenth Regiment, and ten companies of the Fifth Cavalry, eight of which had been redirected from service on the Black Hills Road following their own spirited encounter with Northern Cheyenne Indians at Warbonnet Creek, Nebraska.

Notably serving with the Fifth Cavalry this season were its colonel, Wesley Merritt; its lieutenant colonel, Eugene A. Carr; and two majors, John Upham and Julius Mason. Mason was a troop captain with the Fifth until July 1, when, by seniority, he was promoted major, Third Cavalry, but permitted to serve with his former regiment until the close of the current campaign. The Fifth Cavalry was also noted for having each of its company captains present for duty, a distinction nearly unique among all regiments and portions of regiments engaged in the Great Sioux War and a matter of considerable pride in the Fifth ever after.

With a general officer and nine field-grade officers among twenty-five cavalry and ten infantry companies of the reorganized Big Horn and Yellowstone Expedition, the column's structure was substantially overhauled into one of the most complex organizations during the Great Sioux War. Colonel Merritt commanded a vastly expanded Cavalry Brigade consisting of battalions of the Second and Third Cavalry led by Lieutenant Colonel William B. Royall, Third Cavalry, and Fifth Cavalry, commanded by its lieutenant colonel, Eugene A. Carr. A ten-company Infantry Battalion was again commanded by Major Alexander Chambers, Fourth Infantry, and segmented into three components, reflecting the consolidated companies of the participating regiments (Fourth, Ninth, and Fourteenth).

The expedition's quartermaster, Captain John V. Furey, remained at Goose Creek from August 4 until his recall by Crook in mid-September.

Furey oversaw a force of some two hundred civilian teamsters, wagonmasters, and other irregulars who had freighted for the original and reinforced expedition and Fifth Cavalry. In Furey's corral were hundreds of wagons, now mostly laden with tentage and nonessential clothing and camp gear, which Crook had ordered shed from the column. The expedition itself was provisioned for fifteen days and anticipated being supplemented from Terry's stocks on the Yellowstone.

Crook's and Terry's columns met on August 10 on Rosebud Creek some thirty-six miles above its mouth and marched together for several days, initially exploring portions of the Tongue and Powder rivers en route to the Yellowstone, where they camped for one week. Terry's column, too, had been significantly reinforced with the arrival of elements from the Twenty-second and Fifth Infantry regiments. Crook particularly quietly chafed at the cumbersomeness of the combined operation and the growing obscurity of the Indian trail. Perhaps more importantly, Terry was his senior and they now operated in the Department of Dakota, outside of Crook's jurisdiction.

Crook separated from Terry on August 24 and marched up the Powder River for two days until again crossing the shadowy Indian trail that the combined commands had followed from the Rosebud. Crook tracked that faint trail eastward into Dakota and across the Little Missouri Badlands to the Heart River. There he fatefully turned south. The column's fifteen-day resupply of rations was already nearly exhausted or spoiled by continuous rains. Crook considered but rejected returning to the Yellowstone or advancing eastward to Fort Abraham Lincoln, opting instead to strike for Camp Robinson in his own department, an estimated eleven-day march south, and traveling by way of the Black Hills settlements, perhaps seven days away.

Crook's command was consuming half-rations by September 5. By the seventh its stock of hard bread was fully exhausted, and the men largely subsisted by eating trail-weary horses and mules. Late that day, Crook ordered First Lieutenant John W. Bubb, the expedition's commissary officer, and Captain Anson Mills and 150 selected men from the Third Cavalry, all mounted on the column's strongest horses, forward to Deadwood to purchase supplies for the famished command. En route, Mills chanced on a small Sioux village nestled in the Slim Buttes, some seventy miles north of the Black Hills. Mills attacked the camp at dawn on September 9. Alerted to the action, Crook hurried his weary force to the scene and continued the fight into the next day. The village belonged to American

Horse, a Miniconjou Sioux. He was killed, but his warriors were substantially reinforced from nearby villages and refused to withdraw fully.

Despite having captured provisions in the Indian camp, the worsening condition of the column, exacerbated now by thirteen wounded enlisted men and one officer, obliged Crook's continued advance to Deadwood. Provisions and live cattle from the mining camps finally reached the expedition as it crossed the Belle Fourche River in the shadow of the Black Hills on September 13, ending the almost immediately legendary Starvation March.

On September 16 Crook relinquished command of the Big Horn and Yellowstone Expedition to Merritt. He and many of his staff officers advanced to Fort Laramie via Camp Robinson to confer with Sheridan. Merritt, meanwhile, rested the command in the Black Hills for the next six weeks, welcoming at the end of September the expedition's long-abandoned wagons brimming with camp equipage and additional clothing. The expedition formally disbanded at Camp Robinson on October 24.

The lackluster legacy of the enlarged Big Horn and Yellowstone Expedition was rooted in its modest battlefield success at Slim Buttes but more so by the destructive Starvation March, which debilitated the entire command and rendered its components unfit for renewed service. More important, none of the northern Indians had yet submitted themselves to any of the Sioux agencies. An end to the Great Sioux War was nowhere in sight.[14]

Officers and Organization

Brig. Gen. George Crook, Department of the Platte, Commanding (det. 9-16)
1st Lt. John G. Bourke, Third Cavalry, ADC and AAAG (det. 9-16)
Capt. William S. Stanton, Corps of Engineers, Chief Engineer
1st Lt. John W. Bubb, Fourth Infantry, Chief Commissary of Subsistence
Capt. George M. Randall, Twenty-third Infantry, Commanding Indian Scouts (det. 9-16)
Maj. Thaddeus H. Stanton, Pay Department, Commanding Irregulars and Civilians (det. 9-16)
1st Lt. Walter S. Schuyler, Fifth Cavalry, ADC (det. 9-16)

[14] Primary sources documenting the conformation of the second iteration of Crook's Big Horn and Yellowstone Expedition include Second Cavalry Regimental Returns, July–October 1876; Third Cavalry Regimental Returns, July–October 1876; Fifth Cavalry Regimental Returns, July–October 1876; Fourth Infantry Regimental Returns, July–October 1876; Ninth Infantry Regimental Returns, July–October 1876; and Fourteenth Infantry Regimental Returns, July–October 1876. Among essential primary narratives, Bourke's diary is again especially important, as are King's *Campaigning with Crook* and Finerty's *War-Path and Bivouac*. The principal secondary account is Greene, *Slim Buttes, 1876*.

1st Lt. William P. Clark, Second Cavalry, ADC (joined 8-17; det. 9-16)
Surg. and Maj. Bennett A. Clements, Medical Director
Asst. Surg. and Maj. Albert Hartsuff (det. 9-16)
Asst. Surg. and Capt. Julius H. Patzki
AAS Charles R. Stevens
AAS Valentine T. McGillycuddy
AAS Junius L. Powell
Thomas Moore, Chief of Pack Train
Charles Russell, Chief of Wagon Train

Cavalry Brigade

Col. Wesley Merritt, Fifth Cavalry, Commanding
1st Lt. William C. Forbush, Fifth Cavalry, AAAG
1st Lt. William P. Hall, Fifth Cavalry, AAQM
2nd Lt. Julius H. Pardee, Twenty-third Infantry, ADC
2nd Lt. Robert H. Young, Fourth Infantry, ADC

Second and Third Cavalry

Lt. Col. William B. Royall, Third Cavalry, Commanding
2nd Lt. Henry R. Lemly, Third Cavalry, Battalion Adjutant.
2nd Lt. Charles Morton, Third Cavalry, Acting Regt. Adjutant and AAAG

Second Cavalry Battalion

Capt. Henry E. Noyes, Commanding Battalion and Co. I
Co. A, Capt. Thomas B. Dewees
1st Lt. Martin E. O'Brien
2nd Lt. Daniel C. Pearson
Co. B, 1st Lt. William C. Rawolle
Co. D, 1st Lt. Samuel M. Swigert
2nd Lt. Henry D. Huntington
Co. E, Capt. Elijah R. Wells
2nd Lt. Frederick W. Sibley (det. 9-16)
Co. I, Capt. Henry E. Noyes
1st Lt. Christopher T. Hall (joined 10-3)
2nd Lt. Frederick W. Kingsbury

Third Cavalry

Maj. Andrew W. Evans, Commanding

First Battalion

Capt. Anson Mills, Commanding Battalion and Co. M
Co. A, 1st Lt. Joseph Lawson

Co. B, Capt. Charles Meinhold
 1st Lt. Albert D. King
Co. E, 1st Lt. Adolphus H. Von Luettwitz (WIA, 9-9)
Co. I, Capt. William H. Andrews
 2nd Lt. James E. H. Foster
Co. L, Capt. Peter D. Vroom
 2nd Lt. George F. Chase
Co. M, Capt. Anson Mills
 1st Lt. Augustus C. Paul
 2nd Lt. Frederick Schwatka

Second Battalion

Capt. Frederick Van Vliet, Commanding Battalion and Co. C
Co. C, Capt. Frederick Van Vliet
Co. D, 2nd Lt. James F. Simpson
Co. F, 1st Lt. Alexander D. B. Smead
 2nd Lt. Bainbridge Reynolds
Co. G, 1st Lt. Emmet Crawford

Fifth Cavalry

Lt. Col. Eugene A. Carr, Commanding
1st Lt. Charles King, Acting Regimental Adjutant (det. from Co. K)
Vet. Surg. Charles M. Smith

First Battalion

Maj. John J. Upham, Commanding
2nd Lt. Hoel S. Bishop, Battalion Adjutant (det. from Co. G)
Co. A, Capt. Calbraith P. Rodgers
 2nd Lt. George O. Eaton (disabled 8-10; det. 8-21)
Co. C, Capt. Emil Adam
 2nd Lt. Edward L. Keyes
Co. G, Capt. Edward M. Hayes
Co. I, Capt. Sanford C. Kellogg
 2nd Lt. Satterlee C. Plummer, Fourth Infantry
Co. M, Capt. Edward H. Leib
 1st Lt. Bernard Reilly, Jr. (det. from Co. I)

Second Battalion

Maj. Julius W. Mason, Third Cavalry, Commanding
2nd Lt. Charles D. Parkhurst, Battalion Adjutant (det. from Co. E)
Co. B, Capt. Robert H. Montgomery
 2nd Lt. Eben Swift (joined 10-12)

Co. D, Capt. Samuel S. Sumner
2nd Lt. Robert London (det. from Co. I)
Co. E, Capt. George F. Price
Co. F, Capt. J. Scott Payne
1st Lt. Alfred B. Bache (disabled, det. 10-21)
2nd Lt. Samuel A. Cherry (joined 10-12)
Co. K, Capt. Albert E. Woodson

Infantry Battalion

Maj. Alexander Chambers, Fourth Infantry, Commanding (det. 9-16)
Capt. Samuel Munson, Ninth Infantry, Commanding (since 9-16)
1st Lt. Thaddeus H. Capron, Ninth Infantry, Battalion Adjutant

Fourth Infantry

Co. D, Capt. Avery B. Cain (det. 8-21)
1st Lt. Henry Seton
Co. F, Capt. Gerhard L. Luhn
Co. G, Capt. William H. Powell (det. 9-16)
2nd Lt. Albert B. Crittenden

Ninth Infantry

Co. C, Capt. Samuel Munson (det. 9-16)
2nd Lt. Hayden De Lany
Co. G, Capt. Thomas B. Burrowes (det. 8-23)
1st Lt. William L. Carpenter
Co. H, Capt. Andrew S. Burt (det. 9-16)
2nd Lt. Edgar B. Robertson
2nd Lt. Charles M. Rockefeller (det. from Co. F)

Fourteenth Infantry

Co. B, Capt. James Kennington
2nd Lt. Charles F. Lloyd
Co. C, Capt. Daniel W. Burke
1st Lt. John Murphy (det. from Co. B)
Co. F, Capt. Thomas F. Tobey
2nd Lt. Frederic S. Calhoun
Co. I, 1st Lt. Frank Taylor
2nd Lt. Richard T. Yeatman

Goose Creek/Fort Reno Supply Camp, August 4–September 25, 1876

Capt. John V. Furey, Quartermaster Department, Commanding

AAS Robert B. Grimes
AAS Edward P. Lecompte
Maj. William Arthur, Pay Department (det. 8-3)
Capt. Alexander Sutorius, Third Cavalry (in arrest since 8-3)

DEPLOYMENT NO. 13

Terry's and Gibbon's Column

Montana, August 8–September 26, 1876

After departing Little Big Horn Battlefield, General Terry shepherded his column and Gibbon's column, including the battered remnants of the Seventh Cavalry now led by Major Reno, northward to the broad flats surrounding Fort Pease on the Yellowstone and encamped there for nearly one month. As with Crook's actions after the Rosebud battle, Terry prepared reports, engaged in a lengthy correspondence with Sheridan, and awaited fresh troops deployed to Sioux Country from beyond the bounds of the Department of Dakota.

Anxious to communicate directly with Crook, on July 9 Terry successfully dispatched three enlisted volunteers southward bearing messages, including details on the Little Big Horn Battle. Two of the messengers returned on July 25 with reports from Crook. Both commanders were anxious to resume active campaigning, but not before being reinforced. Troops destined for Terry started appearing in the first several days of August. Six Twenty-second Infantry companies commanded by Lieutenant Colonel Elwell S. Otis arrived on the steamboat *Carroll*, and six companies of Fifth Infantry commanded by Colonel Nelson A. Miles appeared on the steamer *E. H. Durfee*. Otis's troops originated in the Division of the Atlantic and were mostly drawn from Great Lakes posts in Michigan, while Miles's command originated in the Department of the Missouri, largely coming from Fort Leavenworth, Kansas.

In organizing his midsummer movement, Terry first ensured the continued security of the numerous steamboats then operating on the Yellowstone River by affirming protection by squads or whole infantry companies detailed to the boats and also the defense of his supply base, which migrated along the river in synch with the troops. Responsibility for protecting the supply camp reverted to Captain Louis H. Sanger, Seventeenth Infantry, who gained four dismounted companies of Seventh Cavalry to bolster his otherwise meager force. The previous camp guard, three companies of Sixth Infantry commanded by Major Orlando H. Moore, henceforth joined the active campaign.

Unlike the composition of Crook's Big Horn and Yellowstone Expedition, the muscle in Terry's enlarged column was his massed infantry. An infantry brigade was formed under the command of Colonel Gibbon, with Miles commanding a ten-company wing drawn from the Fifth and Sixth regiments and Otis commanding a second wing consisting of twelve companies from the Seventh and Twenty-second regiments. The respective smaller Second and Seventh Cavalry battalions reported to Terry directly.

Anticipating a movement south of the Yellowstone, Terry relocated his command to the mouth of Rosebud Creek by July 30. When the campaign formally resumed on August 8, with wagon transportation available, he permitted carrying tents, bedding, and other camp comforts. These curiosities were quietly lampooned by the bedraggled men of Crook's column, who had departed Goose Creek, Wyoming, with little more than could be carried personally. Terry's wagons also carried thirty days' rations.

When Terry and Crook met on August 10, the combined force numbered nearly four thousand combatants and immediately proved too unwieldy for aggressive movement. The extreme mass of troops was but a momentary condition, however. Fearing that the Indians would escape behind them by crossing the Yellowstone at fords near the mouths of the Tongue or Powder, on the tenth Terry returned Miles and Companies B, E, G, and H, Fifth Infantry, to the Rosebud camp, where they engaged the *Far West* and were transported downriver. Miles positioned companies on the north bank of the Yellowstone several miles below the mouth of the Tongue, at the mouth of the Powder, another near the mouth of O'Fallon's Creek that later moved to opposite the mouth of Glendive Creek, and one aboard the *Far West*. Terry, meanwhile, distributed available rations to Crook's men and returned his wagons to the Rosebud depot, escorted by Companies F and K, Fifth Infantry, which Miles also quickly dispersed along the Yellowstone.

Following Crook's departure from the Yellowstone on August 24, Terry feigned movements in several directions. On the twenty-fifth the majority of his command followed Crook's trail up Powder River but quickly countermarched when learning of Indian movements on the

Yellowstone downstream from O'Fallon's Creek. Terry also learned of Sheridan's intent to winter Miles's and Otis's infantry at the mouth of the Tongue River. In the waning days of August, Terry focused his actions on consolidating and supporting the Fifth and Twenty-second Infantry at Tongue River, investigating reported Indian crossings of the Yellowstone, returning Gibbon's force to its posts in western Montana, and safely disbanding his own command. Portions of the Dakota Column traveled downriver by steamboat, while the Seventh Cavalry and Moore's Sixth Infantry battalion marched via Fort Peck, Montana, to Fort Buford. On September 26 the Seventh finally reached Fort Abraham Lincoln, where they encamped for a month before returning to the field to participate in the disarming and unhorsing actions at the Standing Rock and Cheyenne River Sioux agencies (Deployment No. 18 below).

Terry and the Dakota Column marched vigorously in the summer of 1876, but their contributions to the success of the Great Sioux War were notably meager. The loss of Custer and five companies of the Seventh Cavalry and the dispiriting pall cast over both the Dakota and Montana columns thereafter were never overcome. And yet lessons were learned. Wheeled vehicles (supply wagons and artillery pieces) traveled poorly in the broken landscapes of the Powder, Tongue, and Rosebud. Steamboats were tremendous assets in matters of supply and ferrying troops but were tethers too, and no important battles were fought in their shadows. Massed commands featuring battalions, brigades, and thousands of men earned no laurels. Their contributions were eclipsed by their sheer cumbersomeness, extreme supply issues, and slow movements, no speedier than the slowest of weary men marching afoot or on thoroughly exhausted horses. Terry never again returned to the field during the active phases of the Great Sioux War. But the adaptable and energetic Colonel Miles proved a shrewd student, and under his leadership the war continued and was won.[15]

[15] For the organization of the post–Little Big Horn Terry and Gibbon columns, see Second Cavalry Regimental Returns, June–October 1876; Seventh Cavalry Regimental Returns, June–September 1876; Fifth Infantry Regimental Returns, July–October 1876; Sixth Infantry Regimental Returns, June–September 1876; Seventh Infantry Regimental Returns, June–October 1876; Seventeenth Infantry Regimental Returns, June–September 1876; Twentieth Infantry Regimental Returns, June–September 1876; Twenty-second Infantry Regimental Returns, July–October 1876; and Fort Rice Post Return, July 1876. Willert's *March of the Columns* and *To the Edge of Darkness* are useful in understanding the conformation and movement of this fluid column. The initial conformation of the Fifth Infantry is confirmed in the *Leavenworth Daily Times,* July 13, 1876, reprinted in Davis and Davis, "For the Front." The story of the couriers bearing messages between Terry and Crook is told in Hedren in "'Three Cool, Determined Men.'"

Officers and Organization

Brig. Gen. Alfred H. Terry, Department of Dakota, Commanding
Lt. Col. James W. Forsyth, Division of the Missouri (joined 8-1)
Maj. Beekman Du Barry, Subsistence Department (joined 8-1; det. 8-23)
Capt. Otho E. Michaelis, Ordnance Department, Chief Ordnance Officer
Capt. Robert P. Hughes, Third Infantry, ADC
1st Lt. Eugene B. Gibbs, Sixth Infantry, ADC
1st Lt. Henry J. Nowlan, Seventh Cavalry, AAQM
1st Lt. Edward L. Randall, Fifth Infantry, AAQM (joined 8-11)
1st Lt. Edward Maguire, Corps of Engineers, Chief Engineer Officer
2nd Lt. Henry P. Walker, Seventeenth Infantry, Assistant Engineer Officer
2nd Lt. Richard E. Thompson, Sixth Infantry, ACS
Asst. Surg. and Capt. John W. Williams, Chief Medical Officer
Asst. Surg. and Capt. Philip F. Harvey
Asst. Surg. and Capt. James P. Kimball
Asst. Surg. and 1st Lt. Blair D. Taylor

Second Cavalry

Maj. James S. Brisbin, Commanding and Chief of Cavalry
2nd Lt. Charles B. Schofield, Battalion Adjutant
2nd Lt. Edward J. McClernand, Acting Engineering Officer
AAS Elbert J. Clark
Co. F, 2nd Lt. Charles F. Roe
Co. G, Capt. James N. Wheelan
  1st Lt. Gustavus C. Doane
Co. H, Capt. Edward Ball
  1st Lt. James G. MacAdams
  1st Lt. William P. Clark (joined 8-17; apt. ADC, Big Horn and Yellowstone Expedition, 8-26)
Co. L, 1st Lt. Samuel T. Hamilton

Seventh Cavalry

Maj. Marcus A. Reno, Commanding
1st Lt. George D. Wallace, Regimental Adjutant
1st Lt. Winfield S. Edgerly, RQM
AAS Henry R. Porter

First Battalion

Capt. Frederick W. Benteen, Commanding Battalion and Co. H
Co. C, 1st Lt. Charles A. Varnum, Commanding Co. and Indian Scouts

Co. G, 1st Lt. Francis M. Gibson, Commanding Co. to 8-26 (det. from Co. H)
1st Lt. Ernest A. Garlington, Commanding Co. from 8-26
Co. H, Capt. Frederick W. Benteen (det. 8-26)
1st Lt. Francis M. Gibson, Commanding Co. from 8-26
Co. M, Capt. Thomas H. French
1st Lt. Edward G. Mathey

Second Battalion

Capt. Thomas B. Weir, Commanding Battalion and Co. D
Co. A, Capt. Myles Moylan
Co. B, Capt. Thomas M. McDougall
Co. D, Capt. Thomas B. Weir
Co. K, 1st Lt. Edward S. Godfrey

Infantry Brigade

Col. John Gibbon, Seventh Infantry, Commanding

Right Wing

Col. Nelson A. Miles, Fifth Infantry, Commanding
1st Lt. Frank D. Baldwin, Fifth Infantry, Battalion Adjutant

Fifth Infantry

2nd Lt. Forrest H. Hathaway, Quartermaster
Asst. Surg. and 1st Lt. Louis S. Tesson
AAS William Barbour (det. 10-4)
Co. B, Capt. Andrew S. Bennett
1st Lt. Henry Romeyn
2nd Lt. Thomas M. Woodruff
Co. E, 2nd Lt. James W. Pope
Co. F, Capt. Simon Snyder
1st Lt. Edward L. Randall
2nd Lt. Frank S. Hinkle (joined 8-21)
Co. G, Capt. Samuel Ovenshine
1st Lt. Theodore F. Forbes
Co. H, 1st Lt. Edmund Rice (det. from Co. A)
2nd Lt. Charles E. Hargous
Co. K, 1st Lt. Mason Carter
2nd Lt. James H. Whitten (det. from Co. I)

Sixth Infantry

Maj. Orlando H. Moore
Co. C, Capt. James W. Powell
    2nd Lt. Bernard A. Byrne
Co. D, Capt. Daniel H. Murdock
    1st Lt. Frederick W. Thibaut
Co. I, 2nd Lt. George B. Walker

Left Wing

Lt. Col. Elwell S. Otis, Twenty-second Infantry, Commanding

Seventh Infantry

Capt. Henry B. Freeman, Commanding Battalion and Co. H
1st Lt. Levi F. Burnett, Seventh Infantry, Regimental Adjutant, AAAG, Acting Signal Officer
1st Lt. Joshua W. Jacobs, Seventh Infantry, RQM, AAQM, ACS
1st Lt. James H. Bradley, Seventh Infantry, Chief of Mounted Scouts
Asst. Surg. and 1st Lt. Holmes O. Paulding
Co. A, Capt. William Logan
    1st Lt. Charles A. Coolidge
    2nd Lt. Francis Woodbridge (joined 8-17)
Co. B, Capt. Thaddeus S. Kirtland
    2nd Lt. Charles A. Booth
Co. E, Capt. Walter Clifford
    1st Lt. William I. Reed (joined 8-17)
    2nd Lt. George S. Young
Co. H, Capt. Henry B. Freeman
    2nd Lt. Frederick M. H. Kendrick
Co. I, 1st Lt. William L. English (det. 9-5)
    2nd Lt. Alfred B. Johnson
Co. K, Capt. James M. J. Sanno
    1st Lt. Allan H. Jackson (joined 8-22)

Twenty-second Infantry

Lt. Col. Elwell S. Otis, Commanding
AAS William J. Van Eman
Co. E, Capt. Charles J. Dickey
Co. F, Capt. Archibald H. Goodloe (det. sick since 8-18)
    2nd Lt. Edward W. Casey
Co. G, Capt. Charles W. Miner
    1st Lt. Benjamin C. Lockwood
    2nd Lt. William N. Dykman

Co. H, Capt. De Witt C. Poole (det. 8-25)
1st Lt. Oskaloosa M. Smith, Battalion Adjutant
Co. I, Capt. Francis Clarke
1st Lt. William Conway
2nd Lt. James E. Macklin
Co. K, Capt. Mott Hooton
1st Lt. William J. Campbell
2nd Lt. William H. Kell

Dakota Artillery Detachment

Twentieth Infantry

Provisional Co., 2nd Lt. William H. Low, Jr., Commanding
2nd Lt. Frank X. Kinzie

Montana Artillery Detachment

Seventh Infantry

Co. K (det.), 2nd Lt. Charles A. Woodruff, Commanding and Battalion Adjutant (det. 9-5)

DEPLOYMENT NO. 14

Tongue River Cantonment

Montana, August 28, 1876–September 1, 1877

General Sheridan's newfound intention of prosecuting the Great Sioux War through the winter of 1876–77 from outposts established within Sioux Country played out most effectively and efficiently under the leadership of Colonel Miles, who arrived among Terry's midsummer infantry reinforcements. Sheridan and General of the Army William T. Sherman had gained congressional approval in July for the construction of two new military posts on the Yellowstone River. While the waning boating season hampered permanent construction, Miles's presence served the dual purposes of continuing the war and firmly planting the army in the midst of Indian country in a substantial if momentarily temporary cantonment.

During the fall of 1876, Miles consolidated his entire Fifth Infantry regiment and portions of the Twenty-second Infantry at a sprawling, unpretentious establishment on the west bank of the Tongue River at its junction with the Yellowstone. From this isolated and rustic outpost, Miles kept in motion an array of plainsmen and Indian scouts scouring the landscape for the whereabouts of Sitting Bull, Crazy Horse, and other Indian leaders prominent in the war. The notion of the tribesmen surrendering still had no particular currency at this stage of the conflict, though certainly many of the so-called summer roamers had already quietly returned to the haven of the Missouri and White River agencies or were en route. The northern Indians, meanwhile, sought out the buffalo herds and another season in Sioux Country and in doing so persisted as targets for troops in Montana and Wyoming.

From Tongue River Cantonment, Miles organized four major expeditions against the Sioux that demonstrated, one after another, the government's intention of pushing these tribesmen to their agencies, whatever the human toll. Each of Miles's expeditions disrupted the quietude of the Indian camps and often brought the destruction of stockpiled provisions and conventional camp and personal items. That Miles achieved these ends nearly exclusively with infantry proved the mettle of foot troops in northern plains Indian warfare, regardless of the army's conventional favoring of cavalry.

As spring 1877 overtook the northern plains, Sheridan still believed that the Great Sioux War was not yet won, despite Miles's and Crook's highly visible successes by then, added to the many notable surrenders occurring at the agencies and the evident flight of other Sioux to Canada. The generals feared that many agency Indians would depart seasonally for the buffalo country, as customarily occurred, and thereby continue or renew the war. To support the prospect of renewed summertime campaigning, Miles received the Montana Battalion of Second Cavalry from Fort Ellis. He also loosely coordinated the movements of the reorganized Seventh Cavalry, which returned to the field in May and encamped on Cedar Creek near the Yellowstone, plus a battalion of First Infantry, which had been garrisoned in Department of Dakota posts on the middle Missouri River. Miles also directed the fielding of the Little Missouri Expedition, the army's twenty-seventh and next-to-final organized deployment in the Great Sioux War. Those troops were intent on locating Lame Deer's Miniconjou Sioux holdouts and forcing them into submission. Miles, meanwhile, was soon enmeshed in the Nez Perce troubles invading Montana from Idaho and Oregon. The fighting with the Sioux had all but ended by midsummer 1877, and the field commands were withdrawn or diverted to the Nimiipuu Crisis (Nez Perce War).[16]

Officers and Organization

Col. Nelson A. Miles, Fifth Infantry (joined 9-10)
2nd Lt. James W. Pope, Fifth Infantry, AAAG, Yellowstone Command (until 2-2-77)
1st Lt. George W. Baird, Regimental Adjutant and AAAG, Yellowstone Command (after 2-2-77)
Surg. and Maj. Henry R. Tilton (joined 11-21)
Asst. Surg. and 1st Lt. Louis S. Tesson (joined 9-10; transferred 6-14-77)
AAS William J. Van Eman (joined 10-2; contract annulled 7-30-77)

Fifth Infantry

Lt. Col. Joseph N. G. Whistler (det. 12-19)
Maj. George Gibson (joined 5-23-77)
1st Lt. George W. Baird, Regimental Adjutant (joined 11-2)
2nd Lt. Forrest H. Hathaway, RQM and ACS (joined 7-11-77)
Band (joined 11-3)
Co. A (joined 9-22), Capt. James S. Casey
    1st Lt. Edmund Rice
    2nd Lt. William H. C. Bowen
Co. B (joined 9-19), Capt. Andrew S. Bennett
    1st Lt. Henry Romeyn, Post Adjutant (since 5-17-77)
    2nd Lt. Thomas M. Woodruff (det. 10-17)
Co. C, Capt. Edmond Butler
    2nd Lt. Oscar F. Long, Acting Engineer Officer (joined 11-2)
Co. D (joined 9-22), Capt. Henry B. Bristol (det. sick, 9-7, rejoined 7-7-77)
    1st Lt. Robert McDonald (joined 9-22), ACS (since 7-31-77)
    2nd Lt. Hobart K. Bailey, Post Adjutant (until 11-20)

---

[16] The terminal date provided here reflects the disbanding of the Little Missouri Expedition, loosely overseen by Miles and directly associated with the Great Sioux War. Tongue River Cantonment was succeeded by Fort Keogh, built two miles west of this expedient post.

Tongue River Cantonment/Fort Keogh has no published history despite its long and illustrious existence. Its early garrison composition is detailed in Fifth Infantry Regimental Returns, September 1876–September 1877; Twenty-second Infantry Regimental Returns, September 1876–June 1877; Second Cavalry Regimental Returns, April–September 1877; First Infantry Regimental Returns, May–June 1877; and Fort Keogh Post Returns, September 1876–September 1877. Two useful secondary accounts provide context for Tongue River Cantonment and its early evolution: Robert M. Utley, "War Houses in the Sioux Country," in Hedren, ed., *The Great Sioux War 1876–77*, 252–63; and Greene, *Yellowstone Command*, where the cantonment story is woven through the movements of Miles's perpetually active "Yellowstone Command."

Co. E (joined 9-10), Capt. Ezra P. Ewers (joined 12-15)
1st Lt. Frank D. Baldwin (joined 9-10)
2nd Lt. James W. Pope, Acting Ordnance Officer, Yellowstone Command (since 5-15-77)
Co. F (joined 9-12), Capt. Simon Snyder
1st Lt. Edward L. Randall, aaqm and acs
2nd Lt. Frank S. Hinkle, Post Adjutant (since 12-22; resigned commission 1-31-77)
2nd Lt. Charles B. Thompson (joined 4-28-77)
Co. G (joined 9-10), 1st Lt. Theodore F. Forbes
2nd Lt. David Q. Rousseau
Co. H (joined 9-10), 2nd Lt. James H. Whitten (det. from Co. I, commanding 9-10 to 1-28-77)
1st Lt. Thomas H. Logan (joined 5-24-77)
2nd Lt. Charles E. Hargous
Co. I, Capt. Wyllys Lyman
2nd Lt. James H. Whitten (resigned commission 5-31-77)
Co. K (joined 9-10), Capt. David H. Brotherton (joined 6-27-77)
1st Lt. Mason Carter, Post Adjutant (since 2-1-77)
2nd Lt. George P. Borden (joined 4-29-77)

Twenty-second Infantry

Maj. Alfred L. Hough (joined 5-27-77, det. 6-20-77)
Co. E (joined 10-2, det. 6-3-77), Capt. Charles J. Dickey
Co. F (joined 10-2, det. 6-16-77), 1st Lt. Cornelius C. Cusick
2nd Lt. Edward W. Casey, Post Adjutant (since 11-20)
Co. G (joined 3-12-77, det. 6-16-77), Capt. Charles W. Miner
1st Lt. Benjamin C. Lockwood (det. 6-9)
2nd Lt. William N. Dykman
Co. H (joined 3-12-77, det. 6-16-77), Capt. De Witt C. Poole
1st Lt. Oskaloosa M. Smith
2nd Lt. Alfred C. Sharpe
Co. I (joined 5-27-77, det. 6-16-77), Capt. Francis Clarke
1st Lt. William Conway
Co. K (joined 5-27-77, det. 6-16-77), Capt. Mott Hooton
2nd Lt. William H. Kell (joined 6-3)

Second Cavalry (attached 4-25-77 but never joined post)

Maj. James S. Brisbin
2nd Lt. Charles B. Schofield, Battalion Adjutant
2nd Lt. Samuel R. Douglas, Seventh Infantry, AAQM
Asst. Surg. and 1st Lt. Holmes O. Paulding

Co. F, Capt. George L. Tyler
2nd Lt. Alfred M. Fuller
Co. G, Capt. James N. Wheelan
1st Lt. Gustavus C. Doane
2nd Lt. Edward J. McClernand (joined 7-17-77)
Co. H, Capt. Edward Ball
2nd Lt. Lovell H. Jerome
Co. L, Capt. Randolph Norwood
1st Lt. Samuel T. Hamilton

First Infantry (attached 5-23-77 but never joined post)
Co. B (det. 6-16), 2nd Lt. Hugh T. Reed
Co. G (det. 5-28), Capt. Robert E. Johnston
2nd Lt. Harry C. Johnson
Co. H (det. 6-16) Capt. Thomas M. Tolman
Co. K (det 6-16), Capt. Kinzie Bates
2nd Lt. Frank H. Edmunds

DEPLOYMENT NO. 15

Spring Creek Engagements

Montana, October 10–20, 1876

Four infantry companies commanded by Captain Charles W. Miner, Twenty-second Infantry, attempted to advance construction matériel and quartermaster, ordnance, and commissary supplies from Glendive Cantonment to the Tongue River. They came under attack by Sioux warriors on October 10–11 at the train's camp along Spring Creek, a small Yellowstone tributary, forcing their return to Glendive. On October 14 the train and an enlarged escort commanded now by Lieutenant Colonel Elwell S. Otis, Twenty-second Infantry, consisting of five companies and three Gatling guns, embarked once more for the Tongue River. They were again engaged by aggressive warriors in a running skirmish stretching from the proximity of Spring Creek west some thirty miles to beyond Cedar Creek. Otis's delayed arrival at the Tongue River, in turn, prompted Miles's mustering of the entire Fifth Infantry Regiment in relief. Otis and Miles met on October 18 along Custer Creek. Otis continued west to the Tongue River, off-loaded supplies, and returned to Glendive, while Miles turned north, pursuing the Sioux.[17]

Officers and Organization

Lt. Col. Elwell S. Otis, Twenty-second Infantry
1st Lt. Oskaloosa M. Smith, Twenty-second Infantry, Battalion Adjutant
AAS Charles T. Gibson

Seventeenth Infantry
Co. C, Capt. Malcolm McArthur
  1st Lt. Frank D. Garretty
  2nd Lt. James D. Nickerson
Co. G, Capt. Louis H. Sanger

Twenty-second Infantry
Co. G, Capt. Charles W. Miner
  1st Lt. Benjamin C. Lockwood
Co. H, 1st Lt. William Conway (det. from Co. I)
  2nd Lt. Alfred C. Sharpe
Co. K, Capt. Mott Hooton
  2nd Lt. William H. Kell

DEPLOYMENT NO. 16

Cantonment Reno

Wyoming, October 13, 1876–August 30, 1877

In mid-September 1876 Sheridan affirmed his intention of establishing a sizable cantonment in the Powder River Basin to prevent the Sioux from reoccupying that buffalo-rich landscape and also to enable a continuation of the Great Sioux War from a new post built, like Tongue

[17] The Spring Creek deployments are confirmed in the Seventeenth Infantry Regimental Return, October 1876; Twenty-second Infantry Regimental Return, October 1876; Fifth Infantry Regimental Return, October 1876; Fort Keogh Post Return, October 1876; and Oskaloosa M. Smith and Alfred C. Sharpe, "The Spring Creek Encounters, October 11, 15, and 16, 1876," in Greene, ed., *Battles and Skirmishes of the Great Sioux War,* 116–31. The principal secondary account is Greene, *Yellowstone Command,* 81–91.

River Cantonment in Montana, in the midst of Sioux Country. The new army camp, sited on the west bank of the Powder River a few miles upstream from old Fort Reno of Bozeman Trail renown and immediately dubbed Cantonment Reno to distinguish the two, ultimately played a role quite different from that of Miles's Yellowstone River post. While Miles assembled a large garrison with which he waged a succession of successful campaigns against the northern Indians, Crook detailed only a small complement to the Powder River post and organized his next campaign not there but chiefly at Camp Robinson, Nebraska, where other war-related action was occurring.

Crook's four infantry companies, commanded by Captain Edwin Pollock, Ninth Infantry, served the purposes imagined by Sheridan. A military presence was indeed established in the Powder River Basin, and the little garrison guarded a welter of supplies stockpiled for Crook's use when his Powder River Expedition thrice passed by in November and December. In succeeding months, Pollock's command constructed a bridge across the Powder, retrieved the bodies of two civilians killed by Indians near Pumpkin Buttes, and otherwise performed the "usual garrison and escort duties" common at such posts, as so widely reported in all Post Returns.

Cantonment Reno was unofficially renamed Camp McKinney in mid-June 1877, honoring First Lieutenant John A. McKinney of the Fourth Cavalry, who had been killed in the Red Fork battle on November 25, 1876. The post was officially designated Fort McKinney on August 30 and relocated entirely the following summer to a site in the eastern foothills of the Big Horn Mountains that offered substantial advantages of timber and water while keeping a military garrison in old Sioux Country.[18]

Officers and Organization

Capt. Edwin Pollock, Ninth Infantry, Commanding
2nd Lt. Carver Howland, Fourth Infantry, Post Adjutant

[18] The terminal date provided here reflects the date of the post's name change, when Cantonment Reno became Fort McKinney. This administrative correction is relatively synonymous with the close of the Great Sioux War. The relocated Fort McKinney survived until 1894.

The Cantonment Reno garrison is detailed in Fourth Infantry Regimental Returns, October 1876–August 1877; Ninth Infantry Regimental Returns, October 1876–August 1877; Twenty-third Infantry Regimental Returns, October–December 1876; and Fort McKinney Post Returns, October 1876–August 1877. Two secondary sources provide context for the cantonment's role in the Great Sioux War: Hedren, *Fort Laramie in 1876*, 160–61, 170–71; and Murray, *Military Posts in the Powder River Country of Wyoming*, 110–15. Bollinger's *Fort McKinney 1877 to 1894* places the cantonment within the context of Fort McKinney history.

2nd Lt. John J. O'Brien, Fourth Infantry, Post AAQM and ACS
AAS Edward P. Lecompte (det. 4-18)
Asst. Surg. and 1st Lt. Marshall W. Wood (joined 4-17)

Fourth Infantry
Co. B, Capt. Thomas F. Quinn
1st Lt. Edward L. Bailey
Co. E, Capt. Charles J. Von Herrmann
1st Lt. Butler D. Price
Co. I (joined 1-6-77), Capt. Samuel P. Ferris
1st Lt. John W. Bubb (joined 7-9)
2nd Lt. Charles W. Mason (det. 3-20)

Ninth Infantry
Co. E, 1st Lt. James Regan (joined 11-30; det. 6-15)
2nd Lt. William F. Norris

Twenty-third Infantry
Co. K (trans. 1-8-77), 1st. Lt. Greenleaf A. Goodale (joined 11-20)
2nd Lt. Orlando L. Wieting

DEPLOYMENT NO. 17

Cedar Creek

Montana, October 17–31, 1876

After Miles rendezvoused with Otis late in the episode on Cedar Creek (Deployment No. 15 above), he advanced up that notable Yellowstone affluent that reached the divide separating the Yellowstone and Missouri rivers. Miles's scouts located Sitting Bull's camp at the creek's head. As he continued his advance, troops encountered warriors on distant ridges and saw Indian riders approaching under the cover of a white flag. Those horsemen reported to Miles that Sitting Bull wished to meet and discuss surrendering his people. As the parley was organized, Miles positioned several of his companies on outlying knolls opposite increasingly visible Sioux warriors occupying countering ridges.

The face-to-face meeting on October 20 between Miles and Sitting

Bull amounted to the first occasion during the Great Sioux War when a senior army officer confronted a major leader of the nonagency Indians. The council was tumultuous. Sitting Bull indicated his willingness to yield to the army, but only if all troops vacated the Yellowstone Basin promptly and permanently and the tribesmen were allowed another season of buffalo hunting. Miles was equally unyielding, but both principals agreed to meet again in the morning.

The exchange on October 21 was just as inconclusive and even more filled with tension, as both Miles and Sitting Bull revisited irreconcilable demands from the day before. The council ended with Miles again insisting that Sitting Bull surrender unconditionally or face an immediate attack, which prompted the Hunkpapa chief's abrupt departure.

Miles promptly deployed five companies in skirmish order, fanning the valley and clearing the lateral ridges. Three other companies were held in reserve, while a fourth supported the column's ordnance rifle and a fifth protected the train. A mile of rugged terrain separated the combatants, with the Indians occupying the higher ground. When warriors attempted to fire the prairie, Miles scattered them with volleys from the ordnance rifle and his doughboys' rifles. Casualties were limited. Most of the tribesmen fled northeastward, but their abandoned village yielded tipis, dried meat, and utensils, all of which were destroyed.

The Fifth Infantry occupied the village that evening and endured occasional desultory fire from distant warriors. Miles retired southeastward on October 22 and the next day reached the Yellowstone, where he encamped for several days before returning to Tongue River. While camped, Miles alerted Colonel William B. Hazen at Fort Buford that Sitting Bull was likely bound for the Assiniboine Agency at Fort Peck for food and ammunition. Miles's own dwindling provisions obliged his return to the cantonment, with the last of the command arriving on November 3.

Miles's Cedar Creek fight proved the utility of well-managed infantry in the Great Sioux War and the colonel's own determination to pursue the Indians aggressively, regardless of the weather and his command's increasing fatigue. That determination also registered among the tribesmen, who suffered a second sacked village. Thereafter at least some of their leaders began to question the value of prolonging the war.[19]

---

[19] The Cedar Creek troop deployment is detailed in the Fifth Infantry Regimental Return, October 1876; and Fort Keogh Post Return, October 1876. A useful primary narrative is James W. Pope, "The Battle of Cedar Creek, October 21, 1876," in Greene, ed., *Battles and Skirmishes of the Great Sioux War*, 132–44. Greene also chronicles the Cedar Creek action in *Yellowstone Command*, chapter 5.

Officers and Organization

Fifth Infantry

Col. Nelson A. Miles
1st Lt. Frank D. Baldwin, AAAG (det. from Co. E)
2nd Lt. Hobart K. Bailey, ADC (det. from Co. D)
Asst. Surg. and 1st Lt. Louis S. Tesson
Co. A, Capt. James S. Casey
    2nd Lt. William H. C. Bowen, Wagon Train
Co. B, Capt. Andrew S. Bennett
    2nd Lt. Thomas M. Woodruff
Co. C, Capt. Edmond Butler
Co. D, 1st Lt. Robert McDonald
Co. E, 2nd Lt. James W. Pope
Co. F, Capt. Simon Snyder
    2nd Lt. Frank S. Hinkle
Co. G, 1st Lt. Theodore F. Forbes
    2nd Lt. David Q. Rousseau
Co. H, 2nd Lt. James H. Whitten, Commanding Co. and Pack Train (det. from Co. I)
Co. I, Capt. Wyllys Lyman
Co. K, 1st Lt. Mason Carter

DEPLOYMENT NO. 18

Dismounting and Disarming the Sioux

Dakota and Nebraska, October 20–November 11, 1876

Fearing that residents at the Sioux agencies were collaborators and also that the Missouri and White River agencies served as tacit sanctuaries for northern Indians at a time when the Great Sioux War was far from over, Sheridan ordered the disarming and dismounting of the agency residents in October 1876. Administration of the various agencies had already been transferred from civilian to military control, and the agency garrisons at Standing Rock, Cheyenne River, and Camp Robinson were substantially bolstered that fall to ensure the eventual peaceful transitions of residents from war-making to assimilation.

Colonel Samuel D. Sturgis led a column of cavalry and infantry drawn largely from Fort Abraham Lincoln down the left (east) bank of the Missouri River to the Standing Rock Agency, while Major Reno led a smaller force drawn largely from Fort Rice down the river's west bank to that agency. Both forces confiscated horses and weapons from Hunkpapas and Blackfeet Sioux camped on either side. Terry witnessed the action, traveling with Sturgis from Fort Lincoln to Rice and joining Reno's column from Rice to Standing Rock. Terry rejoined Sturgis as his column continued downriver to the Cheyenne River Agency, administrative home of the Miniconjou Sioux, where they dismounted and disarmed the Indians. Additional infantry at Standing Rock supported Reno's action there, and at Cheyenne River three Twentieth Infantry companies from Fort Sully augmented Sturgis's force. In all, more than 1,200 horses were confiscated at Standing Rock and some 1,900 at Cheyenne River, along with a relatively meaningless cache of obsolete weaponry.

In Nebraska, Crook implemented Sheridan's directive at Red Cloud Agency but not at Spotted Tail Agency, incurring Sheridan's wrath in consequence. But Crook did not want to disrupt the quiet support he was receiving from Spotted Tail and most of his followers. Colonel Ranald S. Mackenzie and battalions of the Fourth and Fifth Cavalry successfully unhorsed and disarmed Red Cloud's Oglala and Red Leaf's Brule Sioux followers encamped near Red Cloud Agency, confiscating some 700 ponies from those bands and an assortment of well-worn weaponry. This was Mackenzie's and the Fourth Cavalry's first formal deployment since arriving on the northern plains in mid-August from the Indian Territory.

In theory the confiscated horses were to be sold on the open market and the proceeds used to purchase stocker cattle benefiting agency residents. Some ponies were sold and others given away, bartered, or stolen, and only a few cattle were purchased. Seemingly, no good accounting of these transactions was ever provided.[20]

---

[20] The diverse actions at the Sioux agencies are documented in Fourth Cavalry Regimental Returns, October 1876; Fifth Cavalry Regimental Return, October 1876; Seventh Cavalry Regimental Returns, October–November 1876; First Infantry Regimental Returns, October–November 1876; Seventeenth Infantry Regimental Returns, October–November 1876; Twentieth Infantry Regimental Returns, October–November 1876; Fort A. Lincoln Post Returns, October–November 1876; Fort Rice Post Returns, October–November 1876; Fort Sully Post Returns, October–November 1876; and Department of Dakota Monthly Returns, October–November 1876. Insightful primary narratives reporting on these respective movements include Theodore W. Goldin, "Dismounting and Disarming the Agency Sioux along the Missouri River," in Greene, ed., *Indian War Veterans*, 147–54; and Eli S. Ricker, "The Surround of Red Cloud and Red Leaf: Interview of William Garnett," in Paul, ed., *The Nebraska Indian Wars Reader*, 157–60. Useful secondary accounts include Daniel, "Dismounting the Sioux"; and Clow, "General Philip Sheridan's Legacy."

Officers and Organization

Standing Rock Agency, Missouri River Left Bank, Dakota, October 18–26, 1876

Col. Samuel D. Sturgis, Seventh Cavalry, Commanding
Brig. Gen. Alfred H. Terry, Department of Dakota (with Reno 10-22 to 10-26)
1st Lt. George D. Wallace, Regimental Adjutant and Commanding Indian Scouts
1st Lt. Winfield S. Edgerly, Seventh Cavalry, RQM
Surg. and Maj. Johnson V. D. Middleton
AAS Robert G. Redd

Seventh Cavalry

Co. B, 1st Lt. William W. Robinson, Jr. (det. from Co. F)
2nd Lt. William J. Nicholson
Co. E, 1st Lt. Charles C. De Rudio
Co. F, Capt. James M. Bell
2nd Lt. John C. Gresham (det. from Co. M)
Co. H, 1st Lt. Francis M. Gibson
2nd Lt. Albert J. Russell
Co. I, 1st Lt. Charles A. Varnum (det. from Co. C)
Co. K, 1st Lt. Edward S. Godfrey (det. from Co. L)
2nd Lt. J. Williams Biddle
Co. L, 2nd Lt. Loyd S. McCormick
Co. M, Capt. Thomas H. French
1st Lt. Edward G. Mathey
Artillery Section, 1st Lt. Luther R. Hare (det. from Co. I)
2nd Lt. Hugh L. Scott (det. from Co. E)

Seventeenth Infantry

Co. A, Capt. William M. Van Horne
Co. H, Capt. Henry S. Howe

Twentieth Infantry

Co. D, Capt. Charles O. Bradley
2nd Lt. Herbert S. Foster
Co. H, Capt. John N. Coe
1st Lt. John Bannister
2nd Lt. George L. Rousseau
Co. I, 2nd Lt. J. Granville Gates

Standing Rock Agency, Missouri River Right Bank, Dakota, October 22–November 3, 1876

Seventh Cavalry

Maj. Marcus A. Reno, Commanding
Brig. Gen. Alfred H. Terry, Department of Dakota (10-22 to 10-26)
Asst. Surg. and 1st Lt. Blair D. Taylor
Co. A, Capt. Myles Moylan
    2nd Lt. Ezra B. Fuller
Co. C, Capt. Henry Jackson
    2nd Lt. Horatio G. Sickel, Jr.
Co. D, 1st Lt. Edwin P. Eckerson
Co. G, 1st Lt. Ernest A. Garlington
    2nd Lt. John W. Wilkinson

First Infantry

Co. K, Capt. Kinzie Bates

Seventeenth Infantry

Lt. Col. William P. Carlin
Co. E, Capt. Edward Collins
    2nd Lt. George H. Roach
Co. F, Capt. Clarence E. Bennett
    1st Lt. Daniel H. Brush

Cheyenne River Agency, Dakota, October 26–November 11, 1876

Col. Samuel D. Sturgis, Seventh Cavalry, Commanding
Brig. Gen. Alfred H. Terry, Department of Dakota
1st Lt. George D. Wallace, Regimental Adjutant
AAS Robert G. Redd

Seventh Cavalry

Co. B, 1st Lt. William W. Robinson, Jr. (det. from Co. F)
    2nd Lt. William J. Nicholson
Co. E, 1st Lt. Charles C. De Rudio
Co. F, Capt. James M. Bell
    2nd Lt. John C. Gresham (det. from Co. M)
Co. H, 1st Lt. Francis M. Gibson
    2nd Lt. Albert J. Russell

Co. I, 1st Lt. Charles A. Varnum, RQM
Co. K, 1st Lt. Edward S. Godfrey (det. from Co. L)
2nd Lt. J. Williams Biddle
Co. L, 1st Lt. Winfield S. Edgerly
2nd Lt. Loyd S. McCormick
Co. M, Capt. Thomas H. French
1st Lt. Edward G. Mathey
Artillery Section, 1st Lt. Luther R. Hare (det. from Co. I)
2nd Lt. Hugh L. Scott (det. from Co. E)

First Infantry

Capt. Leslie Smith, Commanding Battalion and Co. F
Co. C, 1st Lt. Frederick M. Lynde
2nd Lt. Douglas M. Scott
Co. D, 2nd Lt. Marion P. Maus
Co. F, Capt. Leslie Smith

Seventeenth Infantry

Co. A, Capt. William M. Van Horne
Co. H, Capt. Henry S. Howe

Twentieth Infantry

Co. I, 2nd Lt. J. Granville Gates

Red Cloud and Red Leaf Bands, Nebraska, October 22–23, 1876
Col. Ranald S. Mackenzie, Fourth Cavalry, Commanding
Pawnee Scouts, Frank North and Luther North, Commanding
AAS Louis A. La Garde

Fourth Cavalry

Capt. Clarence Mauck, Commanding Battalion
Co. B, 1st Lt. Charles M. Callahan (det. from Co. D)
Co. D, Capt. John Lee
2nd Lt. Stanton A. Mason
Co. E, 1st Lt. David A. Irwin
2nd Lt. Henry H. Bellas
Co. F, Capt. Wirt Davis
2nd Lt. J. Wesley Rosenquest
2nd Lt. Augustus C. Tyler (det. from Co. G)

Co. I, Capt. William C. Hemphill
1st Lt. Otho W. Budd
2nd Lt. Joseph H. Dorst (det. from Co. H)

Fifth Cavalry
Maj. George A. Gordon, Commanding Battalion
Co. H, Capt. John M. Hamilton
1st Lt. Edward W. Ward
2nd Lt. Edwin P. Andrus
Co. L, Capt. Alfred B. Taylor
2nd Lt. Homer W. Wheeler

DEPLOYMENT NO. 19

Fort Peck Sortie

Montana, October 28–November 10, 1876

Colonel William B. Hazen, commander of the Sixth Infantry Regiment and Fort Buford, alerted by Miles of Sitting Bull's movement northward after the clash at Cedar Creek, hurriedly led an infantry battalion to Fort Peck, Sitting Bull's presumed destination. Aside from accompanying a week-long foray with a supply train to Glendive Cantonment in mid-October, Hazen thus far had taken no role in the Great Sioux War, though certainly his Fort Buford garrison was fully and exhaustingly engaged. On this occasion Hazen mustered four companies; his post surgeon, J. A. McKinney; and the services of the steamboat *Peninah,* which in 1876 mostly worked the upper Missouri River between Bismarck and Fort Benton.

Hazen's command boarded the *Peninah* on October 28 and reached Fort Peck on November 1. Word of his approach preceded him, and Sitting Bull, who probably had paused at the agency, was nowhere nearby. The Fort Peck agent told Hazen of issuing rations to 110 lodges of newly arrived Indians and acquiring a number of Indian horses left behind in the tribesmen's abrupt departure. Of those deemed "American horses," Hazen could only find ten that appeared capable of travel to Fort Buford. He left behind a squad from Company F commanded by First Lieutenant

Russell H. Day and returned to Fort Buford, arriving by steamer on November 9, trailed by his command on the tenth.[21]

Officers and Organization

Sixth Infantry

Col. William B. Hazen
1st Lt. Stephen W. Groesbeck, Regimental Adjutant
2nd Lt. Arthur L. Wagner, Artillery Officer
AAS J. A. McKinney
Co. C, 2nd Lt. Bernard A. Byrne
Co. D, Capt. Daniel H. Murdock
Co. F, Capt. William W. Sanders
1st Lt. Russell H. Day, AAQM and ACS
Co. I, 2nd Lt. George B. Walker

DEPLOYMENT NO. 20

Fort Peck Expedition

Montana, November 6–December 23, 1876

Miles's Fifth Infantry had barely recovered from its Cedar Creek foray before being led to the field again, embarking north on November 6 for Fort Peck on the Missouri River, where Sioux Indians were receiving succor. On this campaign his command trailed a three-inch ordnance rifle and twelve-pounder Napoleon, plus a small cattle herd to sustain them. At Fort Peck, Miles consulted with Lieutenant Day, Sixth Infantry, left behind by Hazen the week before. He learned that a conspicuous number of nonagency Sioux were now harbored among the Yanktonais, Assiniboines, and Gros Ventres normally present at this agency. Sitting Bull was not among them, though Miles noted the presence of Iron Dog, prominent in the councils on Cedar Creek in October.

To scour the rugged Missouri River countryside south and southwest

[21] The Fort Peck Sortie is documented in Sixth Infantry Regimental Returns, October–November 1876. Hazen's several reports on the matter appear in *Report of the Secretary of War, 1876*, 481–82; and in Fort Buford Records, vol. 5, 1876–78. See also Kelly, *Fort Buford*, 73.

of Fort Peck more advantageously, Miles divided his command, personally leading Companies A, B, E, G, H, and I, with the Napoleon cannon, into the tortured breaks on the north side of the river, bound westward for the Black Buttes in the high country south of the river and east of the Musselshell. Captain Simon Snyder, meanwhile, led Companies C, D, F, and K south up the Big Dry, exploring carefully and intending to rendezvous with Miles near Black Buttes in eight or ten days.

Snyder's command surveyed the Big Dry and Sunday Creek drainages as directed and awaited Miles at Black Buttes until they had nearly exhausted all rations and forage and then headed south, reaching Tongue River Cantonment on December 10.

Miles, meanwhile, learned from Day at Fort Peck that Sitting Bull was now reportedly east of the agency. This prompted him to detach First Lieutenant Frank D. Baldwin and Companies G, H, and I on December 2 to reconnoiter the country east of Fort Peck, while he continued westward toward the Musselshell and Black Buttes. Upon eventually observing that Snyder had returned to the cantonment, and not encountering any fresh Indian trail, Miles followed.

Baldwin's foray, however, delivered results. New reports from Fort Peck noted that Sitting Bull was encamped on Porcupine Creek near Milk River, east of the agency and north of the Missouri. Baldwin pressed forward, passed through a hastily abandoned camp, and reached fleeing tribesmen as they crossed the iced-over Missouri River near Bark Creek. With noncombatants safely concealed, warriors fired on Baldwin's companies from across the river. A heated exchange lasted several hours but proved inconclusive; as a blizzard set in, Baldwin disengaged and returned to Fort Peck.

Learning that Sitting Bull had fled southeastward into the Redwater Creek drainage, Baldwin returned to the Bark Creek skirmish site on December 11 and continued down the Missouri, crossing at Wolf Point on the fourteenth. Despite enduring continuing blizzard conditions, on December 18 Baldwin discovered Sitting Bull's camp on Ash Creek in the Redwater headlands, barely north over the divide from the Cedar Creek fight site of October 21.

At midday on December 18 Baldwin struck and scattered the village, numbering some 122 lodges. He destroyed the tipis, captured some 60 horses and mules, which he also destroyed, but retained foodstuffs, blankets, and buffalo robes, which were soon fashioned into winter garments at the cantonment for use by the troops.

Miles's Fort Peck Expedition demonstrated his willingness to wage another aggressive campaign in Montana's outback, even in the worst of seasons. And Baldwin's successful engagement at Ash Creek exposed Sitting Bull's people to the ravages of winter once again. After this, the tribesmen sought momentary succor with Crazy Horse's Oglalas, but Indian fortitude, so formidable at Little Big Horn, was growing ever more vulnerable and tenuous.[22]

Officers and Organization

Fifth Infantry

Col. Nelson A. Miles
1st Lt. Frank D. Baldwin, AAAG (det. from Co. E)
2nd Lt. Hobart K. Bailey, ADC (det. from Co. D)
2nd Lt. William H. C. Bowen, Wagon Train (det. from Co. A)
AAS William J. Van Eman
Co. A, Capt. James S. Casey
Co. B, Capt. Andrew S. Bennett
Co. C, Capt. Edmond Butler
    2nd Lt. Oscar F. Long
Co. D, 1st Lt. Robert McDonald
Co. E, 2nd Lt. James W. Pope
Co. F, Capt. Simon Snyder
    2nd Lt. Frank S. Hinkle
Co. G, 2nd Lt. David Q. Rousseau
Co. H, 2nd Lt. James H. Whitten, Pack Train (det. from Co. I)
Co. I, Capt. Wyllys Lyman
Co. K, 1st Lt. Mason Carter

---

[22] The troop deployment associated with Miles's Fort Peck movement is confirmed in the Fifth Infantry Regimental Returns, November–December 1876; and Fort Keogh Post Returns, November–December 1876. An interesting primary narrative is "Regular," "The Fort Peck Expedition, November 6–December 13, 1876," in Greene, ed., *Battles and Skirmishes of the Great Sioux War*, chapter 11. Greene provides the standard secondary account of this expedition and the Ash Creek fight in *Yellowstone Command,* chapter 6.

DEPLOYMENT NO. 21

Powder River Expedition

Wyoming, November 14–December 29, 1876

Crook's third campaign in 1876, the Powder River Expedition of November and December, mirrored the organizational hallmarks of his Big Horn and Yellowstone Expedition just disbanded at Camp Robinson at the end of October. Like that expedition, the new effort was another large and complex orchestration with particular strength in cavalry. No summer units were ordered to this campaign, but the core of Crook's headquarters staff rejoined in the field, as did Company K, Second Cavalry, a participant in the Big Horn Expedition in March, employed all summer on the Cheyenne–Black Hills Road, and now engaged as headquarters provost guard.

The Powder River Expedition featured eleven companies of cavalry commanded by the esteemed Ranald S. Mackenzie, including six from Mackenzie's Fourth regiment, detailed mostly from Fort Sill, Indian Territory, in the Department of the Missouri plus, uniquely, four Fourth Artillery companies deployed as infantry, arriving from posts in the San Francisco Bay area in the Department of California. The artillery battalion and an eleven-company infantry battalion drawn from the Fourth, Ninth, Fourteenth, and Twenty-third regiments were commanded by Lieutenant Colonel Richard I. Dodge, another well-seasoned field-grade officer like Mackenzie. The Powder River Expedition also featured an especially diverse array of Indian auxiliaries, including contingents of Pawnees led by the renowned North brothers, Frank and Luther, provisional companies of Sioux Indians enlisted at Camp Robinson, and even some Northern Cheyennes.

Well-outfitted for winter service, Crook's expedition again marched the deeply rutted Bozeman Trail northward, departing Fort Fetterman on November 14. After pausing at the new Cantonment Reno, still a mere collection of dugouts but scored by mountainous piles of tarpaulined stores, Crook pressed on. He believed that Crazy Horse, his principal target, was then on Rosebud Creek, near the site of their great summer battle. But on November 23 a Cheyenne scout brought a specific report of a very large Northern Cheyenne village secreted in a canyon at or near the head of Crazy Woman's Fork of the Powder River in the foothills of the Big Horn Mountains. At that moment the Powder River Expedition was traveling along Crazy Woman's Fork.

Crook promptly dispatched Mackenzie's cavalry and the Indian scouts to locate and destroy this village. He and the remainder of the column followed in support, much as at Slim Buttes in September and Powder River in March. Mackenzie's column numbered eleven hundred officers and men, one-third that number being Indian auxiliaries. In reality the Northern Cheyenne village was located on the Red Fork of the Powder, a lesser tributary of the Middle Fork of that widely branched stream.

Tracking through the night by the light of the moon, Mackenzie's column pressed westward into the Big Horns, threading its way through the Red Fork's narrow canyon. At dawn on November 25 it came upon the Cheyenne village, nestled in a picturesque mountainous opening several hundred yards wide and perhaps a mile long and completely encircled by steep, mountainous walls. First Lieutenant John Bourke, detached from Crook and serving as an aide-de-camp to Mackenzie, called the landscape an amphitheater. It was wide enough for cavalry companies to gallop front into line and sweep the village, which Mackenzie ordered immediately, to the utter surprise of the inhabitants. The village numbered some twelve hundred people, practically the entire Northern Cheyenne tribe, led by Little Wolf, Old Bear, and Morning Star or Dull Knife, as he was also commonly known.

In the ring and echo of carbine, rifle, and pistol fire, Cheyenne women and children scurried to the nooks and crevices of the mountain flanks while warriors returned a lethal fire, killing First Lieutenant John A. McKinney, Fourth Cavalry, near a gully north of the river. Losses were heavy on both sides, with six soldiers killed (including McKinney) and some forty Cheyennes killed outright. Equally tragic, without shelter and exposed to the horrible cold of the following night, eleven babies froze to death in their mothers' arms.

Mackenzie destroyed some two hundred lodges, each according to Bourke a proverbial "depot of supplies of every mentionable kind." Also uncovered was a surfeit of modern army gear, especially from the Little Big Horn Battle but also the Rosebud fight. Most of the 700 ponies that were also captured were destroyed.

Mackenzie's command camped on the field that evening and on November 26 struck for Cantonment Reno, where his column and Crook's column arrived almost simultaneously. After burying the dead, Crook directed his force northeastward to the headwaters of the Belle

Fourche River and spent most of December ambling through a bleak prairie landscape, suffering from the weather but not for lack of food. This expedition was well provisioned in the extreme as the summer's Big Horn and Yellowstone Expedition had suffered shortages in the extreme. Ultimately the need for animal forage and the persistent brutal cold dictated the close of the campaign. The expedition disbanded at Fort Fetterman on December 29.

Crook's Powder River Expedition was a turning point in the Great Sioux War. The Red Fork clash devastated the Northern Cheyennes, heretofore Sioux allies and participants in most of the war's great battles. The surviving Cheyennes united with Crazy Horse's followers in the coming weeks, and some fought again when Miles collided with the Sioux in the Wolf Mountains in January. Already, however, submission at an agency loomed as the only logical recourse, as became ever clearer in light of Miles's merciless campaigning. Surrenders were not yet occurring, however, and Crook presumed that he would be organizing yet another campaign in the spring.[23]

Officers and Organization

Brig. Gen. George Crook, Department of the Platte, Commanding
1st Lt. John G. Bourke, Third Cavalry, AAAG
Capt. John V. Furey, Quartermaster Department, Chief Quartermaster and Acting Ordnance Officer
1st Lt. Charles H. Rockwell, Fifth Cavalry, Chief Commissary of Subsistence
Capt. George M. Randall, Twenty-third Infantry, Chief of Scouts (joined 12-25)
1st Lt. Walter S. Schuyler, Fifth Cavalry, ADC
Asst. Surg. and Capt. Joseph R. Gibson, Chief Medical Officer
Asst. Surg. and 1st Lt. Curtis E. Price
Asst. Surg. and 1st Lt. Marshall W. Wood

[23] The composition of the Powder River Expedition is outlined in Second Cavalry Regimental Returns, November–December 1876; Third Cavalry Regimental Returns, November–December 1876; Fourth Cavalry Regimental Returns, November–December 1876; Fifth Cavalry Regimental Returns, November–December 1876; Fourth Infantry Regimental Returns, November–December 1876; Ninth Infantry Regimental Returns, November–December 1876; Fourteenth Infantry Regimental Returns, November–December 1876; Twenty-third Infantry Regimental Returns, November–December 1876; and Fourth Artillery Regimental Returns, November–December 1876. Two highly commended primary narratives are Jerry Roche, "The Dull Knife Campaign," in Cozzens, ed., *Eyewitnesses to the Indian Wars,* 414–30; and Bourke, *Mackenzie's Last Fight with the Cheyennes* (quotations on 28). A unique infantry officer's perspective on this campaign is offered by Richard Dodge, commanding the infantry-artillery battalion. See Kime, ed., *The Powder River Expedition Journals of Colonel Richard Irving Dodge.* The standard secondary account is Greene, *Morning Star Dawn.*

AAS William T. Owsley (det. 12-4)
AAS Louis A. La Garde
AAS Charles V. Petteys
Co. K, Second Cavalry, Capt. James Egan, Provost Guard
1st Lt. James N. Allison

Indian Scouts

1st Lt. William P. Clark, Second Cavalry, Commanding
2nd Lt. Hayden De Lany, Ninth Infantry

Cavalry Battalion

Col. Ranald S. Mackenzie, Fourth Cavalry, Commanding
2nd Lt. Joseph H. Dorst, Fourth Cavalry, Regimental Adjutant
1st Lt. Henry W. Lawton, Fourth Cavalry, Battalion QM (det. 11-30)

First Squadron, Fourth Cavalry

Capt. Clarence Mauck, Commanding
Co. B, 1st Lt. Charles M. Callahan (det. from Co. D)
1st Lt. Wentz C. Miller
Co. D, Capt. John Lee
2nd Lt. Stanton A. Mason
Co. E, 1st Lt. Frank L. Shoemaker (det. from Co. F)
2nd Lt. Henry H. Bellas
Co. F, Capt. Wirt Davis
2nd Lt. J. Wesley Rosenquest
2nd Lt. Augustus C. Tyler (det. from Co. G)
Co. I, Capt. William C. Hemphill

Second Squadron

Maj. George A. Gordon, Fifth Cavalry, Commanding (det. 12-4)
Co. H, Third Cavalry, Capt. Henry W. Wessells, Jr.
2nd Lt. Charles L. Hammond
Co. K, Third Cavalry, Capt. Gerald Russell
1st Lt. Oscar Elting
2nd Lt. George A. Dodd
Co. M, Fourth Cavalry, 1st Lt. John A. McKinney (KIA, 11-25)
1st Lt. Henry W. Lawton (since 11-30)
2nd Lt. Harrison G. Otis
Co. H, Fifth Cavalry, Capt. John M. Hamilton
1st Lt. Edward W. Ward (det. 12-4)
2nd Lt. Edwin P. Andrus
Co. L, Fifth Cavalry, Capt. Alfred B. Taylor (det. 12-4)
2nd Lt. Homer W. Wheeler

Artillery and Infantry Battalions

Lt. Col. Richard I. Dodge, Twenty-third Infantry, Commanding
1st Lt. Albert S. Cummins, Fourth Artillery, Battalion Adjutant
1st Lt. William L. Clarke, Twenty-third Infantry, Battalion AAQM

First Battalion (Artillery)

Capt. Joseph B. Campbell, Commanding Battalion and Co. F
Co. C, Capt. Harry C. Cushing
1st Lt. Sydney W. Taylor
2nd Lt. James M. Jones
Co. F, Capt. Joseph B. Campbell
2nd Lt. William Crozier
Co. H, Capt. Frank G. Smith
1st Lt. Harry R. Anderson
Co. K, 1st Lt. George G. Greenough
1st Lt. Walter Howe
2nd Lt. John T. French, Jr.

Second Battalion (Infantry)

Maj. Edwin F. Townsend, Ninth Infantry, Commanding
1st Lt. Morris C. Foote, Ninth Infantry, Battalion Adjutant
Co. A, Ninth Infantry, Capt. William H. Jordan
2nd Lt. Thomas S. McCaleb
Co. B, Ninth Infantry, 1st Lt. William E. Hofman (det. from Co. H)
Co. D, Ninth Infantry, 1st Lt. William B. Pease
2nd Lt. John A. Baldwin
Co. F, Ninth Infantry, 2nd Lt. Charles M. Rockefeller
Co. I, Ninth Infantry, 1st Lt. Jesse M. Lee
Co. K, Ninth Infantry, 1st Lt. Alpheus H. Bowman (joined 11-17)
2nd Lt. George Palmer
Co. D, Fourteenth Infantry, Capt. Joseph H. Van Derslice
1st Lt. Albert Austin
Co. G, Fourteenth Infantry, Capt. David Krause
1st Lt. Patrick Hasson
2nd Lt. William A. Kimball
Co. C, Twenty-third Infantry, Capt. Otis W. Pollock
2nd Lt. J. Rozier Clagett
Co. G, Twenty-third Infantry, Capt. Charles Wheaton
2nd Lt. Charles H. Heyl
Co. I, Twenty-third Infantry, 1st Lt. Frederick L. Dodge
2nd Lt. Edward B. Pratt

DEPLOYMENT NO. 22

Red Fork of the Powder River

Wyoming, November 24–26, 1876

Colonel Ranald S. Mackenzie's pivotal engagement with Northern Cheyenne Indians on November 25 is discussed within the narrative of the encompassing Powder River Expedition (Deployment No. 21).

Officers and Organization

Col. Ranald S. Mackenzie, Fourth Cavalry
2nd Lt. Joseph H. Dorst, Fourth Cavalry, Regimental Adjutant and AAAG
1st Lt. John G. Bourke, Third Cavalry, ADC
1st Lt. Henry W. Lawton, Fourth Cavalry, Battalion QM
AAS Louis A. La Garde

First Battalion

Maj. George A. Gordon, Fifth Cavalry
2nd Lt. Augustus C. Tyler, Fourth Cavalry, Battalion Adjutant
Co. H, Third Cavalry, Capt. Henry W. Wessells, Jr.
    2nd Lt. Charles L. Hammond
Co. K, Third Cavalry, Capt. Gerald Russell
    1st Lt. Oscar Elting
    2nd Lt. George A. Dodd
Co. F, Fourth Cavalry, Capt. Wirt Davis
    2nd Lt. J. Wesley Rosenquest
Co. M, Fourth Cavalry, 1st Lt. John A. McKinney (KIA)
    2nd Lt. Harrison G. Otis
Co. H, Fifth Cavalry, Capt. John M. Hamilton
    1st Lt. Edward W. Ward
    2nd Lt. Edwin P. Andrus
Co. L, Fifth Cavalry, Capt. Alfred B. Taylor
    2nd Lt. Homer W. Wheeler

Second Battalion

Capt. Clarence Mauck, Fourth Cavalry
1st Lt. Wentz C. Miller, Fourth Cavalry, Battalion Adjutant
Co. B, Fourth Cavalry, 1st Lt. Charles M. Callahan
Co. D, Fourth Cavalry, Capt. John Lee
    2nd Lt. Stanton A. Mason

Co. E, Fourth Cavalry, 1st Lt. Frank L. Shoemaker
2nd Lt. Henry H. Bellas
Co. I, Fourth Cavalry, Capt. William C. Hemphill
2nd Lt. James N. Allison, Second Cavalry
2nd Lt. James M. Jones, Fourth Artillery

Indian Scouts

Sioux and Arapaho
1st Lt. William P. Clark, Second Cavalry
2nd Lt. Hayden De Lany, Ninth Infantry

Pawnee
Frank North
Luther North

Shoshone
1st Lt. Walter S. Schuyler, Fifth Cavalry

DEPLOYMENT NO. 23

Wolf Mountains

Montana, December 27, 1876–January 18, 1877

Miles attributed persistent Indian harassment of mail carriers and herders throughout December in the proximity of Tongue River Cantonment to Crazy Horse's Oglala Sioux and was increasingly determined to move against Crazy Horse. On December 29 he led three companies and a makeshift mounted infantry detachment southward up the Tongue following the trail of four other companies that had started two days earlier. The combined force again included the cantonment's ordnance rifle and Napoleon cannon that Miles had used to good effect in earlier movements.

The party chanced on stray oxen on January 3 and detached four soldiers and a guide to round them up. But when the column advanced out of sight, Indians attacked these soldiers and killed one of them. Indian signs grew increasingly common in the upper Tongue Valley, including smoldering fires and gaunt ponies abandoned in the camps. Some in Miles's command suggested that this was a ruse.

In fact, Crazy Horse's warriors were well aware of Miles's advance and were planning an attack. In gloomy weather on January 7 Miles's civilian scouts came upon a small group of Cheyenne women and children searching for relatives. They had come forth supposedly unknowingly, lured by the smoke from Miles's cooking fires. Miles fed and detained them. As his scouts continued exploring the valley ahead, they stumbled into an ambush being prepared by Sioux and Cheyenne warriors. Hearing the exchange of fire, Miles forwarded several companies, which skirmished with the Indians until nightfall.

After a cold, uncertain night, Miles advanced cautiously southward and from a prominence overlooking the valley ahead observed hundreds of Indians coming forward and making no pretense at hiding. Miles dispersed his command to a key knoll alongside the river in his front and on the ridgeline east of the Tongue and loosed several rounds from the Napoleon, to no immediate effect. The tribesmen, meanwhile, gained the crest of another knoll and other eastern ridges and pressed the soldiers. The fighting from the knolls grew particularly vicious. Neither side gained advantage, although a prominent Northern Cheyenne medicine man, Big Crow, was killed. Eventually the steady press of the infantry and well-aimed artillery fire from both guns drove the Indians from their positions.

After nearly five hours of continuous fighting, a blinding snowstorm ended the engagement. The warriors fled up the valley. Miles remained on the field for the remainder of the day and on January 9 probed southward, passing through the Indians' abandoned camp several miles from the battlefield. Lacking supplies to continue a pursuit and fearful of the weather, Miles turned back for the cantonment, which the command reached on January 18.

The Wolf Mountains Battle was yet another blow to the Sioux, this time chiefly Crazy Horse's Oglala and Miniconjou followers, and also Northern Cheyennes who had joined the Sioux after their own devastating fight with troops in the Big Horn Mountains. For these people, offensive warfare was virtually over. Crazy Horse and Sitting Bull never again united. Miles's aggressiveness on the Yellowstone, despite the weather, was bringing an end to the Great Sioux War.[24]

---

[24]The troop deployment associated with Miles's Wolf Mountains campaign is confirmed in Fifth Infantry

Officers and Organization

Col. Nelson A. Miles, Fifth Infantry, Commanding
1st Lt. Frank D. Baldwin, Fifth Infantry, AAAG
2nd Lt. Oscar F. Long, Fifth Infantry, Acting Engineer Officer
Surg. and Major Henry R. Tilton
Asst. Surg. and 1st Lt. Louis S. Tesson

Fifth Infantry

Co. A, Capt. James S. Casey
Co. C, Capt. Edmond Butler
Co. D, 1st Lt. Robert McDonald
2nd Lt. Hobart K. Bailey
Co. E, Capt. Ezra P. Ewers
Co. K, 1st Lt. Mason Carter
Mounted Infantry Detachment, 2nd Lt. Charles E. Hargous
Artillery Detachment, 2nd Lt. James W. Pope

Twenty-second Infantry

Co. E, Capt. Charles J. Dickey
Co. F, 1st Lt. Cornelius C. Cusick
2nd Lt. Edward W. Casey

DEPLOYMENT NO. 24

Muddy Creek

Montana, April 29–May 14, 1877

Throughout the spring of 1877 a flurry of diplomatic engagements involving Miles in the Yellowstone River countryside and Chiefs Spotted Tail and Red Cloud from the White River agencies induced the surrender of many Sioux and Northern Cheyenne bands, particularly in Nebraska.

Regimental Returns, December 1876–January 1877; Twenty-second Infantry Regimental Returns, December 1876–January 1877; and Fort Keogh Post Returns, December 1876–January 1877. Two compelling primary narratives of this campaign are provided by Henry R. Tilton and Edmond Butler, "The Wolf Mountains Expedition and the Battle of Wolf Mountains, January 8, 1877," in Greene, ed., *Battles and Skirmishes of the Great Sioux War,* chapter 14. Useful secondary accounts are provided by Greene, *Yellowstone Command,* chapter 7; and Pearson, "Nelson A. Miles, Crazy Horse, and the Battle of Wolf Mountains."

Sitting Bull, meanwhile, encouraged his followers and others to cross into Canada and find sanctuary there. These movements had fairly well emptied the Yellowstone and Powder River basins of the northern Indians, except for a body of Miniconjou Sioux under Lame Deer, who steadfastly rejected notions of surrender or flight.

Scouts kept Miles alert to the presence of Lame Deer's followers in the Tongue and Rosebud valleys, but he deferred an advance until he was resupplied when river navigation resumed. With replenishments finally at hand, and word that Lame Deer's camp was supposedly swelling with like-minded Indians, he advanced against them. Segments of Miles's command departed the cantonment beginning on April 29. The column all told tallied six infantry companies from the Fifth and Twenty-second regiments and the Montana Battalion of the Second Cavalry, recently transferred to Tongue River Cantonment from Fort Ellis.

Miles's march revisited well-worn trails from other movements, including his own in January and Terry's and Crook's in August 1876. Lame Deer's trail was equally pronounced: it crossed from the Tongue into the Rosebud Valley and headed up Rosebud Creek. Miles detached three infantry companies and his wagons in the Tongue Valley and continued west over the divide. From heights west of Rosebud Creek, Miles's scouts located the Indian camp on Muddy Creek, a small Rosebud tributary. In a night march Miles closed on the village, numbering sixty-one lodges, and prepared for an attack at daybreak on May 7.

Second Lieutenant Edward W. Casey, Twenty-second Infantry, leading scouts and mounted infantry, and Second Lieutenant Lovell H. Jerome, leading Company H, Second Cavalry, charged the village and stampeded the pony herd. When Miles subsequently entered the camp, one of his scouts pointed out Lame Deer. They attempted to communicate. For a moment the firing stopped while scouts urged Lame Deer's surrender, but a scuffle ensued and shooting resumed. A bullet narrowly missed Miles, killing the orderly at his side. Pandemonium erupted. Lame Deer fled and was struck down by a soldier fusillade.

Miles then fully deployed the cavalry, who swept the village and chased fleeing Indians into the hillsides west of the creek, where they inflicted many casualties. When Miles's infantry companies arrived on the scene, the fighting was all but over, aside from sporadic long-range shooting. The troops occupied the camp that evening and methodically destroyed its contents and the ponies. At mid-morning on May 10 the column commenced its return to the cantonment, arriving on the fourteenth.

At Muddy Creek, also known as the Lame Deer Fight, Miles engaged the last of the Sioux who were visibly resisting surrender and the consequent imposition of the Rule of 1876. The generals and colonels who waged the Great Sioux War saw its end at hand.[25]

Officers and Organization

Col. Nelson A. Miles, Fifth Infantry
1st Lt. George W. Baird, Fifth Infantry, AAAG
2nd Lt. Oscar F. Long, Fifth Infantry, Acting Engineer Officer
2nd Lt. Samuel R. Douglas, Seventh Infantry, AAQM
2nd Lt. Edward W. Casey, Twenty-second Infantry, Commanding Scouts and Mounted Infantry
Asst. Surg and 1st Lt. Paul R. Brown
AAS William J. Van Eman

Fifth Infantry

Co. B, Capt. Andrew S. Bennett
2nd Lt. Thomas M. Woodruff
Co. H, 2nd Lt. Charles E. Hargous

Twenty-second Infantry

Co. E, Capt. Charles J. Dickey
Co. F, 1st Lt. Cornelius C. Cusick
Co. G, Capt. Charles W. Miner
1st Lt. Benjamin C. Lockwood
Co. H, Capt. De Witt C. Poole
1st Lt. Oskaloosa M. Smith
2nd Lt. Alfred C. Sharpe

Second Cavalry

Capt. Edward Ball, Commanding Battalion and Co. H
2nd Lt. Charles B. Schofield, Battalion Adjutant
Co. F, Capt. George L. Tyler
2nd Lt. Alfred M. Fuller (WIA)
Co. G, Capt. James N. Wheelan

[25] The troop composition associated with Miles's Muddy Creek or Lame Deer expedition is confirmed in Fifth Infantry Regimental Returns, April–May 1877; Twenty-second Infantry Regimental Returns, April–May 1877; Second Cavalry Regimental Returns, April–May 1877; and Fort Keogh Post Returns, April–May 1877. An important primary narrative is John F. McBlain, "The Lame Deer Fight, May 7, 1877," in Greene, ed., *Battles and Skirmishes of the Great Sioux War,* 204–12. The standard secondary account is Greene, *Yellowstone Command,* chapter 9.

Co. H, Capt. Edward Ball
2nd Lt. Lovell H. Jerome (WIA)
Co. L, Capt. Randolph Norwood
1st Lt. Samuel T. Hamilton

DEPLOYMENT NO. 25

In the Field near the Yellowstone River
Montana, May 1–August 12, 1877

Anticipating renewed campaigning in 1877 in consort with Miles, eleven companies of the reorganized Seventh Cavalry, commanded this season by its colonel, Samuel D. Sturgis, took the field in May. They traveled along the Missouri River overland to Fort Buford, which they reached on the seventeenth, and then the Yellowstone Valley to the mouth of Cedar Creek, Montana, where the regiment established a summer camp on May 29. Thus far Sturgis had participated in only one Great Sioux War deployment, the unhorsing and disarming of the Standing Rock and Cheyenne River Sioux. While his experience in Indian campaigning was considerable, it was largely limited to action in the West before the Civil War.

From camps variously located on Cedar and Sunday creeks, Seventh Cavalry companies participated in scouting and escort duty in the Big Open country and along the Yellowstone. No northern Indians were encountered. Company B led by Captain Thomas M. McDougall was detached on June 13 and joined the Little Missouri Expedition under Major Henry M. Lazelle, First Infantry, formed in mid-May to chase Lame Deer's shattered band. And Company I led by Captain Henry J. Nowlan was dispatched on June 17 to the Little Big Horn Battlefield to support Lieutenant Colonel Michael V. Sheridan's efforts at policing that field and exhuming the remains of a number of officers, including George Custer, for reburial elsewhere. It was readily apparent to everyone that the Great Sioux War was all but over. These troops would soon be diverted to the Nez Perce conflict, where they played a prominent role in confrontations with those tribesmen at Canyon Creek and Bear's Paw Mountains in western and northern Montana, respectively.[26]

Officers and Organization

Seventh Cavalry

Col. Samuel D. Sturgis, Commanding
Lt. Col. Elmer Otis, Commanding First Battalion (det., sick, 7-27)
Maj. Lewis Merrill, Commanding Second Battalion
1st Lt. George D. Wallace, Regimental Adjutant (resigned position 6-6)
1st Lt. Ernest A. Garlington, Regimental Adjutant (since 6-6)
1st Lt. Charles A. Varnum, RQM
1st Lt. Francis M. Gibson, AACS (det. from Co. H)
1st Lt. Luther R. Hare, Engineer Officer (det. from Co. I)
Asst. Surg. and Capt. Valery Havard
Asst. Surg. and 1st Lt. Edwin F. Gardner
Asst. Surg. and 1st Lt. Holmes O. Paulding
Band
Co. A, Capt. Myles Moylan
 2nd Lt. Ezra B. Fuller
Co. B (det. 6-13), Capt. Thomas M. McDougall
 1st Lt. William W. Robinson, Jr. (det. from Co. F)
Co. D, Capt. Edward S. Godfrey
 1st Lt. Edwin P. Eckerson
Co. E, 1st Lt. Charles C. De Rudio
 2nd Lt. Edwin P. Brewer (det. from Co. D)
Co. F, Capt. James M. Bell
 2nd Lt. Herbert J. Slocum
Co. G, 1st Lt. Ernest A. Garlington (until 6-6)
 1st Lt. George D. Wallace (since 6-6)
 2nd Lt. William J. Nicholson
Co. H, Capt. Frederick W. Benteen
 2nd Lt. Albert J. Russell
Co. I (det. 6-17 to 7-19), Capt. Henry J. Nowlan
 2nd Lt. Hugh L. Scott
Co. K, Capt. Owen Hale
 2nd Lt. J. Williams Biddle
Co. L, 1st Lt. John W. Wilkinson
 2nd Lt. Loyd S. McCormick (det., sick, 5-25)
Co. M, Capt. Thomas H. French
 2nd Lt. John C. Gresham

---

[26] This field movement along the Yellowstone River in summer 1877 is documented in Seventh Cavalry Regimental Returns, May–August 1877; Fort A. Lincoln Post Returns, May–August 1877; First Infantry Regimental Returns, May–June 1877; and Twenty-second Infantry Regimental Return, June 1877. Secondary accounts are few and skimpy but include Greene, *Yellowstone Command,* 216–18, 220; and Chandler, *Of Garryowen in Glory,* 74–76.

First Infantry (joined 5-28, det. 7-24)
Co. G, Capt. Robert E. Johnston
2nd Lt. Harry C. Johnson

Twenty-second Infantry (joined 6-3, det. 6-16)
Co. E, Capt. Charles J. Dickey

DEPLOYMENT NO. 26

In the Field near the Tongue River
Wyoming and Montana, May 29–September 1, 1877

As with the deployment of the Seventh Cavalry in the Department of Dakota, in May 1877 General Crook ordered five Fifth Cavalry companies to the field from Fort D. A. Russell, Wyoming, for preemptive patrolling of the buffalo country east of the Big Horn Mountains. In early June Company L and Assistant Surgeon Julius H. Patzki detached from this column at Fort Fetterman to escort Generals Sheridan and Crook from Camp Brown, Wyoming, across the Big Horns to the Tongue River. There they joined companies A, B, and I, now commanded by Major Verling K. Hart, and continued to Custer's Battlefield, a location of extreme interest to Sheridan. After the Little Big Horn visit, Hart's Battalion continued to probe in all directions from its camp on the Tongue but encountered no Indians. The Fifth Cavalry's Sioux War service ceased at the end of August when Colonel Wesley Merritt summoned this battalion to the Nez Perce campaign.[27]

Officers and Organization

Fifth Cavalry
Capt. John M. Hamilton, Commanding Battalion and Co. H (until 6-23)

[27] This 1877 field movement is documented in Fifth Cavalry Regimental Returns, May–September 1877. Two primary narratives chronicle this obscure deployment: Price, *Across the Continent with the Fifth Cavalry;* and Hedren, "Eben Swift's Army Service on the Plains."

Maj. Verling K. Hart, Commanding (joined 6-23)
2nd Lt. Robert London, Battalion AAQM
Asst. Surg. and Capt. Julius H. Patzki
Asst. Surg. and 1st Lt. Robert W. Shufeldt
AAS Edward P. Lecompte
Co. A, Capt. Calbraith P. Rodgers
Co. B, Capt. Robert H. Montgomery (det. 7-14)
  2nd Lt. Eben Swift, Battalion Adjutant (until 7-4)
Co. H, Capt. John M. Hamilton
  2nd Lt. Edwin P. Andrus, Battalion Adjutant (since 7-4)
Co. I, Capt. Sanford C. Kellogg
Co. L, 1st Lt. Charles H. Rockwell
  2nd Lt. Homer W. Wheeler

DEPLOYMENT NO. 27

Little Missouri Expedition

Montana and Dakota, June 16–September 1, 1877

For nearly three months in midsummer 1877 Colonel Miles loosely directed several subordinate commands that relentlessly scoured southeastern Montana and western Dakota for Sioux, particularly the followers of the deceased Lame Deer, killed at Muddy Creek in May. While Sturgis's Seventh Cavalry maneuvered north of the Yellowstone, the co-called Little Missouri Expedition, led initially by Major Henry M. Lazelle, First Infantry, focused its efforts south and east of the river.

Lazelle commanded an amorphic infantry and cavalry column drawn from units at Tongue River Cantonment, plus one company of Sturgis's Seventh Cavalry from Cedar Creek. Initially marching with the expedition were the six companies of Twenty-second Infantry that traveled eastward with Lazelle to the Little Missouri River but detached there. They continued to Fort Abraham Lincoln and from there returned to the Division of the Atlantic, from whence they had come one year earlier.

Spurred by news from Lazelle of his having encountered evidence of a fresh Indian movement and his subsequent request for cavalry support, Miles dispatched companies of the Second Cavalry and mounted Fifth Infantry from Tongue River on July 2, commanded by Captain Edward

Ball, Second Cavalry. Meanwhile, on the Little Missouri River on July 3, scouts from Lazelle's column traded shots with warriors from a small Sioux camp, this amounting to the last recorded exchange of gunfire in the Great Sioux War.

The enlarged column was soon commanded by Major James S. Brisbin, Second Cavalry, Lazelle's senior in grade by nearly six years. Brisbin reorganized the troops into three battalions and kept them in perpetual motion throughout a landscape stretching from the headwaters of the Heart, Cannonball, and Grand rivers east of the Little Missouri badlands to O'Fallon's Creek and the Powder River drainage in eastern Montana. Occasionally troops passed through abandoned Indian campsites, but after July 3 they encountered no tribesmen. Meanwhile, family by family, Lame Deer's followers trickled into the Spotted Tail Agency in Nebraska, beginning in late July. The last group, a small band led by Fast Bull, surrendered on September 9. There were no other warring Indians in the Sioux Country of old. The active phase of the Great Sioux War had come to a quiet close.[28]

Officers and Organization

Initial Organization, June 16–July 26, 1877

Maj. Henry M. Lazelle, First Infantry
2nd Lt. Marion P. Maus, First Infantry, Acting Topographical Officer
2nd Lt. Frank H. Edmunds, First Infantry, Wagonmaster
2nd Lt. Edward W. Casey, Twenty-second Infantry, Cattle herd (joined 6-18)
Asst. Surg. and 1st Lt. Paul R. Brown (det. 7-10)

First Infantry

Co. B, 2nd Lt. Hugh T. Reed
Co. H, Capt. Thomas M. Tolman
Co. K, Capt. Kinzie Bates

Twenty-second Infantry (det. 7-10)

Co. E, Capt. Charles J. Dickey
Co. F, 1st Lt. Cornelius C. Cusick

[28] The Little Missouri Expedition is documented in First Infantry Regimental Returns, June–September 1877; Fifth Infantry Regimental Returns, June–September 1877; Twenty-second Infantry Regimental Returns, June–July 1877; Second Cavalry Regimental Returns, July–September 1877; Seventh Cavalry Regimental Returns, June–September 1877; Fort Keogh Post Returns, June–September 1877; and Fort Sully Post Returns, June–September 1877. Two interesting enlisted men's narratives report on this final field movement of the Great Sioux War: Cox, *Five Years in the United States Army;* and Zimmer, *Frontier Soldier.* The standard secondary source on this movement is Greene, "Out with a Whimper."

Co. G, Capt. Charles W. Miner
Co. H, Capt. De Witt C. Poole
    1st Lt. Oskaloosa M. Smith
Co. I, Capt. Francis Clarke
    1st Lt. William Conway
Co. K, Capt. Mott Hooten
    2nd Lt. William H. Kell

Seventh Cavalry

Co. B (joined 6-17), Capt. Thomas M. McDougall
    1st Lt. William W. Robinson, Jr. (det. from Co. F)

Second Cavalry (joined 7-3)

Capt. Edward Ball, Commanding Battalion and Co. H
Co. F, Capt. George L. Tyler
Co. G, Capt. James N. Wheelan
    2nd Lt. Edward J. McClernand, Battalion Adjutant (joined 7-17)
Co. H, Capt. Edward Ball
    2nd Lt. Lovell H. Jerome (joined 7-18)

Fifth Infantry (joined 7-3)

Co. A (mounted), Capt. James S. Casey
    1st Lt. Henry Romeyn
Co. H (mounted), 1st Lt. Thomas H. Logan

Reorganization, July 27–September 1, 1877

Maj. James S. Brisbin, Second Cavalry, Commanding
2nd Lt. Edward J. McClernand, Second Cavalry, Battalion Adjutant
1st Lt. Frank D. Baldwin, Fifth Infantry, ADC and Chief of Scouts
2nd Lt. Charles E. Hargous, Fifth Infantry, Commanding Crow Scouts
2nd Lt. Samuel R. Douglas, Seventh Infantry, AAQM
AAS Victor Biart

First Battalion

Capt. Edward Ball, Second Cavalry, Commanding Battalion and Co. H

Second Cavalry

Co. F, Capt. George L. Tyler
Co. G, Capt. James N. Wheelan
Co. H, Capt. Edward Ball
    2nd Lt. Lovell H. Jerome

Seventh Cavalry

Co. B, Capt. Thomas M. McDougall
 1st Lt. William W. Robinson, Jr.

Second Battalion

Capt. James S. Casey, Fifth Infantry, Commanding Battalion and Co. A

Fifth Infantry

Co. A (mounted), Capt. James S. Casey
 1st Lt. Henry Romeyn
Co. H (mounted), 1st Lt. Thomas H. Logan

Third Battalion

Maj. Henry M. Lazelle, First Infantry, Commanding
2nd Lt. Marion P. Maus, First Infantry, Acting Topographical Officer
2nd Lt. Frank H. Edmunds, First Infantry, Wagonmaster
Capt. Andrew S. Bennett, Fifth Infantry, Crow Scouts (joined 7-30)
 2nd Lt. Charles E. Hargous

First Infantry

Co. B, 2nd Lt. Hugh T. Reed
Co. G (joined 7-28), Capt. Robert E. Johnston
 2nd Lt. Harry C. Johnson
Co. H, Capt. Thomas M. Tolman
Co. K, Capt. Kinzie Bates

Hotchkiss Gun, 1st Lt. Samuel T. Hamilton, Second Cavalry

Seventh Cavalry (joined 8-21)

Capt. Owen Hale, Commanding Battalion and Co. K
Co. A, Capt. Myles Moylan
Co. H, Capt. Frederick W. Benteen
 2nd Lt. Albert J. Russell
Co. K, Capt. Owen Hale
 2nd Lt. J. Williams Biddle

Fifth Infantry (joined 8-21)

Capt. Simon Snyder, Commanding Battalion and Co. F
Co. B (mounted), 2nd Lt. Thomas M. Woodruff
Co. F (mounted), Capt. Simon Snyder
 2nd Lt. Charles B. Thompson

DEPLOYMENT NO. 28

Big Horn Post

Montana, July 5–September 1, 1877

Sherman's and Sheridan's vision of troops occupying the buffalo country of the northern plain—yesterday's Sioux Country—was partly fulfilled in 1876 with the founding of cantonments on the Yellowstone River in Montana and Powder River in Wyoming, both of which evolved into sizable, enduring forts. So, too, did the post established in July 1877 on the Big Horn River. In Sherman's words, each fort ensured that "these Sioux Indians can never again regain this country."

The founding of the Big Horn Post, or Post No. 2 as it was also initially called, fell to Lieutenant Colonel George P. Buell and six companies of the Eleventh Infantry, redirected to this duty from agency service on the middle Missouri River. Buell chose to construct on an imposing plateau overlooking the confluence of the Big Horn and Little Big Horn rivers, barely fifteen miles from Custer's Battlefield. As steamboat pilot Grant Marsh had demonstrated a year earlier when evacuating wounded Seventh Cavalrymen, the Big Horn River was occasionally navigable as far as the mouth of the Little Big Horn. This allowed transportation of troops, construction crews, structural matériel, and army wherewithal directly to the site, at least for a short while in 1877. Buell also constructed a way station on the Yellowstone River just above the mouth of the Big Horn to receive freight and passengers bound for his post.

Big Horn Post, soon called Fort Custer, received the headquarters contingent and eight companies of the Second Cavalry in October 1877 and quickly gained a reputation as one of the finest cavalry stations in the nation. Despite lingering uncertainties with Indians in the initial months of construction, duty at Fort Custer focused almost wholly on relations with the Crow Indians and the care of Custer National Cemetery, established in 1879. As related to the Sioux and the Great Sioux War, Sheridan's vision of a transformed Sioux Country was indeed fulfilled.[29]

---

[29] The terminal date provided here reflects a date relatively synonymous with the close of the Great Sioux War. Fort Custer functioned until April 1898.

The Big Horn Post/Fort Custer garrison is confirmed in Eleventh Infantry Regimental Returns, June–September 1877; and Fort Custer Post Returns, June–September 1877. The Sherman quotation appears in a letter to secretary of war George W. McCrary written from the Big Horn River, July 25, 1877, in *Reports of Inspection Made in the Summer of 1877*, 44. An anthology brimming with useful information about this post is Upton, *Fort Custer on the Big Horn*.

Officers and Organization

Eleventh Infantry

Lt. Col. George P. Buell
1st Lt. George Ruhlen, Seventeenth Infantry, AAQM and ACS
Asst. Surg. and Capt. Louis S. Tesson (joined 7-17)
AAS Andrew C. Bergen (joined 7-17)
Co. A (joined 7-24), 1st Lt. John Whitney
2nd Lt. James E. Macklin
Co. B (joined 7-16), Capt. Joseph Conrad
2nd Lt. Albert L. Myer (det. 7-21)
Co. C (joined 7-29), 2nd Lt. William H. Wheeler
Co. F, 2nd Lt. Harry Tiffany, Commanding Co. and Post Adjutant
Co. G, Capt. Theodore Schwan
1st Lt. Leon A. Matile (joined 7-24)
2nd Lt. John J. Dougherty (det. 7-30)
Co. H (joined 7-24, det. 7-25), Capt. Erasmus C. Gilbreath
1st Lt. Ogden B. Read

Part III

What Went Right and Wrong?

Reflection and Analysis

From the exhausting and politically charged wintertime relief of Fort Pease in February 1876 and the first volleys of carbine and rifle fire at Powder River just weeks afterward through the brief exchange of gunshots on the Little Missouri River a year and a half later, the Great Sioux War had become one of the most difficult, prolonged, intriguing, costly Indian wars in American history. This conflict was waged on twenty-seven different battlefields, with financial costs exceeding $2.3 million.[1] Rosebud Creek on June 17, 1876, was the largest Indian battle that ever occurred in the Trans-Mississippi West. The Battle of Little Big Horn on June 25 was marked by the phenomenal efforts of tribesmen allied for cultural and societal survival and the unimaginable deaths of five companies of cavalry and the nation's most visible and charismatic military leader. The war also featured the unconscionable physical and cultural devastation of the Northern Cheyennes at Red Fork of the Powder River on November 25, the destruction of five other Indian villages, and the almost mythic materialization of Sitting Bull and Crazy Horse in spiritual and warrior roles.

The U.S. Army ultimately prevailed in the Great Sioux War and in doing so furthered its capacity to wage these so-called unconventional wars. In subsequent decades veteran officers published compelling memoirs of their service on the northern plains wherein they reflected on the triumphs in the cause of "winning the West," the notion that largely framed their view of this great national saga, and discussed the lessons

[1] In December 1877 the Senate asked the president for an estimation of the costs associated with the "late war with the Sioux Indians." The War Department in turn requested details from the Departments of Dakota and Platte pertinent to quartermaster, subsistence, ordnance, and medical expenditures. The respective departments provided costs of $992,807.78 and $1,319,723.46, for a sum of $2,312,531.24. "Cost of the Late War with the Sioux Indians"; and "Further Information in Relation to the Cost of the Sioux War."

evident in this abject warfare.[2] In this era of reflection, one of the army's young, ambitious scholars, Second Lieutenant Edward S. Farrow of the Twenty-first Infantry, not a Sioux War but a Nez Perce War veteran, penned a warmly received, almost encyclopedic practical guide to field service against Indians. It brimmed with useful suggestions on packing, forced marching, living off the land, skirmishing with the tribesmen, and much more.[3] And very specific matters germane to Indian warfare, including issues of weapons and tactics, were discussed and analyzed by Sioux War veterans like John Gibbon, Charles King, and Edward S. Godfrey in essays appearing in the army's new professional journals.[4]

The army finally institutionalized the study of its American wars, including these Plains Indian wars, at new branch schools of application such as the Infantry and Cavalry School established at Fort Leavenworth in May 1881. It was patterned after the already highly successful Artillery School at Fort Monroe, Virginia, and Engineer School of Application at Willett's Point, New York. This new school had as its first commander Great Sioux War veteran Colonel Elwell S. Otis, then of the Twentieth Infantry, and soon included among its permanent faculty some of the army's able young scholars. First Lieutenant Arthur L. Wagner, Sixth Infantry, was a veteran of Great Sioux War service along the Yellowstone River. Captain Eben Swift, Fifth Cavalry, was another veteran of the Great Sioux War at the close of the Big Horn and Yellowstone Expedition and a participant in other northern plains Indian campaigns, including the interception of the Northern Cheyennes in 1878. At this and other schools lieutenants drawn from the line regiments received classroom instruction in military history, army administration, strategy, and tactics and considerable practical field drill in matters of reconnaissance, security, attack, and defense.[5]

The British military paid heed to the lessons of the Great Sioux War too, introducing the study of irregular warfare to its officers in the late 1880s

---

[2] The extraordinary outpouring of nineteenth-century officer reminiscences and memoirs of the Great Sioux War includes John Gibbon, "Last Summer's Expedition against the Sioux Indians and Its Great Catastrophe" and "Hunting Sitting Bull"; King, *Campaigning with Crook,* "Custer's Last Battle," and *Trials of a Staff-Officer;* Bourke, *Mackenzie's Last Fight with the Cheyennes* and *On the Border with Crook;* Baird, "General Miles's Indian Campaigns"; Godfrey, "Custer's Last Battle"; Hughes, "The Campaign against the Sioux in 1876"; and Miles, *Personal Recollections and Observations of General Nelson A. Miles.*

[3] Farrow, *Mountain Scouting.*

[4] Gibbon, "Arms to Fight Indians"; King, "Arms or Tactics"; Godfrey, "Cavalry Fire Discipline."

[5] Nenninger, *The Leavenworth Schools and the Old Army,* 22–29; Brereton, *Educating the U.S. Army,* 13–14; King, "The Leavenworth School"; Utley, "The Contribution of the Frontier to the American Military Tradition," 528.

and drawing on experiences of British, French, Russian, and American soldiers in both classroom study and an insightful text titled *Small Wars: Their Principles and Practices* that perfectly captured the tenets of Sheridan's unwritten doctrine for Indian warfare on the American Plains.[6]

Despite these commendable advances in continuing education in matters directly associated with the arts of war and the high visibility that the Indian wars and especially the Great Sioux War gained in the outpouring of war-related memoirs and essays in the final quarter of the nineteenth century, the army's strategic thinkers continued to view the Indian conflicts as an anomaly that would soon be something of the American past. And, of course, they soon were. In the army's eyes, the next real war would be a conventional one with another developed nation. In the long run the lessons on unconventional warfare learned on the plains and studied in the branch schools were never deeply engrained. The army could hardly imagine the Philippine Insurrection lying in its not too distant future.[7]

Sheridan's Army certainly deployed fully to the Great Sioux War. Under Crook's and Terry's initial direction, fifty-five companies representing three cavalry and six infantry regiments, drawn exclusively from their respective departments, were currently or had already been deployed to the war by June 1, 1876. The majority of these initial companies formed three columns converging on the landscape south of the Yellowstone River, while others tended supply caches or safeguarded trails. These were experienced troops, including elements of the Second and Third and entire Seventh Cavalry, which was widely regarded as perhaps *the* most experienced and best-led Indian fighting regiment in the American Army. This initial deployment engaged almost thirteen percent of the entire American Army. While Crook's and Terry's troops fought phenomenal battles with the Sioux at Rosebud and Little Big Horn, however, they faltered, and the initial effort collapsed.

By September 30, 1876, Sheridan and his department commanders had infused those summer commands with new troops drawn largely from beyond the immediate departments and led by energetic officers like Miles, Elwell Otis, Merritt, Carr, and Mackenzie who had not suffered the stings of Powder River, Rosebud, or Little Big Horn. By then some ninety-nine companies representing five cavalry regiments, ten infantry regiments, and one artillery regiment were engaged on the northern plains, with one more new infantry regiment momentarily sidelined at

[6] Trinque, "Small Wars and the Little Bighorn"; Callwell, *Small Wars*.

[7] Cosmas, *An Army for Empire*, 8–9.

two Missouri River agencies but destined to join the fray before its end. At that stage of the conflict, nearly one-fourth (24.18 percent) of the American Army's line companies had or were currently engaged in the Great Sioux War. Before the war's end nearly one-third (31.62 percent) of the army's line companies could call themselves Great Sioux War veterans. They included all twelve companies of the Third, Fifth, and Seventh Cavalry, all ten companies of the Fifth and Ninth Infantry, and ultimately five of the army's ten cavalry regiments, twelve of the army's twenty-five infantry regiments, and a battalion of the Fourth Artillery.

Each of the commanders organizing major movements in the Great Sioux War (including Brisbin, Reynolds, Crook, Gibbon, Terry, Merritt, Miles, Pollock, Sturgis, Lazelle, and Buell) did so logically. Their plans were consistent with an orthodoxy of organization and detail not so much learned at West Point or from some manual as simply based on observable common practice throughout the army, whether at the departments, on military posts, or within regiments. Expeditions and columns invariably had adjutants tending communications and paperwork, quartermasters and commissaries of subsistence tending supplies and provisions, chiefs of scouts, and medical officers. Some columns had engineers and ordnance officers. Sometimes generals and colonels had aides-de-camp. Common sense drove the structures of the headquarters components and management of the line companies that composed the expeditions. Sometimes battalions were formed by aligning companies from the same regiment, and sometimes by mixing them. Sometimes battalions were composed of two companies, as in Reynolds's Big Horn Expedition, while battalions in Crook's Big Horn and Yellowstone Expedition included five and six companies. On several of Miles's sorties, the entire ten companies of the Fifth Infantry Regiment campaigned. The simple objectives of any of these parcelings or divisions were the streamlining of the command structures and the equitable division of oversight. Sometimes the structures were relatively complex due to the extreme sizes of the columns, as with the Big Horn and Yellowstone Expedition, Terry's late-summer orchestration, and Lazelle's and Brisbin's Little Missouri Expedition, and sometimes they were exceedingly simple. Lieutenant Colonel Elwell Otis's six-company battalion of the Twenty-second Infantry was a unique extreme of simplicity. In his October 26, 1876, report to Terry and Sheridan on his duty at Glendive Cantonment and his engagements along Spring Creek, Otis noted that he was "ably assisted by Lieut. O. M. Smith, my only staff-officer. All other officers were serving with their companies, and furnished to their men examples of fearless exposure and great endurance."[8]

No discernible reason explains why Crook specifically named his respective columns while no other field commander did—although Miles called his burgeoning eastern Montana force the "Yellowstone Command" in the dateline of correspondence originating at Cantonment Tongue River. Crook's Big Horn Expedition, Big Horn and Yellowstone Expedition, and Powder River Expedition were each formally named in a General Order at the commencement of the movement, an action not uncommon during the Civil War, where command names variously reflected rivers or landscapes being protected. Every other column and movement associated with the Great Sioux War came to be known informally by a geographic place-name or by the name of the officer in command, thus giving history the Fort Pease Relief, Terry's Column, Reno's Scout, and the Fort Peck Expedition, among others. No particular name emerged at all for a handful of movements, such as Merritt's distinguished action in eastern Wyoming leading to the Warbonnet Creek skirmish and Hazen's Fort Peck sortie.

The orthodoxy of total war and each of the tactical elements of Sheridan's unwritten doctrine for Indian warfare played a conclusive role in the Great Sioux War, although less by grand scheme than by simple persistence, diligence, and repetition evinced by the many field commanders. Upon reflection, Sheridan acknowledged in the fall of 1876 the lost opportunity of a quick wintertime strike against Sitting Bull's and Crazy Horse's warriors seven months earlier, when the formidable northern plains winter impeded the orchestration of columns from three distant sectors converging on the Little Missouri countryside and lower Powder River Basin. Only Reynolds successfully mustered an initial late-winter column and engaged Indians, attacking a Cheyenne village at daybreak in mid-March but suffering unmanageable consequences. Gibbon by then had organized a column bound for the Lower Yellowstone but moved timidly and ultimately to no consequence at all. By the time Crook and Terry fielded major columns in late spring, the three forces (theirs and Gibbon's) faced the prospect of a summer war. They also confronted the unimagined ascendancy of the Lakotas and their allies, who fought audaciously and with marked determination at Rosebud Creek and heroically and with pronounced numerical superiority at Little Big Horn.

During the remainder of the summer of 1876, the Great Sioux War was

[8] "Report of Lt. Col. E. S. Otis," in *Report of the Secretary of War, 1876*, 518.

characterized by flailing, aimless movements and small chance encounters with Indians. Near Red Cañon, Dakota, on August 1 Captain William S. Collier repulsed attackers at a nearby stage station. At the Powder River Depot site on August 2 Major Orlando Moore successfully repulsed Sioux scavengers. And on September 9 Captain Anson Mills rousted a small Sioux village in the Slim Buttes. Mills attacked at dawn and captured the camp and pony herd and with Crook's support successfully repulsed a series of counterattacks soon thereafter. These circumstances at Slim Buttes were strikingly similar at the onset to those faced by Reynolds at Powder River, but Reynolds's smaller cavalry force could not withstand the Cheyenne counterattacks and yielded the camp and later the captured ponies. Crook deployed a substantially larger force at Slim Buttes, including infantry. He held and destroyed the camp and ponies and repulsed the counterattacks but withdrew before inflicting any additional damage to nearby camps, one of which evidently belonged to Crazy Horse.

Merritt's action at Warbonnet Creek was the army's one lustrous accomplishment in the post-Rosebud summer war. Upon learning that a sizable body of Northern Cheyennes had bolted from the Red Cloud Agency, he forced-marched and positioned seven companies of his Fifth Cavalry in front of the Indians, surprising the camp's scouts in a dawn encounter at Warbonnet Creek and driving the villagers back to Red Cloud. Merritt's feat was aggressive and achieved visible results, not yet an army hallmark in the Great Sioux War.

What Merritt and Moore probably did not realize and Crook perhaps only barely perceived as they engaged Indians respectively at Warbonnet Creek, Powder River Depot, and Slim Buttes was the inevitable splintering of the great Little Big Horn coalition. After Little Big Horn the consolidated encampment had trailed relatively en masse southward up the river to the foothills of the Big Horns, where they hunted and celebrated their great victory. Lieutenant Frederick Sibley chanced upon scouts and hunters from this Big Horn Mountain camp in early July while making his way to the Crow Agency. In mid-July the tribesmen scattered widely from that camp. All bands were intent on eluding troops but mostly interested simply in laying in winter provisions of game, chiefly buffalo. The Cheyennes encountered by Merritt at Warbonnet Creek were an anomaly, being among the last of the agency residents lured to the northern camps while such travel was still reasonably possible and the excitement of war was still vibrant. They too, of course, needed to hunt. With the Little Big Horn coalition dispersed, the nature of the Great Sioux

War changed dramatically for the army and ominously for the tribesmen. The Indians were henceforth relentlessly hunted until they surrendered at the agencies or the bands fled America and joined Sitting Bull's defectors north of the Medicine Line.

Actions in the fall of 1876 by Miles on the Yellowstone and Mackenzie on the Red Fork of the Powder River crushed the Indians' capacity to continue their resistance. Within weeks of one another, three villages were struck and destroyed, casualties were inflicted, particularly among the Cheyennes, and all the people were exposed to winter without shelter and food. This was classic offensive warfare exercised by the army with fierce resolve, and total war precisely as Sheridan embraced and encouraged it. Crazy Horse had played a version of offensive war too, at Tongue River, Wyoming, and Rosebud Creek in June 1876, and had helped lead an audacious defense at Little Big Horn that had strong overtones of offense. But by the time he invoked offensive war once more in the Wolf Mountains in January 1877, the tenor of the Great Sioux War had changed. The Wolf Mountains fight played to a draw, but by now Crazy Horse's followers were weary, resources were scarce, and suffering was widespread. Miles, well equipped and provisioned, had already demonstrated the capacity to strike violently and whenever opportunity beckoned, irrespective of the drawbacks of winter.

In meaningful and obvious ways, the army controlled Sioux Country by midwinter 1876–77, and its position was strengthening with each passing month. Troops moved supplies at will on the Yellowstone from Fort Buford and Glendive Cantonment to Tongue River Cantonment and in the Powder River Basin from Fort Fetterman to Cantonment Reno. They responded to Indian incursions with haste: not just Miles at Tongue River and Major Alfred L. Hough replacing Otis at Glendive Cantonment, but also Hazen at Fort Buford, First Lieutenant Frank Taylor at Sage Creek, Wyoming, Captain Peter D. Vroom from Camp Robinson, and Major Andrew W. Evans at Fort Laramie. The army functioned now from three new, increasingly stable installations in Sioux Country, plus two camps on the Black Hills Road. The Tongue River and Reno cantonments would evolve into permanent forts in 1877 and were joined by the Big Horn Post in July and others in subsequent years.

The army also controlled the Sioux agencies, governing with commendable fairness but also a firm hand. Few movements went unnoticed. As if to confirm that the lands beyond the Great Sioux Reservation no longer belonged to the Sioux, Sheridan again flooded the unceded country with troops in the spring of 1877, rendering that landscape perfectly unwelcome. Of three substantial commands maneuvering in the buffalo country in the summer of 1877, only Lazelle's troops closed with Indians, inconsequential as that encounter was. Aside from those with Sitting Bull in Canada, the Sioux and Northern Cheyennes were now reservation people. Cattle ranchers eyed the northern plains with increasing interest, and railroaders itched to lay track west of the Missouri River. The Black Hills gold rush was maturing too, as placer mining in the streams gave way to capital-intensive hard-rock mining in a mountainscape without Indians. The Great Sioux War was over.

When the Senate asked the army in December 1877 for a tally of the financial costs associated with the Great Sioux War, as noted above, it also inquired about the "casualties of rank and file among the soldiers engaged in said Sioux war." The Adjutant General's Office quickly tabulated the commissioned officers and enlisted men killed and wounded in the Medical Department, the various cavalry and infantry regiments, and Indian scouts, for the period of February 1876 through November 1877. This accounting listed 16 officers killed and 2 wounded and 265 enlisted men killed and 122 wounded, for an aggregate of 405 killed and wounded, or 408 including 2 Indian scouts killed and 1 wounded. That tally was adjusted slightly in another enumeration prepared by the Adjutant General's Office in 1891, and both tallies have been updated again in appendix E in a list that more carefully accounts for military casualties across the board, especially wounded officers and enlisted men. This was an era when so-called walking wounded were rarely added to any tally unless they were incapacitated, and yet battle reports, regimental returns, and muster rolls invariably acknowledged these additional injured soldiers. Studies by the Great Sioux War's leading historians also always reflected and adjusted these varied primary sources and statistics. The current tabulation acknowledges 16 officers killed and 7 wounded and 266 enlisted men killed and 132 wounded, for an aggregate of 421 killed and wounded in the Great Sioux War, or 431 including civilian and Indian scouts and interpreters killed or wounded in military action.[9]

In his 1877 annual report to General Sherman, Sheridan commented

[9] "Cost of the Late War with the Sioux Indians," 3; *Chronological List of Actions.* Other key sources are provided in the source note in appendix E.

on the casualties suffered by the men in his division in the preceding two years, calling the "ratio of loss of officers and men in proportion to the number engaged . . . equal to or greater than the ratio of loss on either side in the present Russo-Turkish campaign, or in the late civil war in this country."[10] Reflecting on Sheridan's statement, Charles A. Woodruff, who had served in the Seventh Infantry in 1876, noted that "the number of soldiers killed in the department[s] commanded by Generals Terry, C[r]ook and Howard was greater than the number killed in the Philippines from May 1, 1898, to Sept. 30, 1899, and nearly twice the number of soldiers and sailors, regulars and volunteers, killed in Cuba and P[ue]rto Rico during the same period."[11]

Confirming these statements by Sheridan and Woodruff is beyond the scope of this work. Woodruff included figures from the Nez Perce War and particularly his own Seventh Infantry, mauled in the Battle of the Big Hole in August 1877, which further complicates comparisons. But indeed both statements reflected the serious nature and heavy toll of the campaign. For one unit certainly, the Seventh Cavalry, the ratio of officers and men lost in proportion to the number engaged clearly was extraordinary and may have been what Sheridan imagined as he made his declaration. Of the 660 men marching with the regiment into battle at Little Big Horn, 301 were killed or wounded, amounting to a casualty rate of 45.6 percent, an astonishing figure indeed.[12] No other regiment suffered comparably in the Great Sioux War. But such staggering numbers were not, in fact, uncommon during the Civil War. Among Regular Army regiments engaged at Gettysburg, for instance, losses exceeded 29 percent for the Sixth Infantry, 25 percent for the Fourteenth Infantry, 50 percent for the Seventh Infantry, and 57 percent for the Seventeenth Infantry.[13] One of the benchmark Civil War battle casualty rates belongs to the First Minnesota Infantry Regiment, which suffered a casualty rate of 58.3 percent at Gettysburg.[14]

---

[10] "Report of Lieutenant-General P. H. Sheridan," in *Report of the Secretary of War, 1877*, 58.

[11] "Indian Warfare Losses Severe"; Woodruff, "Historical Sketch of the 7th Infantry," 181.

[12] "Report of Lieutenant-General P. H. Sheridan," in *Report of the Secretary of War, 1877*, 58.

[13] Reese, *Regulars!* 208.

[14] The First Minnesota statistic is provided because its casualty rate at Gettysburg has long been heralded as "the greatest regimental loss in any battle, in proportion to the number engaged," supposedly amounting to 82 percent of men available for duty and participating in a heroic charge on the battle's second day (Leehan, *Pale Horse at Plum Run*, 154). But that tally is misleading and would be analogous to reporting only the casualty rate of the five Seventh Cavalry companies following Custer at the Little Big Horn (99 percent fatalities) instead of a rate computed for the regiment as a whole in a two-day battle. More recent accountings of the First Minnesota refine this figure. Moe, *The Last Full Measure*, 296, reports a 70 percent casualty rate. Leehan, *Pale Horse at Plum Run*, 169–88, reports the 58.39 percent casualty rate given here.

Accounting for Indian casualties in the Great Sioux War has long perplexed historians. Officers reporting on actions they variously commanded or participated in were customarily specific about casualties suffered by the troops in their control but usually general, at best, or vague on the casualties inflicted. They sometimes used simple rounded numbers like ten, twenty-five, or thirty and noted that Indians invariably carried off their killed and wounded, which thus made better tallies impossible. These statistics found their way into accountings that are still widely referenced today but at face value provide only a questionable estimate of Lakota and Northern Cheyenne casualties incurred in this war. Furthermore, through the years the fixation on all matters related to the Little Big Horn tended to blind many researchers who, when this was still possible, queried Indian and white participants and informants vigorously on that battle but probed less aggressively into the encompassing story. Fortunately, these researchers amassed valuable information on Indian casualties at Little Big Horn, mostly fatalities. Newer scholarship, however, is allowing a more complete and accurate assessment of Indians killed and wounded in the Great Sioux War, especially with the surfacing and examination of additional tribal accounts of the other actions. The figures provided in appendix E for Indians killed and wounded in this war are the most comprehensive yet assembled. Indian casualties were recorded in seventeen of the war's twenty-seven actions. The conflict's three largest battles accounted for the greatest numbers: 99 killed and wounded at Rosebud, 103 killed and wounded at Little Big Horn, and 120 killed and wounded at Red Fork of the Powder River, among a total of 162 Indians killed in the Great Sioux War and 236 wounded.[15]

❧ ❧ ❧

Left unanswered to the last is the question of what went wrong for Sheridan's Army at Powder River and especially Little Big Horn. By the conventional measures and evidence, the army in 1876 was very well led by an educated, veteran officer corps tested on the battlefields of the Civil War and Western frontier. These officers commanded a capable and seasoned body of troops whose own Civil and Indian war experiences were the norm. The noncommissioned officers in particular were older

[15] Russell, "How Many Indians Were Killed?" Indian casualty counts for Little Big Horn have been skillfully collected and analyzed by Hardorff in *Hokahey!* Other key sources are provided in the source note in appendix E.

soldiers who reflected the élan of their companies and regiments, taught common men to be soldiers, and instilled fighting trim in the ranks. This army was also outfitted with new uniforms and equipment reasonably well tailored for the campaign needs of the West and carried weapons as advanced and deadly as those available anywhere in the world. And this army employed a doctrine, written and unwritten, perfectly suited to the unconventional nature of Indian warfare. Upton's tactics were well drilled into the line soldiers, and precepts of converging columns, winter war, dawn attacks, native trackers, offensive war, and total war were well understood by the general and field-grade officers organizing and leading the war's many deployments. These tactics already had been successfully implemented in warfare against Indians elsewhere in the West by many of these very officers.

But for all that was right and probable about Sheridan's Army, the Great Sioux War presented circumstances and situations that sometimes defied these well-seasoned, veteran soldiers. Battles may have not only an order but also a disorder, where judgment and leadership fail as officers confront battlefield circumstances beyond their experiences or outside the anticipated norm and where being well schooled, well drilled, and well armed was simply not enough. By the conventional measures, Colonel Joseph Reynolds, a Civil War major general of volunteers twice breveted for gallant and meritorious service in fierce combat at Chickamauga, Georgia, and Missionary Ridge, Tennessee, was equal to the challenge presented at Powder River. But his performance there was dismal. This village was not reconnoitered before the attack, and distances of travel and synchronization became issues as the engagement unfolded. Reynolds did not command the battlefield as Crook, Miles, and Mackenzie so expertly did at Rosebud Creek, Cedar Creek, and Red Fork of the Powder, respectively, but instead dallied among the tipis and plunder. He did not maintain control over his battalions. Some troops fought desperately with warriors pouring down devastating enfilading fire from high ground, while others remained out of the fighting almost entirely. Their counterfire unnerved Reynolds: instead of driving off these warriors, he abruptly abandoned the field, even leaving behind two of his casualties. In the enveloping confusion and haste, they had no time to destroy the pony herd. Reynolds trailed the ponies with his column to their evening bivouac some twenty-two miles away but then left them unguarded, allowing the Cheyennes to recover their animals quietly in the darkness. Crook was furious and filed court-martial charges against Reynolds and two others for mismanaging the engagement. Respective courts found the officers guilty as charged.

Reynolds's indecisive leadership at Powder River was a great personal failing that stigmatized him for the few remaining months of his career and the final twenty-two years of his life. In fact, he had confronted circumstances at Powder River that were nearly the norm in the realm of total war against Indian populations. His six companies of some three hundred men were certainly the numerical equal of the Cheyenne warriors. But the Cheyennes were defending women and children, their village, and their way of life, and they fought with a resolve quite different from that of Reynolds's troopers and prevailed that day. The Cheyennes' success at Powder River proved to be ominous in the course of the Great Sioux War, emboldening the northern bands and steeling their resolve to unite and resist and luring agency people west and north to join them. A chance encounter along the Powder River Trail near Sage Creek, Wyoming, in late May was telling. There Captain James Egan and Company K, Second Cavalry, who were veterans of the Powder River fight, brushed with some 700 or 800 Sioux harassing a civilian wagon train bound for the Black Hills. As Egan came on, the Indians withdrew to the north. As later reported to Crook and Sheridan, Egan "did not think it prudent to attack and they did not molest him." In May not every Indian was an enemy, but almost certainly these Sioux found Crazy Horse, and on June 25 Custer found them.[16]

Crook's withdrawal from the Rosebud Creek battlefield in mid-June to his base camp in northern Wyoming, two days' march to the south, further emboldened the northern tribesmen. They viewed this fight as their victory because it removed an immediate threat to their security and bolstered their confidence. The northerners maintained cohesiveness as their village continued to swell with the arrival of momentous numbers of agency people. In a dramatic vision gained from the Sun Dance on Rosebud Creek in early June, Sitting Bull prophesied that soldiers would bear down on this village but come in upside down, their feet in the sky, their heads to the earth, with hats falling off. "These soldiers do not possess ears. They are to die," Sitting Bull exclaimed.[17]

Custer's attack on the massed northerners at Little Big Horn fulfilled Sitting Bull's amazing prophesy. Custer's abrupt decision to attack on the afternoon of June 25 was made in spite of his command's weariness after

---

[16] Utley, *Frontier Regulars,* 254; Hedren, *Fort Laramie in 1876,* 100 (quotation).

[17] Utley, *The Lance and the Shield,* 138.

several days of steady riding up Rosebud Creek and a night march to the divide separating the Rosebud and Little Big Horn. And he knew that Terry and Gibbon at that same time were marching up the Big Horn, intending to position themselves for some version of a coordinated or supported attack on June 26. Custer's haste is in part rightly explained by the knowledge that his column had been seen by hunters from the village and by other Indians who were rummaging through ration crates dropped during the night march. Custer presumed that when the Indians learned of his nearness to their village they would break camp and flee, which was conventional thinking and reaction on the plains in these situations. But Custer's innate impulsiveness and self-confidence also drove his decision, despite forewarnings from his scouts and from the trail evidence itself that this was an Indian camp of profound size.

Before departing the Yellowstone, Custer had declined Terry's offer of Brisbin's Montana Battalion of Second Cavalry. That was a fit battalion, ably led, and certainly would have altered Custer's deployment strategy significantly, whether augmenting the conceived battalions or, equally likely, functioning as a fourth strike group. The scenarios posed by the availability of four additional companies, attacking the village separately and perhaps from a different quarter or bolstering Reno's or Custer's forces, are tantalizing but moot. Custer rejected the offer, limiting the attack and its consequences to his regiment alone.

Custer's deployment of the Seventh Cavalry and his decisions as the battle unfolded were all logical. He was encouraged when he paused on a bluff overlooking the valley and saw Reno's men engaged on a skirmish line at the southern margins of the camp, which he still could not exactly see. What he saw directly below him, however, resembled a diagram in Upton's tactics manual. This was how his men were trained to fight, and these were good soldiers who had fought well with him before. But only after Custer pulled back from the river bluff and continued north, seeking a place where he too could cross and strike the village at its flank, did matters unravel. His correct decision to recall Captain Frederick Benteen's battalion, off scouting south of the battle action and the pack train proved of no consequence to him. Custer's appearance in Medicine Tail Coulee, which funneled straight to the Little Big Horn and a shallow river crossing that led to the heart of the village, triggered an overwhelming response from the camp, which rose up and seemingly quickly engulfed and destroyed him. By that time Reno and Benteen were of no value to Custer. Pandemonium had overwhelmed Reno and his decimated command as he retreated from the valley to the bluffs. Benteen and the pack train were simply absorbed by that chaos when they came on.[18]

Seemingly missing in all retellings of Custer's, Reno's, and Benteen's actions at Little Big Horn is how these commanders and their battalions never particularly influenced the battle beyond its initiation. Instead they were driven by the actions of the Sioux and Northern Cheyennes, who seized tactical advantage and put these companies on the defensive until they were neutralized or destroyed. Warriors streaming from the southern end of the great village halted Reno's charge and brought such pressure to bear that he yielded his initial skirmish line and withdrew to a position on his right flank in cottonwoods and dense underbrush along the Little Big Horn. And then these warriors infiltrated this second position and inflicted such lethalness that he yielded again, this time retreating with reckless abandon to the high bluffs east of the river.

We know less about Custer's maneuvering in Medicine Tail Coulee and beyond. But clearly his movements were rebuffed by warriors, some of whom already had repulsed Reno and joined many others rallying to this new threat. One and all poured out of the village and made uncanny use of terrain and sagebrush cover as they pressed, surrounded, and shattered these five companies. The locations of bodies after the fight and cartridge case evidence methodically unearthed a century later suggest tantalizing details about the fighting here. Custer or his company commanders engaged or defended in Deep Coulee north of Medicine Tail Coulee and formed intermittent semblances of skirmish lines to protect themselves and meet oncoming warriors. Indian accounts suggest that these soldiers fought bravely: 42 of 210, including Custer, found their way to the highest point in this sector of the battlefield, ever after known as Last Stand or Custer Hill, where they fought until all perished.[19]

Ultimately, Custer and his company commanders never controlled their fate. Battalions fragmented, leadership collapsed, and discipline evaporated. While individual soldiers may indeed have fought bravely, they were met by equally courageous Sioux and Northern Cheyenne warriors who were united and angry and fought with supreme confidence and numerical superiority. War leaders like Crazy Horse, Gall, Crow King, White

---

[18] Custer had been tactically disadvantaged in combat before and yet always prevailed. For insightful commentary on this aspect of his mind-set and deportment, see Urwin, "Was the Past Prologue?"

[19] Fox, *Archaeology, History, and Custer's Last Battle*, 200–202; Scott et al., *Archaeological Perspectives on the Battle of the Little Bighorn*, 17–20.

Bull, Hump, and Two Moon exerted powerful influence as they rallied and led followers in a live-or-die fight. Reno and Custer posed immediate threats to women, children, and the elderly, of course, and warriors rallied foremost for their safety. But on this day at Greasy Grass these Sioux and Northern Cheyenne fighters were also emotionally charged to defend their homeland, freedom, and way of life. These circumstances at Little Big Horn were without parallel in the North American West and existed for a mere moment before vaporizing. This day belonged to the Lakotas and Northern Cheyennes. Custer and Sheridan's Army's well-drilled soldiers, splendid tactics, and superior weapons were no match at all.[20]

❧ ❧ ❧

At the annual meeting of the Order of Indian Wars of the United States convened on February 26, 1921, at the Army and Navy Club in Washington, D.C., Brigadier General Charles King, then of the Wisconsin National Guard, regaled thirty-six companions and twelve guests with stories from the Sioux Campaign of 1876. King delivered stirring word pictures of a phenomenal Indian war, drawn as always from personal experience and delivered with a soldierly rhythm and cadence perfected over many years in countless National Guard and military academy lecture halls and fashioned in dozens of army novels, histories, and short stories penned over an equally long and productive writing career. King was a Fifth Cavalry first lieutenant in 1876, and his address was most rousing when recounting scouting in Wyoming's Hat Creek Breaks and Cheyenne River countryside, the Fifth's dramatic Indian fights at Warbonnet Creek and Slim Buttes, and the need to shoot horses to ease soldier hunger pangs during the never-to-be-forgotten Starvation March. King closed his address that evening with a poignant homage to this fraternity of veterans of the old frontier:

> A more thankless task, a more perilous service, a more exacting test of leadership, soldiership, morale and discipline no army in Christendom has ever been called upon to undertake than that which for eighty years was the lot of the little fighting force of regulars who cleared the way across the continent for the emigrant and settler, who summer and winter stood guard over the wide frontier, whose lives were spent in almost utter isolation, whose lonely

---

[20] Utley, *The Lance and the Shield*, 162; Larson, *Gall*, 129–35; Utley, *Frontier Regulars*, 262.

> death was marked and mourned only by sorrowing comrade, or mayhap grief-stricken widow and children left destitute and despairing. There never was a warfare on the face of the earth in which the soldier, officer or man, had so little to gain, so very much to lose. There never was a warfare which, like this, had absolutely nothing to hold the soldier stern and steadfast to the bitter end, but the solemn sense of Soldier Duty.[21]

King's notion of "soldier duty" was perhaps the only earthly honor earned by the United States Army from the Great Sioux War. They had asked for and received no more.

---

[21] King, "Address," 38.

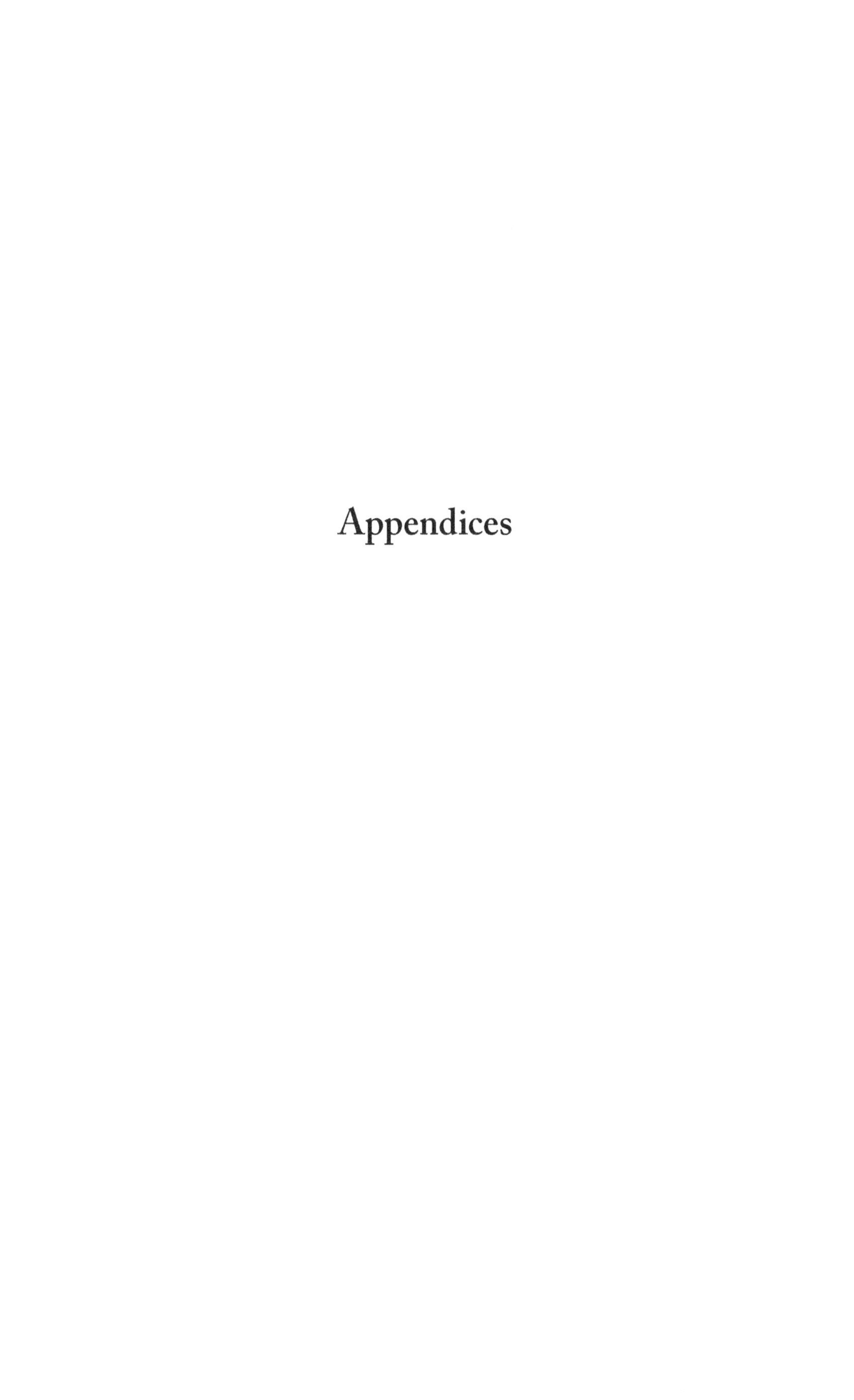

Appendices

APPENDIX A

Participating Great Sioux War Regiments and Companies and Instances of Post-Civil War/Pre-1876 Indian Campaign Experience

Second Cavalry
  Companies A, B, D, E, F, G, H, I, K, L

Third Cavalry
  Companies A, B, C, D, E, F, G, H, I, K, L, M

Fourth Cavalry
  Companies B, D, E, F, I, M

Fifth Cavalry
  Companies A, B, C, D, E, F, G, H, I, K, L, M

Seventh Cavalry
  Band, Companies A, B, C, D, E, F, G, H, I, K, L, M

First Infantry
  Companies B, C, D, F, G, H, K

Fourth Infantry
  Companies B, C, D, E, F, G, I, K

Fifth Infantry
  Band, Companies A, B, C, D, E, F, G, H, I, K

Sixth Infantry
  Companies B, C, D, E, F, G, H, I

Seventh Infantry
  Companies A, B, C, E, H, I, K

Ninth Infantry
  Companies A, B, C, D, E, F, G, H, I, K

Eleventh Infantry
  Companies A, B, C, F, G, H

Fourteenth Infantry
Companies B, C, D, F, G, I

Seventeenth Infantry
Companies A, C, E, F, G, H

Twentieth Infantry
Provisional Company, Companies D, H, I

Twenty-second Infantry
Companies E, F, G, H, I, K

Twenty-third Infantry
Companies C, G, H, I, K

Fourth Artillery
Companies C, B, H, K

❧ ❧ ❧

Second Cavalry
A, Wyoming 1868, 1870
B, Nebraska, 1868, Wyoming 1871–72, 1874
D, Wyoming 1867, 1869–70, 1875, Kansas 1869
E, Wyoming 1866–67, Nebraska 1870
F, Montana 1870, 1872
G, Montana 1870, 1872
H, Kansas 1868, Montana 1870, 1872
I, Wyoming 1870
K, Nebraska 1869–70, Wyoming 1869, 1873–74
L, Kansas 1869, Montana 1870, 1872

Third Cavalry
A, Indian Territory 1868, Arizona 1870–71
B, New Mexico 1869, Texas 1870, Arizona 1870–71, Nebraska 1872
C, Indian Territory 1868, Arizona 1870
D, New Mexico 1867, Indian Territory 1868, Arizona 1871
E, New Mexico 1867–68, Arizona 1870–71
F, Indian Territory 1868, New Mexico 1869, Texas 1869, Arizona 1870–71
G, Colorado 1866, New Mexico 1867–68, Indian Territory 1868, Arizona 1870–71, Nebraska 1875
H, New Mexico 1867–69, Arizona 1871
I, New Mexico 1867–68, Indian Territory 1868
K, New Mexico 1867, New Mexico 1869, Arizona 1870–71
L, Arizona 1870
M, Arizona 1870

Fourth Cavalry
B, Texas 1872–74, Mexico 1873
D, Texas 1867–70, 1872, 1874
E, Texas 1870, 1874, Mexico 1873
F, Texas, 1869–72, 1874
I, Texas 1872–74, Mexico 1873, Indian Territory 1876
M, Texas 1870–71, Mexico 1873

Fifth Cavalry
A, Kansas 1868–69, Nebraska 1869, Colorado 1869, Arizona 1873–75, Texas 1875
B, Kansas 1868–69, Nebraska 1869, Arizona 1872–75
C, Colorado 1869, Kansas 1869, Arizona 1872–74
D, Colorado 1869
E, Colorado 1869, Kansas, 1869, Arizona 1872–74
F, Kansas 1868–69, Nebraska 1869, Arizona 1872–74
G, Colorado 1869, Nebraska 1871, Arizona 1872–74, Indian Territory 1876
H, Kansas 1868–69, 1875, Nebraska 1869, 1871, Colorado 1869, Arizona 1872–74
I, Kansas 1868–69, Nebraska 1869–71, Arizona 1873–75
K, Arizona 1872–75
L, Kansas 1868–69, Nebraska 1869, 1871, Arizona 1872–74
M, Kansas 1868–69, Nebraska 1869, Colorado 1869, Arizona 1872–74

Seventh Cavalry
A, Kansas 1867, 1869, Indian Territory 1868, Montana 1873, Dakota 1874
B, Kansas 1867–69, Indian Territory 1868, Montana 1873, Dakota 1874
C, Colorado 1867, Kansas 1867, 1869, Indian Territory 1868
D, Kansas 1867, 1869, Indian Territory 1868
E, Kansas 1867, 1869, Indian Territory 1868, Montana 1873, Dakota 1874
F, Kansas 1867, 1869, Indian Territory 1868, Montana 1873, Dakota 1874
G, Kansas 1867, 1869, Indian Territory 1868, Montana 1873, Dakota 1874
H, Kansas 1867–69, Indian Territory 1868
I, Kansas 1867, 1869, Indian Territory 1868
K, Kansas 1867–69, Indian Territory 1868, Montana 1873
L, Colorado 1868, Montana 1873, Dakota 1874
M, Kansas 1867–70, Indian Territory 1868, Montana 1873

First Infantry
G, Dakota 1875

Fourth Infantry
B, Wyoming 1869
D, Wyoming 1869
E, Wyoming 1869
F, Wyoming 1869
G, Colorado 1867, Wyoming 1869
K, Wyoming 1869

Fifth Infantry
B, Kansas 1869
C, Kansas 1869, Texas 1874
D, Kansas 1869, Texas 1874, Indian Territory 1874
E, Kansas 1868–69, Texas 1874
F, Arizona 1865, Kansas 1875
G, Kansas 1869
H, Indian Territory 1875
I, Texas 1874
K, Kansas 1867

Sixth Infantry
B, Dakota 1872–73
C, Dakota 1872–73

Seventh Infantry
A, Montana 1874
B, Wyoming 1869
C, Montana 1872
E, Montana 1872
I, Wyoming 1869, Montana 1872
K, Montana 1875

Ninth Infantry
C, California 1867, Oregon 1868
D, California 1866

Eleventh Infantry
A, Texas 1874
F, Texas 1874
G, Texas 1874
H, Texas 1872, 1874

Fourteenth Infantry
B, Arizona 1866–69
C, Arizona 1866–69
D, Arizona 1866–67, Wyoming 1872
F, Arizona 1866–69, Wyoming 1872
G, Arizona 1867–68, Wyoming 1872

Seventeenth Infantry
A, Montana 1872
C, Montana 1872
H, Dakota 1872–73

Twenty-second Infantry
E, Dakota 1869
F, Dakota 1869, Montana 1872

G, Dakota 1872, Montana 1872
H, Dakota 1868, 1872
I, Dakota 1868
K, Dakota 1868, 1872

Twenty-third Infantry
C, Oregon 1866, 1868, Idaho 1866
G, Arizona 1872–73
H, Idaho 1868, Arizona 1873
I, Arizona 1872–73
K, Oregon 1867–68

Fourth Artillery
H, California 1873
K, California 1873

Sources: Chronological List of Actions, 23–61; Heitman, *Historical Register and Dictionary of the United States Army,* 2:426–42.

APPENDIX B

Staff and Field-Grade Officers Engaged in the Great Sioux War

Note: The columns in appendices B and C report whether the named officer actually commanded troops in the Great Sioux War, as opposed to service in that war in a staff or support capacity, as evidenced in the Deployment chapters; the year of graduation from West Point or "yes" if the officer attended but did not graduate; and whether the officer was a Civil War veteran, received a Civil War brevet for gallant and meritorious service, or was a veteran of an Indian campaign before the Great Sioux War. The Comments column indicates whether an officer held a colonel or general of volunteers commission in the Civil War, participated in one or more of the Civil War's prominent battles, or participated in specific Indian warfare on the northern plains prior to the 1876 conflict.

Name of Officer	Command?	West Point?	Civil War?	CW Brevet?	Indian Wars?	Comments
Arthur, William			yes	yes		
Brisbin, James S.	yes		yes	yes		brig. gen. CW
Buell, George P.	yes		yes	yes	yes	col. CW
Carlin, William P.	yes	'50	yes	yes		brig. gen. CW
Carr, Eugene A.	yes	'50	yes	yes	yes	brig. gen. CW
Chambers, Alexander	yes	'53	yes	yes	yes	brig. gen. CW; Vicksburg
Crook, George	yes	'52	yes	yes	yes	maj. gen. CW; Antietam
Custer, George A.	yes	'61	yes	yes	yes	maj. gen. CW; Gettysburg; Yellowstone R. '73

Name of Officer	Command?	West Point?	Civil War?	CW Brevet?	Indian Wars?	Comments
Dodge, Richard I.	yes	'48	yes			
Du Barry, Beekman		'49	yes	yes		
Evans, Andrew W.	yes	'52	yes	yes	yes	col. CW
Forsyth, James W.		'56	yes	yes		brig. gen. CW
Gibbon, John	yes	'47	yes	yes		maj. gen. CW; Antietam, Gettysburg
Gibson, George			yes	yes		Gettysburg
Gordon, George A.	yes	'54	yes	yes		Antietam, Gettysburg
Hart, Verling K.	yes		yes	yes	yes	Yellowstone R. '73
Hazen, William B.	yes	'55	yes	yes	yes	maj. gen. CW
Hough, Alfred L.	yes		yes	yes		
Lazelle, Henry M.	yes	'55	yes	yes	yes	col. CW; Yellowstone R. '71, '72
Mackenzie, Ranald S.	yes	'62	yes	yes	yes	brig. gen. CW; Gettysburg
Mason, Julius W.	yes		yes	yes	yes	
Merrill, Lewis	yes	'55	yes	yes	yes	col. CW; Bozeman Trail
Merritt, Wesley	yes	'60	yes	yes		maj. gen. CW; Gettysburg
Miles, Nelson A.	yes		yes	yes	yes	brig. gen. CW
Moore, Orlando H.	yes		yes	yes	yes	col. CW
Otis, Elmer	yes	'53	yes			
Otis, Elwell S.	yes		yes	yes		

Name of Officer	Command?	West Point?	Civil War?	CW Brevet?	Indian Wars?	Comments
Reno, Marcus A.	yes	'57	yes	yes		col. CW
Reynolds, Joseph J.	yes	'43	yes	yes		maj. gen. CW
Royall, William B.	yes		yes	yes	yes	Mex. War
Stanton, Thaddeus H.	yes		yes			
Sturgis, Samuel D.	yes	'46	yes	yes		Mex. War; brig. gen. CW
Terry, Alfred H.	yes		yes	yes		maj. gen. CW; Thanks of Congress
Townsend, Edwin F.	yes	'54	yes	yes		
Upham, John J.	yes	'59	yes	yes		Gettysburg
Whistler, Joseph N. G.	yes	'46	yes	yes	yes	Mex. War; col. CW; Yellowstone R. '71

Sources: Heitman, *Historical Register and Dictionary of the United States Army,* vol. 1; *Chronological List of Actions;* Altshuler, *Cavalry Yellow & Infantry Blue; Record of Engagements with Hostile Indians within the Military Division of the Missouri;* Price, *Across the Continent with the Fifth Cavalry;* Rodenbough, *From Everglade to Cañon with the Second Dragoons;* Lubetkin, *Jay Cooke's Gamble;* Mills, *Rosters from 7th U.S. Cavalry Campaigns;* Johnson, *That Body of Brave Men.*

APPENDIX C

Company-Grade Officers Engaged in the Great Sioux War

Name of Officer	Command Co./Batt.?	West Point?	Civil War?	CW Brevet?	Indian Wars?	Comments
Adam, Emil	yes		yes		yes	
Allison, James N.		'71				
Anderson, Harry R.		yes	yes			
Andrews, William H.	yes		yes	yes	yes	
Andrus, Edwin P.		'75				
Austin, Albert			yes			
Bache, Alfred B.					yes	
Bailey, Edward L.			yes	yes		col. CW; Gettysburg
Bailey, Hobart K.					yes	
Baird, George W.			yes			col. CW
Baker, Stephen	yes		yes			
Baldwin, Frank D.					yes	
Baldwin, John A.						
Ball, Edward	yes		yes		yes	Marias R.; Yellowstone R. '71, '72

Name of Officer	Command?	West Point?	Civil War?	CW Brevet?	Indian Wars?	Comments
Bannister, John			yes	yes		
Bates, Kinzie	yes		yes	yes		Vicksburg
Bell, James M.			yes	yes	yes	Yellowstone R. '73
Bellas, Henry H.						
Bennett, Andrew S.	yes		yes		yes	
Bennett, Clarence E.	yes	'55				
Benteen, Frederick W.	yes		yes	yes	yes	col. CW; Yellowstone R. '73
Biddle, J. Williams	yes					
Bishop, Hoel S.		'73			yes	
Booth, Charles A.		'72				
Borden, George P.		yes	yes			
Bourke, John G.		'69	yes		yes	
Bowen, William H. C.	yes					
Bowman, Alpheus H.	yes		yes			
Bradley, Charles O.	yes		yes			
Bradley, James H.	yes		yes		yes	Bozeman Trail
Brewer, Edwin P.		yes				
Bristol, Henry B.	yes				yes	
Britton, Thomas	yes		yes	yes		Gettysburg; Yellowstone R. '73
Bronson, Nelson	yes		yes		yes	Yellowstone R. '73

Name of Officer	Command?	West Point?	Civil War?	CW Brevet?	Indian Wars?	Comments
Brotherton, David H.		'54	yes	yes		
Brown, Rufus P.	yes	'66				
Brush, Daniel H.		'71	yes			
Bubb, John W.			yes			
Budd, Otho W.						
Burke, Daniel W.	yes		yes	yes		Gettysburg
Burnett, Levi F.			yes	yes		Antietam
Burrowes, Thomas B.	yes		yes	yes	yes	Bozeman Trail
Burt, Andrew S.	yes		yes	yes	yes	Bozeman Trail
Butler, Edmond	yes				yes	
Byrne, Bernard A.	yes					
Cain, Avery B.	yes		yes	yes		
Calhoun, Frederic S.			yes		yes	Yellowstone R. '73
Calhoun, James	yes				yes	Yellowstone R. '73
Callahan, Charles M.	yes		yes	yes		
Campbell, Joseph B.		'61	yes	yes		Antietam
Campbell, William J.			yes			
Capron, Thaddeus H.			yes			
Carland, John	yes		yes			
Carpenter, William L.			yes			

Name of Officer	Command?	West Point?	Civil War?	CW Brevet?	Indian Wars?	Comments
Carter, Mason	yes		yes		yes	
Casey, Edward W.	yes	'73				
Casey, James S.	yes		yes	yes		
Chance, Josiah			yes			
Chase, George F.		'71				
Cherry, Samuel A.		'75				
Clagett, J. Rozier						
Clark, William P.	yes	'68				
Clarke, Francis	yes		yes	yes	yes	Vicksburg; Yellowstone R. '73
Clarke, William L.						
Clifford, Walter	yes		yes	yes		
Coates, Edwin M.	yes		yes	yes		
Coe, John N.	yes		yes			
Collier, William S.	yes		yes	yes		Gettysburg
Collins, Edward	yes		yes			
Conrad, Joseph	yes		yes	yes		col. CW
Conway, William			yes		yes	Yellowstone R. '73
Cooke, William W.	yes		yes	yes	yes	
Coolidge, Charles A.						

Name of Officer	Command?	West Point?	Civil War?	CW Brevet?	Indian Wars?	Comments
Crawford, Emmet	yes		yes		yes	
Crittenden, Albert B.						
Crittenden, John J.						
Crozier, William		'76				
Cummings, Joseph F.	yes	'76				
Cummins, Albert S.		'73				
Cushing, Harry C.	yes		yes	yes		
Cusick, Cornelius C.	yes		yes		yes	
Custer, Thomas W.	yes		yes	yes	yes	2 CW Medals of Honor; Yellowstone R. '73
Davis, Wirt	yes		yes	yes	yes	
Day, Russell H.	yes		yes		yes	Yellowstone R. '73
De Lany, Hayden		yes	yes		yes	
De Rudio, Charles C.	yes		yes		yes	Yellowstone R. '73
Dewees, Thomas B.	yes		yes	yes	yes	Bozeman Trail
Dickey, Charles J.	yes		yes	yes	yes	Vicksburg; Yellowstone R. '73
Doane, Gustavus C.			yes		yes	Marias R.
Dodd, George A.		'76				
Dodge, Frederick L.	yes		yes			

Name of Officer	Command?	West Point?	Civil War?	CW Brevet?	Indian Wars?	Comments
Dorst, Joseph H.		'73			yes	
Dougherty, John J.		'72				
Douglas, Samuel R.		'76				
Drew, George A.			yes	yes	yes	
Dykman, William N.		'75				
Eaton, George O.		'73	yes		yes	
Eckerson, Edwin P.	yes				yes	
Edgerly, Winfield S.		'70				
Edmunds, Frank H.		'71				
Egan, James	yes		yes	yes	yes	
Elting, Oscar			yes		yes	
English, William L.	yes		yes			
Eskridge, Richard I.	yes		yes		yes	
Ewers, Ezra P.	yes		yes	yes		
Ferris, Samuel P.	yes	'61	yes	yes		col. CW
Fitzgerald, Michael J.	yes					
Foote, Morris C.	yes		yes	yes		
Forbes, Theodore F.	yes		yes	yes		
Forbush, William C.		'68			yes	
Foster, Herbert S.		'76				

Name of Officer	Command?	West Point?	Civil War?	CW Brevet?	Indian Wars?	Comments
Foster, James E. H.			yes			
Freeman, Henry B.	yes		yes	yes	yes	Bozeman Trail
French, John T., Jr.		'76				
French, Thomas H.	yes		yes	yes	yes	Yellowstone R. '73
Fuller, Alfred M.		'76				
Fuller, Ezra B.		'73	yes			
Furey, John V.	yes		yes			
Garlington, Ernest A.	yes	'76				
Garretty, Frank D.			yes	yes		
Gates, J. Granville						
Gibbs, Eugene B.						
Gibson, Francis M.	yes				yes	Yellowstone R. '73
Gilbreath, Erasmus C.	yes		yes			
Godfrey, Edward S.	yes	'67	yes		yes	Yellowstone R. '73
Goodale, Greenleaf A.	yes		yes	yes		Gettysburg
Goodloe, Archibald H.	yes	'65				
Greenough, George G.	yes	'65				
Gresham, John C.		'76				
Groesbeck, Stephen W.			yes			

Name of Officer	Command?	West Point?	Civil War?	CW Brevet?	Indian Wars?	Comments
Gurley, Charles L.	yes					
Hale, Owen	yes		yes	yes	yes	Yellowstone R. '73
Hall, Christopher T.		'68			yes	
Hall, William P.		'68			yes	
Hamilton, John M.	yes		yes	yes	yes	
Hamilton, Samuel T.	yes		yes			
Hammond, Charles L.		'76				
Hare, Luther R.	yes	'74				
Hargous, Charles E.	yes		yes	yes		
Harrington, Henry M.	yes	'72			yes	Yellowstone R. '73
Hasson, Patrick					yes	
Hathaway, Forrest H.			yes	yes		
Hawley, William	yes		yes		yes	Vicksburg
Hayes, Edward M.	yes		yes	yes	yes	
Hemphill, William C.	yes		yes		yes	
Henry, Guy V.	yes	'61	yes	yes	yes	col. CW
Heyl, Charles H.					yes	Grace Creek, Neb.
Hinkle, Frank S.			yes		yes	
Hodgson, Benjamin H.		'70			yes	Yellowstone R. '73

Name of Officer	Command?	West Point?	Civil War?	CW Brevet?	Indian Wars?	Comments
Hofman, William E.			yes			
Hooton, Mott	yes		yes	yes	yes	Yellowstone R. '73
Howe, Henry S.	yes		yes			
Howe, Walter	yes	'67				
Howland, Carver		'76				
Hughes, Robert P.			yes	yes		
Huntington, Henry D.		'75				
Irwin, David A.	yes		yes		yes	
Jackson, Allan H.			yes	yes		Gettysburg
Jackson, Henry	yes		yes		yes	
Jacob, Richard T., Jr.	yes				yes	Yellowstone R. '73
Jacobs, Joshua W.			yes			
Jerome, Lovell H.	yes	'70			yes	Yellowstone R. '71
Johnson, Alfred B.						
Johnson, Charles A.	yes		yes			
Johnson, Harry C.						
Johnson, John B.	yes		yes			
Johnston, Robert E.	yes		yes	yes		
Jones, James M.		'75				

Name of Officer	Command?	West Point?	Civil War?	CW Brevet?	Indian Wars?	Comments
Jordan, William H.	yes	'60	yes	yes		
Kell, William H.			yes		yes	Yellowstone R. '73
Kellogg, Sanford C.	yes		yes	yes	yes	Yellowstone R. '72
Kendrick, Frederick M. H.	yes		yes			
Kennington, James	yes		yes	yes		
Keogh, Myles W.	yes		yes	yes	yes	Gettysburg
Keyes, Edward L.					yes	
Kimball, William A.		yes				
King, Albert D.						
King, Charles		'66	yes		yes	
Kingsbury, Frederick W.	yes	'70				
Kinzie, Frank X.	yes					
Kirtland, Thaddeus S.	yes		yes		yes	Bozeman Trail
Krause, David	yes		yes	yes		Gettysburg
Lawson, Joseph	yes		yes			
Lawton, Henry W.			yes	yes	yes	
Lee, Jesse M.	yes		yes			
Lee, John	yes		yes	yes		
Leib, Edward H.	yes		yes	yes	yes	
Lemly, Henry R.		'72				

Name of Officer	Command?	West Point?	Civil War?	CW Brevet?	Indian Wars?	Comments
Lloyd, Charles F.						
Lockwood, Benjamin C.			yes			
Logan, Thomas H.	yes		yes	yes		Gettysburg
Logan, William	yes				yes	Yellowstone R. '72
London, Robert		'73			yes	
Long, Oscar F.		'75				
Low, William H., Jr.	yes	'72				
Luhn, Gerhard L.	yes		yes	yes		
Lyman, Wyllys	yes		yes	yes	yes	
Lynde, Frederick M.	yes		yes			
MacAdams, James G.			yes		yes	
Macklin, James E.			yes			
Maguire, Edward		'67				
Martin, John W.		yes				
Mason, Charles W.						
Mason, Stanton A.		'75				
Mathey, Edward G.			yes		yes	Yellowstone R. '73
Matile, Leon A.			yes			
Mauck, Clarence	yes		yes	yes	yes	

Name of Officer	Command?	West Point?	Civil War?	CW Brevet?	Indian Wars?	Comments
Maus, Marion P.	yes	'74				
McArthur, Malcolm	yes	'65			yes	Yellowstone R. '72
McCaleb, Thomas S.		'75				
McClernand, Edward J.		'70			yes	Yellowstone R. '71, '72
McCormick, Loyd S.		'76				
McDonald, Robert	yes					
McDougall, Thomas M.	yes		yes	yes	yes	Yellowstone R. '73
McIntosh, Donald	yes				yes	Yellowstone R. '73
McKinney, John A.	yes	'71			yes	
Meinhold, Charles	yes		yes	yes	yes	Vicksburg
Merriam, Lewis			yes			
Michaelis, Otho E.						
Miller, Wentz C.	yes	'69	yes		yes	
Mills, Anson	yes	yes	yes	yes		
Miner, Charles W.	yes		yes			
Monahan, Deane	yes		yes	yes	yes	
Montgomery, Robert H.	yes		yes	yes	yes	Antietam, Gettysburg
Moore, Alexander	yes		yes	yes	yes	Antietam, Gettysburg
Morton, Charles	yes	'69	yes		yes	
Moylan, Myles	yes		yes	yes	yes	Yellowstone R. '73

Name of Officer	Command?	West Point?	Civil War?	CW Brevet?	Indian Wars?	Comments
Munson, Samuel	yes		yes		yes	
Murdock, Daniel H.	yes		yes			
Murphy, John			yes			
Myer, Albert L.						
Nicholson, William J.						
Nickerson, Azor H.			yes	yes	yes	Antietam, Gettysburg
Nickerson, James D.			yes			
Norris, William F.		'72				
Norwood, Randolph	yes		yes		yes	Antietam
Nowlan, Henry J.		*	yes		yes	*Sandhurst grad.
Noyes, Henry E.	yes	'61	yes	yes	yes	Bozeman Trail
O'Brien, John J.			yes			
O'Brien, Martin E.			yes		yes	
O'Connell, William	yes		yes	yes	yes	
Otis, Harrison G.			yes	yes		
Ovenshine, Samuel	yes					
Palmer, George		'76				
Pardee, Julius H.		'71				
Parkhurst, Charles D.		'72			yes	

Name of Officer	Command?	West Point?	Civil War?	CW Brevet?	Indian Wars?	Comments
Paul, Augustus C.			yes	yes		
Payne, J. Scott	yes	'66				
Peale, James T.	yes		yes	yes	yes	
Pearson, Daniel C.		'70			yes	
Pease, William B.	yes		yes			
Penney, Charles G.	yes		yes	yes		Vicksburg
Plummer, Satterlee C.		'65				
Pollock, Edwin	yes		yes			
Pollock, Otis W.	yes		yes			
Poole, De Witt C.	yes		yes		yes	Yellowstone R. '73
Pope, James W.	yes	'68				
Porter, James E.		'69				
Powell, James W.	yes		yes	yes		
Powell, William H.	yes		yes	yes	yes	Antietam, Gettysburg
Pratt, Edward B.						
Price, Butler D.			yes			
Price, George F.	yes				yes	
Quinn, Thomas F.	yes		yes	yes		
Quinton, William			yes			

Name of Officer	Command?	West Point?	Civil War?	CW Brevet?	Indian Wars?	Comments
Randall, Edward L.			yes			
Randall, George M.	yes		yes	yes	yes	Antietam
Rawn, Charles C.	yes		yes		yes	Yellowstone R., '72
Rawolle, William C.	yes		yes	yes		Antietam
Read, Ogden B.			yes	yes		
Reed, Hugh T.	yes	'73				
Reed, William I.						
Regan, James	yes				yes	Bozeman Trail
Reilly, Bernard, Jr.			yes		yes	
Reily, William Van W.						
Reynolds, Bainbridge	yes	'73				
Rice, Edmund	yes		yes	yes		Antietam, Gettysburg
Roach, George H.			yes			
Robertson, Edgar B.		'74				
Robinson, Frank U.			yes		yes	
Robinson, William W., Jr.	yes	'69	yes			
Rockefeller, Charles M.	yes		yes			
Rockwell, Charles H.	yes	'69			yes	
Rodgers, Calbraith P.	yes					

Name of Officer	Command?	West Point?	Civil War?	CW Brevet?	Indian Wars?	Comments
Roe, Charles F.		'68				
Rogers, William W.	yes		yes	yes		Gettysburg
Romeyn, Henry			yes	yes		
Rosenquest, J. Wesley						
Rousseau, David Q.	yes		yes			
Rousseau, George L.						
Ruhlen, George		'72				
Russell, Albert J.		'76				
Russell, Gerald	yes		yes	yes	yes	Vicksburg
Sanders, William W.	yes		yes	yes		col. CW
Sanger, Louis H.	yes		yes	yes		Gettysburg
Sanno, James M. J.	yes	'63				
Schindel, Jeremiah P.	yes		yes	yes		Gettysburg
Schofield, Charles B.		'70			yes	Yellowstone R. '72
Schuyler, Walter S.	yes	'70			yes	
Schwan, Theodore	yes		yes	yes		
Schwatka, Frederick		'71				
Scott, Douglas M.						
Scott, Hugh L.		'76				

Name of Officer	Command?	West Point?	Civil War?	CW Brevet?	Indian Wars?	Comments
Seton, Henry			yes			
Sharpe, Alfred C.		yes				
Shoemaker, Frank L.	yes	'68				
Sibley, Frederick W.		'74				
Sickel, Horatio G., Jr.		'76				
Simpson, James F.	yes		yes	yes		Gettysburg
Slocum, Herbert J.		yes				
Smead, Alexander D. B.	yes					
Smith, Algernon E.	yes		yes	yes	yes	Yellowstone R. '73
Smith, Edward W.			yes	yes		
Smith, Frank G.	yes		yes	yes		
Smith, Leslie	yes		yes			
Smith, Oskaloosa M.			yes		yes	Yellowstone R. '73
Snyder, Simon	yes				yes	
Stanton, William S.		'65				
Sturgis, James G.		'75				
Sumner, Samuel S.	yes		yes	yes	yes	Antietam, Vicksburg
Sutorius, Alexander	yes		yes	yes	yes	
Swift, Eben		'76				

Name of Officer	Command?	West Point?	Civil War?	CW Brevet?	Indian Wars?	Comments
Swigert, Samuel M.	yes	’68			yes	Marias R.
Taylor, Alfred B.	yes		yes	yes	yes	
Taylor, Frank	yes					
Taylor, George McM.	yes		yes		yes	
Taylor, Sydney W.					yes	
Thibaut, Frederick W.	yes		yes	yes	yes	Antietam; Yellowstone R. ’73
Thompson, Charles B.						
Thompson, Lewis	yes		yes	yes	yes	Marias R.; Yellowstone R. ’72
Thompson, Richard E.		’68				
Tiffany, Harry	yes					
Tobey, Thomas F.			yes			
Tolman, Thomas M.	yes	’65				
Tyler, Augustus C.		’73				
Tyler, George L.	yes		yes	yes	yes	Yellowstone R. ’71
Van Derslice, Joseph H.	yes		yes	yes		Antietam
Van Horne, William M.	yes		yes			
Van Vliet, Frederick	yes		yes	yes		
Varnum, Charles A.	yes	’72			yes	Yellowstone R. ’73

Name of Officer	Command?	West Point?	Civil War?	CW Brevet?	Indian Wars?	Comments
Von Herrmann, Charles J.	yes		yes	yes		
Von Luettwitz, Adolphus H.	yes		yes			
Vroom, Peter D.	yes		yes	yes	yes	
Wagner, Arthur L.		'75				
Walker, George B.	yes	'72			yes	Yellowstone R. '73
Walker, Henry P.		'74				
Wallace, George D.	yes	'72			yes	Yellowstone R. '73
Ward, Edward W.			yes		yes	
Watts, Charles H.		'72			yes	
Weir, Thomas B.	yes		yes	yes	yes	
Wells, Elijah R.	yes		yes	yes	yes	
Wessells, Henry W., Jr.	yes	*				*cadet, Naval Academy, did not graduate
Wheaton, Charles	yes		yes			
Wheelan, James N.	yes		yes	yes	yes	
Wheeler, Homer W.	yes					
Wheeler, William H.		'74				
Whitman, Royal E.			yes	yes		col. CW
Whitney, John	yes		yes	yes		

Name of Officer	Command?	West Point?	Civil War?	CW Brevet?	Indian Wars?	Comments
Whitten, James H.	yes					
Wieting, Orlando L.		'70	yes			
Wilkinson, John W.	yes	'72				
Wilson, James L.		'74	yes			
Wilson, Robert P.	yes		yes	yes	yes	
Woodbridge, Francis						
Woodruff, Charles A.	yes	'71	yes			
Woodruff, Thomas M.		'71				
Woodson, Albert E.	yes				yes	
Yates, George W.	yes		yes	yes	yes	Gettysburg; Yellowstone R. '73
Yeatman, Richard T.		'72				
Young, George S.						
Young, Robert H.			yes		yes	

Sources: Heitman, *Historical Register and Dictionary of the United States Army,* vol. 1; Altshuler, *Cavalry Yellow & Infantry Blue; Records of Living Officers of the United States Army; Record of Engagements with Hostile Indians within the Military Division of the Missouri;* Price, *Across the Continent with the Fifth Cavalry;* Rodenbough, *From Everglade to Cañon with the Second Dragoons;* Carter, *On the Border with Mackenzie;* Lubetkin, *Jay Cooke's Gamble;* Greene, *Washita;* Mills, *Rosters from 7th U.S. Cavalry Campaigns.*

APPENDIX D

Medical Officers and Contract Surgeons Engaged in the Great Sioux War

Ashton, Isaiah H., AAS
Barbour, William, AAS
Bergen, Andrew C., AAS
Biart, Victor, AAS
Boyer, Samuel S., AAS
Brown, Paul R., Asst. Surg. and 1st Lt.
Chenoweth, Albert, AAS
Clark, Elbert J., AAS
Clements, Bennett A., Surg. and Maj.
DeWolf, James M., AAS (KIA)
Frick, Abraham P., AAS
Gardner, Edwin F., Asst. Surg. and 1st Lt.
Gibson, Charles T., AAS
Gibson, Joseph R., Asst. Surg. and Capt.
Grimes, Robert B., AAS
Hart, C. H., AAS
Hartsuff, Albert, Surg. and Maj.
Harvey, Philip F., Asst. Surg. and Capt.
Havard, Valery, Asst. Surg. and Capt.
Kimball, James P., Asst. Surg. and Capt.
La Garde, Louis A., AAS
Lecompte, Edward P., AAS
Lord, George E., Asst. Surg. and 1st Lt. (KIA)
McGillycuddy, Valentine T., AAS
McKinney, J. A., AAS
Middleton, Johnson V. D., Surg. and Maj.
Munn, Curtis E., Asst. Surg. and Capt.
Owsley, William T., AAS
Patzki, Julius H., Asst. Surg. and Capt.

Paulding, Holmes O., Asst. Surg. and 1st Lt.
Petteys, Charles V., AAS
Porter, Henry R., AAS
Powell, Junius L., AAS
Price, Curtis E., Asst. Surg. and 1st Lt.
Redd, Robert G., AAS
Reynolds, Richard M., AAS
Ridgely, John V., AAS
Shufeldt, Robert W., Asst. Surg. and 1st Lt.
Stevens, Charles R., AAS
Taylor, Blair D., Asst. Surg. and 1st Lt.
Tesson, Louis S., Asst. Surg. and 1st Lt.
Tilton, Henry R., Surg. and Maj.
Van Eman, William J., AAS
Williams, John W., Asst. Surg. and Capt.
Wood, Marshall W., Asst. Surg. and 1st Lt.

Sources: Personal History of Surgeons Serving in the Department of the Platte, 1876–77; Parker, *Records of the Association of Acting Assistant Surgeons of the United States Army.*

APPENDIX E

Battles, Skirmishes, and Casualties of the Great Sioux War

Date	Engagement	Officers		Enlisted Men		Civilians		Indians	
		KIA	WIA	KIA	WIA	KIA	WIA	KIA	WIA
1876									
Mar. 5	Powder River, Wyo.				1				
Mar. 17	Powder River, Mont.		1	4	5			1	
June 9	Tongue River, Wyo.				1				
June 17	Rosebud Creek, Mont.		1	9	20	1		36	63
June 22	Elkhorn Creek, Wyo.							1	
June 25–26	Little Big Horn, Mont.	15	2	235	44	5		43	60
July 7	Tongue River, Wyo.								5
July 17	Warbonnet Creek, Neb.							1	
July 29	Mouth of Powder River, Mont.				1				
Aug. 1	Cheyenne River, Dak.							1	
Aug. 2	Mouth of Powder River, Mont.					1		1	
Aug. 14	Missouri River, Dak								
Aug. 23	Yellowstone River, Mont.			1					
Sept. 9–10	Slim Buttes, Dak.		1	3	13	1	1	10	2
Sept. 14	Owl Creek, Dak.			1					
Oct. 11	Spring Creek, Mont.								
Oct. 14	Richard Creek, Wyo.			1					
Oct. 15–16	Clear/Spring creeks, Mont.				3			1	3
Oct. 21	Cedar Creek, Mont.				2			5	

Date	Engagement	Officers		Enlisted Men		Civilians		Indians	
		KIA	WIA	KIA	WIA	KIA	WIA	KIA	WIA
Nov. 25	Red Fork Powder River, Wyo.	1		6	21			40	80
Dec. 7	Bark Creek, Mont.							1	
Dec. 18	Ash Creek, Mont.							1	
1877									
Jan. 3	Tongue River, Mont.			1					
Jan. 7–8	Wolf Mountains, Mont.			1	9			5	3
Jan. 13	Elkhorn Creek, Wyo.				3				
Feb. 23	Crow Creek, Dak.							1	
May 7	Muddy Creek, Mont.		2	4	9	1		14	20
July 3	Little Missouri River, Dak.								
Totals		16	7	266	132	9	1	162	236

Sources: Chronological List of Actions, 61–64; augmented by Vaughn, *The Reynolds Campaign on Powder River,* 160; Vaughn, *With Crook at the Rosebud,* 214, 216; Bray, *Crazy Horse,* 234, 258; Mangum, *Battle of the Rosebud,* 88, 167*n*25–26; Sklenar, *To Hell with Honor,* 327–28; Hardorff, *Hokahey!* 57, 82, 97, 113, 154–55; Utley, *Frontier Regulars,* 256, 261, 276, 280; *Report of the Secretary of War, 1876,* 480–81; Hedren, *Fort Laramie in 1876,* 139, 183, 218; Greene, *Slim Buttes, 1876,* 87–88, 170–71; Greene, *Yellowstone Command,* 88, 90, 104, 136, 142, 162, 171, 176, 206, 211–13; Greene, *Morning Star Dawn,* 139–40. With respect to Indians killed and wounded, numbers vary, sometimes greatly. At Little Big Horn, for instance, Utley reports Indian fatalities ranging from 30 to 300; Sklenar reports 30 to 50 killed and says that Two Moon estimated about 100 wounded. Hardorff documents 43 fatalities and wounded ranging from 30 to 160, excluding extremes, with two informants reporting 60 and another reporting 64. I have tended to report Indian numbers conservatively.

APPENDIX F

Officers Killed or Wounded in the Great Sioux War (Alphabetical by Grade)

Custer, George A., Lt. Col., Seventh Cavalry (KIA)

Benteen, Frederick W., Capt., Seventh Cavalry (WIA)
Custer, Thomas W., Capt., Seventh Cavalry (KIA)
Henry, Guy V., Capt., Third Cavalry (WIA)
Keogh, Myles W., Capt., Seventh Cavalry (KIA)
Yates, George W., Capt., Seventh Cavalry (KIA)

Calhoun, James, 1st Lt., Seventh Cavalry (KIA)
Cooke, William W., 1st Lt., Seventh Cavalry (KIA)
Lord, George E., Asst. Surg. and 1st Lt. (KIA)
McIntosh, Donald, 1st Lt., Seventh Cavalry (KIA)
McKinney, John A, 1st Lt., Fourth Cavalry (KIA)
Porter, James E., 1st Lt., Seventh Cavalry (KIA)
Rawolle, William C., 1st Lt., Second Cavalry (WIA)
Smith, Algernon E., 1st Lt., Seventh Cavalry (KIA)
Von Luettwitz, Adolphus H., 1st Lt., Third Cavalry (WIA)

Crittenden, John J., 2nd Lt., Twentieth Infantry (KIA)
Fuller, Alfred M., 2nd Lt., Second Cavalry (WIA)
Harrington, Henry M., 2nd Lt., Seventh Cavalry (KIA)
Hodgson, Benjamin H., 2nd Lt., Seventh Cavalry (KIA)
Jerome, Lovell H., 2nd Lt., Second Cavalry (WIA)
Reily, William Van W., 2nd Lt., Seventh Cavalry (KIA)
Sturgis, James G., 2nd Lt., Seventh Cavalry (KIA)
Varnum, Charles A., 2nd Lt., Seventh Cavalry (WIA)

APPENDIX G

Glossary of Critical Military Terms (Adapted to 1876)

Acting (e.g., *Acting* Assistant Adjutant General [AAAG], *Acting* Commissary of Subsistence [ACS or AACS], or *Acting* Assistant Quartermaster [AAQM]). An officer temporarily performing the duties pertaining to a staff branch of the American Army.

Acting Assistant Surgeon (AAS). A physician employed in civil life engaged to perform the duties required of commissioned medical officers when the number of the latter was insufficient.

Adjutant. At the regiment and field level, a staff officer with the rank of lieutenant appointed by a field, regimental, or post commander to assist in the execution of all details associated with a field movement, regiment, or post. This officer was the channel of official communication, tended the commanding officer for orders or instructions of any sort, and promulgated such orders in writing after making a complete record thereof. The adjutant had charge of the books, files, and men of the headquarters; kept the rosters; and paraded and inspected escorts, guards, and other armed parties prior to their proceeding on duty.

Adjutant General (AG). The principal assistant to the general of the army and the principal staff officer of the American Army. The comparable position at the division and department level was an assistant adjutant general (AAG). Duties were similar to those of an adjutant, though of greater complexity and sensitivity.

Aide-de-camp (ADC). An officer selected by a general to carry orders and represent him in correspondence and in directing movements.

Assistant (e.g., *Assistant* Adjutant General or *Assistant* Quartermaster). The second grade in the staff branches of the American Army.

Battalion. An aggregation of from two to twelve companies.

Brigade. A body of troops, whether cavalry, artillery, or infantry, or a mixed command, consisting of two or more regiments.

Commissary of Subsistence. An officer usually of the Subsistence Department charged with the administration of the subsistence affairs of the department or command, including the requisition of stores, the obligation of subsistence funds, and the purchasing of subsistence stores.

Company. A body of men commanded by a captain and two lieutenants: one-tenth of a regiment in the American infantry and one-twelfth of a regiment in the American cavalry and artillery.

Engineer Officer. An officer whose duties in the field were principally the construction of fortifications, making surveys, and facilitating the passage of an army by constructing roads and bridges.

Field Officer. A colonel, lieutenant colonel, or major of a battalion or regiment, as distinguished from general officers, who are superior to field officers in rank; from line officers, who are inferior; and from staff officers, general or regimental, who may be of rank superior, equivalent, or inferior to that of field officers.

General Officer. An officer whose authority extends beyond the immediate command of a regiment and who may have a separate district or department. In the staff corps the word "general" is also used (such as surgeon general, quartermaster general, adjutant general) to denote that the officeholder has charge of his special department but does not ordinarily imply that he is a general officer.

Line Officer. A captain, first lieutenant, or second lieutenant typically in charge of a company.

Ordnance. A general name for all kinds of weapons employed in war and the appliances necessary for their use. Included are all guns, howitzers, projectiles, gun-carriages, limbers, caissons, small-arms, side-arms, and accoutrements for artillery, cavalry, and infantry and all ammunition for cannon and small-arms. Harness and horse equipments are also furnished by the ordnance department.

Ordnance Officer. An officer whose duties in the field were principally the requisitioning of ordnance stores and the accounting for all ordnance and ordnance stores on hand.

Provost Guard. The interior guard of a camp or army, in charge of arms, property, tents, and prisoners.

Quartermaster (QM). An officer whose duties in the field included the requisitioning and provisioning of clothing; camp and garrison equipage; cavalry and artillery horses; and fuel, forage, straw, and stationery as well as the marking out of the camp when on the march.

Regiment. A body of troops commanded by a colonel, whose strength in the American Army was about 1,200 in a cavalry regiment, about 600 in an artillery regiment, and about 500 in an infantry regiment.

Squad. A small section of a company or battery, placed in the charge of an officer or noncommissioned officer for purposes of inspection and supervision.

Squadron. Two companies of cavalry.

Staff Officer. An officer not attached to a regiment whose duties extended over the whole division or department, or a large section of it, with duties such as adjutant general, quartermaster, or commissary of subsistence. Regimental staff officers were limited to the adjutant and quartermaster; incumbents were not attached to companies.

Subsistence. The necessary provisions for an army, including prescribed rations of pork or bacon; fresh or salt beef; bread, flour, hard bread, or corn meal; peas, beans, or rice; and coffee, sugar, salt, and vinegar.

Sources: Adapted from Wilhelm, *A Military Dictionary and Gazetteer;* Farrow, *Farrow's Military Encyclopedia;* Boatner, *The Civil War Dictionary;* and Everly et al., *Preliminary Inventory of the Records of United States Army Continental Commands.*

Bibliography

Archival Materials

Fourth Artillery Regimental Returns, 1871–77. National Archives Microfilm Publication M727, roll 30. Washington, D.C.

❦ ❦ ❦

Second Cavalry Regimental Returns, 1872–79. National Archives Microfilm Publication M744, roll 19. Washington, D.C.

Third Cavalry Regimental Returns, 1876–84. National Archives Microfilm Publication M744, roll 31. Washington, D.C.

Fourth Cavalry Regimental Returns, 1872–76. National Archives Microfilm Publication M744, roll 42. Washington, D.C.

Fifth Cavalry Regimental Returns, 1872–76. National Archives Microfilm Publication M744, roll 53. Washington, D.C.

Fifth Cavalry Regimental Returns, 1877–85. National Archives Microfilm Publication M744, roll 54. Washington, D.C.

Seventh Cavalry Regimental Returns, 1874–81. National Archives Microfilm Publication M744, roll 72. Washington, D.C.

❦ ❦ ❦

First Infantry Regimental Returns, 1874–81. National Archives Microfilm Publication M665, roll 7. Washington, D.C.

Fourth Infantry Regimental Returns, 1876–85. National Archives Microfilm Publication M665, roll 47. Washington, D.C.

Fifth Infantry Regimental Returns, 1870–79. National Archives Microfilm Publication M665, roll 58. Washington, D.C.

Sixth Infantry Regimental Returns, 1869–78. National Archives Microfilm Publication M665, roll 70. Washington, D.C.

Seventh Infantry Regimental Returns, 1874–84. National Archives Microfilm Publication M665, roll 83. Washington, D.C.

Ninth Infantry Regimental Returns, 1870–79. National Archives Microfilm Publication M665, roll 104. Washington, D.C.

Eleventh Infantry Regimental Returns, 1873–82. National Archives Microfilm Publication M665, roll 126. Washington, D.C.

Fourteenth Infantry Regimental Returns, 1873–82. National Archives Microfilm Publication M665, roll 155. Washington, D.C.

Seventeenth Infantry Regimental Returns, 1872–80. National Archives Microfilm Publication M665, roll 184. Washington, D.C.

Twentieth Infantry Regimental Returns, 1874–81. National Archives Microfilm Publication M665, roll 212. Washington, D.C.

Twenty-second Infantry Regimental Returns, 1874–81. National Archives Microfilm Publication M665, roll 228. Washington, D.C.

Twenty-third Infantry Regimental Returns, 1874–82. National Archives Microfilm Publication M665, roll 237. Washington, D.C.

Fort Abraham Lincoln Post Returns, 1872–80. National Archives Microfilm Publication M617, roll 628. Washington, D.C.

Fort Custer Post Returns, 1877–98. National Archives Microfilm Publication M617, roll 277. Washington, D.C.

Fort Keogh Post Returns, 1876–86. National Archives Microfilm Publication M617, roll 572. Washington, D.C.

Fort Laramie Post Returns, 1861–76. National Archives Microfilm Publication M617, roll 596. Washington, D.C.

Fort McKinney Post Returns, 1876–87. National Archives Microfilm Publication M617, roll 703. Washington, D.C.

Fort Rice Post Returns, 1871–78. National Archives Microfilm Publication M617, roll 1007. Washington, D.C.

Fort Sully Post Returns, 1875–84. National Archives Microfilm Publication M617, roll 1239. Washington, D.C.

"Cost of the Late War with the Sioux Indians." 45th Cong., 2d Sess., 1878. Sen. Ex. Doc. 33. Part 2. Serial 1780.

Department of Dakota Monthly Returns, 1876. RG393, Entry 1205, Records of U.S. Army Continental Commands, National Archives, Washington, D.C.

Fort Buford Records, vol. 5, 1876–78. Fort Union Trading Post National Historic Site, Williston, North Dakota.

"Further Information in Relation to the Cost of the Sioux War." 45th Cong., 2d Sess., 1878. Sen. Ex. Doc. 33. Part 2. Serial 1780.

Nelson A. Miles Papers. U.S. Army Military History Institute, Carlisle Barracks, Pennsylvania.

Personal History of Surgeons Serving in the Department of the Platte, 1876–77. RG393,

Entry 3931. Records of U.S. Army Continental Commands, National Archives, Washington, D.C.

"Sioux Campaign." Special Files of Headquarters, Division of the Missouri. National Archives Microfilm Publication 1495, roll 5. Washington, D.C.

Books

Alberts, Don E. *Brandy Station to Manila Bay: A Biography of General Wesley Merritt.* Austin, Tex.: Presidial Press, 1980.

Altshuler, Constance W. *Cavalry Yellow & Infantry Blue: Army Officers in Arizona between 1851 and 1886.* Tucson: Arizona Historical Society, 1991.

Bad Heart Bull, Amos, and Helen H. Blish. *A Pictographic History of the Oglala Sioux.* Lincoln: University of Nebraska Press, 1967.

Bailey, John W. *Pacifying the Plains: General Alfred Terry and the Decline of the Sioux, 1866–1890.* Westport, Conn.: Greenwood Press, 1979.

Barnett, Louise. *Touched by Fire: The Life, Death, and Mythic Afterlife of George Armstrong Custer.* New York: Henry Holt & Company, 1996.

Boatner, Mark M., III. *The Civil War Dictionary.* Revised ed. New York: David McKay Company, Inc., 1988.

Bollinger, Gill. *Fort McKinney 1877 to 1894: A Wyoming Frontier Post.* Buffalo, Wyo.: Jim Gatchell Memorial Museum Press, 2006.

Bourke, John G. *Mackenzie's Last Fight with the Cheyennes.* Governor's Island, N.Y.: Military Service Institution, 1890. Reprint ed. Bellevue, Neb.: Old Army Press, 1970.

———. *On the Border with Crook.* New York: Charles Scribner's Sons, 1891.

Bradley, James H. *The March of the Montana Column: A Prelude to the Custer Disaster.* Norman: University of Oklahoma Press, 1961.

Bray, Kingsley M. *Crazy Horse: A Lakota Life.* Norman: University of Oklahoma Press, 2006.

Brereton, T. R. *Educating the U.S. Army: Arthur L. Wagner and Reform, 1875–1905.* Lincoln: University of Nebraska Press, 2000.

Buecker, Thomas R. *Fort Robinson and the American West, 1874–1899.* Lincoln: Nebraska State Historical Society, 1999.

Buecker, Thomas R., and R. Eli Paul, eds. *The Crazy Horse Surrender Ledger.* Lincoln: Nebraska State Historical Society, 1994.

Callwell, Charles E. *Small Wars: Their Principles and Practices.* London: Harrison & Sons, 1896.

Carroll, John M., ed. *The Papers of the Order of Indian Wars.* Fort Collins, Colo.: Old Army Press, 1975.

Carroll, John M., and Byron Price, eds. *Roll Call on the Little Big Horn, 28 June 1876.* Fort Collins, Colo.: Old Army Press, 1974.

Carter, R. G. *On the Border with Mackenzie, or Winning West Texas from the Comanches.* Mattituck, N.Y.: J. M. Carroll & Company, [1935].

Chandler, Melbourne C. *Of Garryowen in Glory: The History of the 7th U.S. Cavalry.* Annandale, Va.: Turnpike Press, Inc., 1960.

Chronological List of Actions, &c., with Indians from January 15, 1837 to January, 1891. [Washington, D.C.]: Adjutant General's Office, [1891]. Reprint ed. Fort Collins, Colo.: Old Army Press, 1979.

Coffman, Edward M. *The Old Army: A Portrait of the American Army in Peacetime, 1784–1898.* New York: Oxford University Press, 1986.

Cosmas, Graham A. *An Army for Empire: The United States Army in the Spanish American War.* Columbia: University of Missouri Press, 1971.

Cox, John E. *Five Years in the United States Army.* New York: Sol Lewis, 1973.

Cozzens, Peter, ed. *Eyewitnesses to the Indian Wars, 1876–1890, Vol. Four: The Long War for the Northern Plains.* Mechanicsburg, Penn.: Stackpole Books, 2004.

Custer, George A. *My Life on the Plains, or Personal Experiences with Indians.* New York: Sheldon and Company, 1874.

DeMontravel, Peter R. *A Hero to His Fighting Men: Nelson A. Miles, 1839–1925.* Kent, Ohio: Kent State University Press, 1998.

Dodge, Richard I. *The Black Hills.* New York: James Miller, 1876.

Donovan, James. *A Terrible Glory: Custer and the Little Bighorn—The Last Great Battle of the American West.* New York: Little, Brown & Company, 2008.

Dunlay, Thomas W. *Wolves for the Blue Soldiers: Indian Scouts and Auxiliaries with the United States Army, 1860–90.* Lincoln: University of Nebraska Press, 1982.

Everly, Elaine, et al. *Preliminary Inventory of the Records of United States Army Continental Commands, 1821–1920.* Washington, D.C.: National Archives & Records Service, 1973.

Farrow, Edward S. *Farrow's Military Encyclopedia: A Dictionary of Military Knowledge.* 3 vols. New York: Military-Naval Publishing Company, 1895.

———. *Mountain Scouting: A Handbook for Officers and Soldiers on the Frontiers.* New York: privately printed, 1881. Reprint ed. Norman: University of Oklahoma Press, 2000.

Finerty, John F. *War-Path and Bivouac, or the Conquest of the Sioux.* Chicago: Donohue & Henneberry, 1890.

Forsyth, George A. *The Story of a Soldier.* New York: D. Appleton and Company, 1900.

Fox, Richard A., Jr. *Archaeology, History, and Custer's Last Battle.* Norman: University of Oklahoma Press, 1993.

Frasca, Albert J., and Robert H. Hill. *The .45-70 Springfield.* Northridge, Calif.: Springfield Publishing Company, 1980.

Gray, John S. *Custer's Last Campaign: Mitch Boyer and the Little Bighorn Reconstructed.* Lincoln: University of Nebraska Press, 1991.

Greene, Jerome A., ed. *Battles and Skirmishes of the Great Sioux War, 1876–1877.* Norman: University of Oklahoma Press, 1993.

———, ed. *Indian War Veterans: Memories of Army Life and Campaigns in the West, 1864–1898.* New York: Savas Beatie, 2007.

———. *Morning Star Dawn: The Powder River Expedition and the Northern Cheyennes, 1876.* Norman: University of Oklahoma Press, 2003.

———. *Slim Buttes, 1876: An Episode of the Great Sioux War.* Norman: University of Oklahoma Press, 1982.

———. *Stricken Field: The Little Bighorn since 1876.* Norman: University of Oklahoma Press, 2008.

———. *Washita: The U.S. Army and the Southern Cheyennes, 1867–1869.* Norman: University of Oklahoma Press, 2004.

———. *Yellowstone Command: Colonel Nelson A. Miles and the Great Sioux War, 1876–1877.* Lincoln: University of Nebraska Press, 1991.

Haley, James L. *The Buffalo War.* Garden City, N.Y.: Doubleday & Company, 1976.

Hanson, Joseph M. *The Conquest of the Missouri, Being the Story of the Life and Exploits of Captain Grant Marsh.* Chicago: A. C. McClurg, 1909.

Hardorff, Richard G. *Hokahey! A Good Day to Die! The Indian Casualties of the Custer Fight.* Spokane, Wash.: Arthur H. Clark Company, 1993.

Harrigan, Ed. *The Regular Army O!* New York: Wm. A. Pond & Company, 1874. Reprint ed. with additions and glossary. N.p.: Don Rickey, Jr., 1962.

Hattaway, Herman, and Archer Jones. *How the North Won: A Military History of the Civil War.* Urbana: University of Illinois Press, 1983.

Hedren, Paul L. *First Scalp for Custer: The Skirmish at Warbonnet Creek, Nebraska, July 17, 1876.* Revised ed. Lincoln: Nebraska State Historical Society, 2005.

———. *Fort Laramie in 1876: Chronicle of a Frontier Post at War.* Lincoln: University of Nebraska Press, 1988.

———, ed. *The Great Sioux War 1876–77: The Best from* Montana The Magazine of Western History. Helena: Montana Historical Society Press, 1991.

———. *Sitting Bull's Surrender at Fort Buford: An Episode in American History.* Williston, N.Dak.: Fort Union Association, 1997.

———. *We Trailed the Sioux: Enlisted Men Speak on Custer, Crook, and the Great Sioux War.* Mechanicsburg, Pa.: Stackpole Books, 2003.

Heitman, Francis B. *Historical Register and Dictionary of the United States Army.* 2 vols. Washington, D.C.: Government Printing Office, 1903. Reprint ed. Urbana: University of Illinois Press, 1965.

Hutchins, James S. *Boots & Saddles at the Little Bighorn: Weapons, Dress, Equipment, Horses, and Flags of General Custer's Seventh U.S. Cavalry in 1876.* Fort Collins, Colo.: Old Army Press, 1976.

Hutton, Paul A. *Phil Sheridan and His Army.* Lincoln: University of Nebraska Press, 1985.

———, ed. *Soldiers West: Biographies from the Military Frontier.* Lincoln: University of Nebraska Press, 1987.

Jamieson, Perry D. *Crossing the Deadly Ground: United States Army Tactics, 1865–1899.* Tuscaloosa: University of Alabama Press, 1994.

Jensen, Richard E., ed. *The Indian Interviews of Eli S. Ricker, 1903–1919.* Voices of the American West, Volume 1. Lincoln: University of Nebraska Press, 2005.

———, ed. *The Settler and Soldier Interviews of Eli S. Ricker, 1903–1919.* Voices of the American West, Volume 2. Lincoln: University of Nebraska Press, 2005.

Johnson, Mark W. *That Body of Brave Men: The U.S. Regular Infantry and the Civil War in the West.* Cambridge, Mass.: Da Capo Press, 2003.

Kane, Lucile M., trans. and ed. *Military Life in Dakota: The Journal of Philippe Régis de Trobriand.* St. Paul, Minn.: Alvord Memorial Commission, 1951.

Kappler, Charles J., ed. *Indian Affairs: Laws and Treaties.* Washington, D.C.: Government Printing Office, 1903. Reprinted as *Indian Treaties, 1778–1883.* Mattituck, N.Y.: Amereon House, 1972.

Kelly, Carla. *Fort Buford: Sentinel at the Confluence.* Williston, N.Dak.: Fort Union Association, 2009.

Kime, Wayne R. *Colonel Richard Irving Dodge: The Life and Times of a Career Army Officer.* Norman: University of Oklahoma Press, 2006.

———, ed. *The Powder River Expedition Journals of Colonel Richard Irving Dodge.* Norman: University of Oklahoma Press, 1997.

King, Charles. *Campaigning with Crook and Stories of Army Life.* New York: Harper & Brothers, 1890.

———. *Trials of a Staff-Officer.* Philadelphia: L. R. Hamersley & Company, 1891.

King, James T. *War Eagle: A Life of General Eugene A. Carr.* Lincoln: University of Nebraska Press, 1963.

Lamar, Howard R., ed. *The New Encyclopedia of the American West.* New Haven: Yale University Press, 1998.

Larson, Robert W. *Gall: Lakota War Chief.* Norman: University of Oklahoma Press, 2007.

Lazarus, Edward. *Black Hills/White Justice: The Sioux Nation versus the United States, 1775 to the Present.* New York: HarperCollins Publishers, 1991.

Leehan, Brian. *Pale Horse at Plum Run: The First Minnesota at Gettysburg.* St. Paul: Minnesota Historical Society Press, 2002.

Liddic, Bruce R. *Vanishing Victory: Custer's Final March.* El Segundo, Calif.: Upton & Sons, Publishers, 2004.

Lubetkin, M. John. *Jay Cooke's Gamble: The Northern Pacific Railroad, the Sioux, and the Panic of 1873.* Norman: University of Oklahoma Press, 2006.

Mangum, Neil C. *Battle of the Rosebud: Prelude to the Little Bighorn.* El Segundo, Calif.: Upton & Sons, 1987.

McChristian, Douglas C. *An Army of Marksmen: The Development of United States Army Marksmanship in the Nineteenth Century.* Fort Collins, Colo.: Old Army Press, 1981.

———. *The U.S. Army in the West, 1870–1880: Uniforms, Weapons, and Equipment.* Norman: University of Oklahoma Press, 1995.

McDermott, John D. *Circle of Fire: The Indian War of 1865.* Mechanicsburg, Penn.: Stackpole Books, 2003.

Michno, Gregory F. *Lakota Noon: The Indian Narrative of Custer's Defeat.* Missoula, Mont.: Mountain Press Publishing Company, 1997.

Miles, Nelson A. *Personal Recollections and Observations of General Nelson A. Miles.* Chicago: Werner Company, 1896.

Mills, Charles K. *Rosters from 7th U.S. Cavalry Campaigns, 1866–1898.* Mattituck, N.Y.: J. M. Carroll & Company, 1983.

Moe, Richard. *The Last Full Measure: The Life and Death of the First Minnesota Volunteers.* New York: Henry Holt & Company, 1993.

Murray, Robert A. *Military Posts in the Powder River Country of Wyoming, 1865–1894.* Lincoln: University of Nebraska Press, 1968.

Nenninger, Timothy K. *The Leavenworth Schools and the Old Army: Education, Professionalism, and the Officer Corps of the United States Army, 1881–1918.* Westport, Conn.: Greenwood Press, 1978.

Nichols, Ronald H. *In Custer's Shadow: Major Marcus Reno.* Fort Collins, Colo.: Old Army Press, 1999.

———, ed. *Reno Court of Inquiry: Proceedings of a Court of Inquiry in the Case of Major Marcus A. Reno.* Crow Agency, Mont.: Custer Battlefield Historical & Museum Association, [1992].

Noyes, C. Lee. *The Guns "Long Hair" Left Behind: The Gatling Gun Detachment and the Little Big Horn.* London: English Westerners' Society, 2000.

Ostler, Jeffrey. *The Plains Sioux and U.S. Colonialism from Lewis and Clark to Wounded Knee.* New York: Cambridge University Press, 2004.

Parker, W. Thornton, ed. *Records of the Association of Acting Assistant Surgeons of the United States Army.* Salem, Mass.: Salem Press Publishing & Printing Company, 1891.

Paul, R. Eli, ed. *The Nebraska Indian Wars Reader, 1865–1877.* Lincoln: University of Nebraska Press, 1998.

Powell, Peter J. *Sweet Medicine: The Continuing Role of the Sacred Arrows, the Sun Dance, and the Sacred Buffalo Hat in Northern Cheyenne History.* 2 vols. Norman: University of Oklahoma Press, 1969.

Price, George F. *Across the Continent with the Fifth Cavalry.* New York: Antiquarian Press, Ltd., 1959.

Prucha, Francis P. *Guide to the Military Posts of the United States.* Madison: State Historical Society of Wisconsin, 1964.

Rankin, Charles E., ed. *Legacy: New Perspectives on the Battle of the Little Bighorn.* Helena: Montana Historical Society Press, 1996.

Record of Engagements with Hostile Indians within the Military Division of the Missouri, from 1868 to 1882. Washington, D.C.: Government Printing Office, 1882. Reprint ed. Bellevue, Neb.: Old Army Press, 1969.

Records of Living Officers of the United States Army. Philadelphia: L. R. Hamersley & Company, 1884.

Reese, Timothy J. *Regulars!: A History of Gen. George Sykes' U.S. Regular Infantry Division of the Fifth Army Corps, 1861–1864.* Revised ed. Burkittsville, Md.: by the author, 2006.

Report of the Secretary of War, 1875. Washington, D.C.: Government Printing Office, 1875.

Report of the Secretary of War, 1876. Washington, D.C.: Government Printing Office, 1876.

Report of the Secretary of War, 1877. Washington, D.C.: Government Printing Office, 1877.

Reports of Inspection Made in the Summer of 1877 by Generals P. H. Sheridan and W. T. Sherman of Country North of the Union Pacific Railroad. Washington, D.C.: Government Printing Office, 1878. Reprint ed. Fairfield, Wash.: Ye Galleon Press, 1984.

Rickey, Don, Jr. *Forty Miles a Day on Beans and Hay: The Enlisted Soldier Fighting the Indian Wars.* Norman: University of Oklahoma Press, 1963.

Robinson, Charles M., III. *Bad Hand: A Biography of General Ranald S. Mackenzie.* Austin, Tex.: State House Press, 1993.

———, ed. *The Diaries of John Gregory Bourke, Volume One: November 20, 1872–July 28, 1876.* Denton: University of North Texas Press, 2003.

———, ed. *The Diaries of John Gregory Bourke, Volume Two: July 29, 1876–April 7, 1878.* Denton: University of North Texas Press, 2005.

———. *General Crook and the Western Frontier.* Norman: University of Oklahoma Press, 2001.

———. *A Good Year to Die: The Story of the Great Sioux War.* New York: Random House, 1995.

Rodenbough, Theo F. *From Everglade to Cañon with the Second Dragoons (Second United States Cavalry).* New York: D. Van Nostrand, 1875. Reprint ed. Norman: University of Oklahoma Press, 2000.

Rodenbough, Theo F., and William L. Haskins. *The Army of the United States.* New York: Maynard, Merrill & Company, 1896. Reprint ed. New York: Argonaut Press, Ltd., 1966.

Scott, Douglas D., Richard A. Fox, Jr., Melissa A. Conner, and Dick Harmon. *Archaeological Perspectives on the Battle of the Little Bighorn.* Norman: University of Oklahoma Press, 1989.

Sears, Stephen W. *Gettysburg.* Boston/New York: Houghton Mifflin Company, 2003.

Sklenar, Larry. *To Hell with Honor: Custer and the Little Big Horn.* Norman: University of Oklahoma Press, 2000.

Stewart, Edgar I. *Custer's Luck.* Norman: University of Oklahoma Press, 1955.

Taunton, Francis B. *Army Failures against the Sioux in 1876: An Examination.* British Custeriana Series. N.p.: Westerners Publications Limited, 2001.

Thain, Raphael P. *Notes Illustrating the Military Geography of the United States, 1813–1880.* Washington, D.C.: Government Printing Office, 1881. Reprint ed. Austin: University of Texas Press, 1979.

Trudeau, Noah A. *Gettysburg: A Testing of Courage.* New York: HarperCollins Publishers, 2002.

Under the Maltese Cross, Antietam to Appomattox, the Loyal Uprising in Western Pennsylvania, 1861–1865: Campaigns of the One Hundred and Fifty-fifth Pennsylvania. Pittsburg, Pa.: 155th Regimental Association, 1910.

Upton, Emory. *Infantry Tactics, Double and Single Rank, Adapted to American Topography and Improved Fire-Arms.* New York: D. Appleton & Company, 1874. Reprint ed. New York: Greenwood Press, 1968.

Upton, Richard, ed. *Fort Custer on the Big Horn, 1877–1898.* Glendale, Calif.: Arthur H. Clark Company, 1973.

Utley, Robert M. *Cavalier in Buckskin: George Armstrong Custer and the Western Military Frontier.* Norman: University of Oklahoma Press, 1988.

———. *Frontier Regulars: The United States Army and the Indian, 1866–1890.* New York: Macmillan Publishing Company, Inc., 1973.

———. *Frontiersmen in Blue: The United States Army and the Indian, 1848–1865.* New York: Macmillan Company, 1967.

———. *The Lance and the Shield: The Life and Times of Sitting Bull.* New York: Henry Holt and Company, 1993.

Vaughn, J. W. *The Reynolds Campaign on Powder River.* Norman: University of Oklahoma Press, 1961.

———. *With Crook at the Rosebud.* Harrisburg, Pa.: Stackpole Company, 1956.

Wagner, David E. *Patrick Connor's War: The 1865 Powder River Expedition.* Norman, Okla.: Arthur H. Clark Company, 2010.

———. *Powder River Odyssey: Nelson Cole's Western Campaign of 1865, the Journals of Lyman G. Bennett and Other Eyewitness Accounts.* Norman, Okla.: Arthur H. Clark Company, 2009.

White, Leonard D. *The Republican Era, 1869–1901: A Study in Administrative History.* New York: Macmillan Company, 1958.

Wilhelm, Thomas. *A Military Dictionary and Gazetteer.* Philadelphia: L. R. Hamersley & Company, 1881.

Willert, James. *Little Big Horn Diary: Chronicle of the 1876 Indian War.* La Mirada, Calif.: James Willert, Publisher, 1977.

———. *March of the Columns: Chronicle of the 1876 Indian War, June 27–September 16, 1876.* El Segundo. Calif.: Upton & Sons, Publishers, 1994.

———. *To the Edge of Darkness, a Chronicle of the 1876 Indian War: General Gibbon's Montana Column and the Reno Scout, March 14–June 20, 1876.* El Segundo, Calif.: Upton & Sons, Publishers, 1998.

Wooster, Robert. *The Military and United States Indian Policy, 1865–1903.* New Haven: Yale University Press, 1988.

———. *Nelson A. Miles and the Twilight of the Frontier Army.* Lincoln: University of Nebraska Press, 1993.

Zimmer, William F. *Frontier Soldier: An Enlisted Man's Journal of the Sioux and Nez Perce Campaigns, 1877.* Edited by Jerome A. Greene. Helena: Montana Historical Society Press, 1998.

Articles and Essays

Abrams, Marc H. "The Green Factor at the Little Bighorn." *Research Review: The Journal of the Little Big Horn Associates* 20 (Winter 2006): 17–21.

Anderson, Harry H. "Indian Peace Talkers and the Conclusion of the Sioux War of 1876." *Nebraska History* 44 (December 1963): 233–55.

Athearn, Robert G., ed. "A Winter Campaign against the Sioux." *Mississippi Valley Historical Review* 35 (September 1948): 272–84.

Baird, George W. "General Miles's Indian Campaigns." *Century Magazine* 42 (July 1891): 351–70.

Bourke, John. "Mackenzie's Last Fight with the Cheyennes: A Winter Campaign in Wyoming and Montana." *Journal of the Military Service Institution* 11 (January 1890): 29–49 and (March 1890): 198–221.

Brown, Lisle G. "The Yellowstone Supply Depot." *North Dakota History* 40 (Winter 1973): 24–33.

Buecker, Thomas R. "'Can You Send Us Immediate Relief?': Army Expeditions to the Northern Black Hills, 1876–1878." *South Dakota History* 25 (Summer 1995): 95–115.

Clow, Richmond L. "General Philip Sheridan's Legacy: The Sioux Pony Campaign of 1876." *Nebraska History* 57 (Winter 1876): 460–77.

Daniel, Forrest W. "Dismounting the Sioux." *North Dakota History* 41 (Summer 1974): 8–13.

Davis, E. Elden, and Karen L. Davis, eds. "For the Front." *Bighorn Yellowstone Journal* 1 (Summer 1992): 18–22.

Gibbon, John. "Arms to Fight Indians." *United Service* 1 (April 1879): 237–44.

———. "Hunting Sitting Bull." *American Catholic Quarterly Review* 2 (October 1877): 665–94.

———. "Last Summer's Expedition against the Sioux Indians and Its Great Catastrophe." *American Catholic Quarterly Review* 2 (April 1877): 271–304.

Godfrey, Edward S. "Cavalry Fire Discipline." *Journal of the Military Service Institution* 19 (September 1896): 252–59.

———. "Custer's Last Battle." *Century Magazine* 43 (January 1892): 357–87.

Greene, Jerome A. "Out with a Whimper: The Little Missouri Expedition and the Close of the Great Sioux War." *South Dakota History* 35 (Spring 2005): 1–39.

Hardorff, R. "Dutch." "The Reno Scout." *Little Big Horn Associates Research Review* 11 (December 1977): 3–12.

Hedren, Paul L. "Eben Swift's Army Service on the Plains, 1876–1879." *Annals of Wyoming* 50 (Spring 1978): 141–55.

———. "Garrisoning the Black Hills Road: The United States Army's Camps on Sage Creek and Mouth of Red Canyon, 1876–77." *South Dakota History* 37 (Spring 2007): 1–45.

———. "'Three Cool, Determined Men': The Sioux War Heroism of Privates Evans, Stewart, and Bell." *Montana The Magazine of Western History* 41 (Winter 1991): 14–27.

———, ed. "'The Worst Campaign I Ever Experienced': Sergeant John Zimmerman's Memoir of the Great Sioux War." *Annals of Wyoming* 76 (Winter 2004): 2–14.

Heski, Tom. "Camp Powell: The Powder River Depot." *Research Review: The Journal of the Little Big Horn Associates* 17 (Winter 2003): 13–24, 30–31.

———. "Soldiers, Surveyors, Steamboats & Stanley's Stockade." *Research Review: The Journal of the Little Big Horn Associates* 13 (Winter 1999): 19–31.

Hughes, Robert P. "The Campaign against the Sioux in 1876." *Journal of the Military Service Institution* 18 (January 1896): 1–44.

"Indian Warfare Losses Severe." *Rocky Mountain Husbandman* (Great Falls, Mont.), December 12, 1940.

King, Charles. "Address." In *Proceedings of the Annual Meeting and Dinner of the Order of Indian Wars of the United States*, 20–39. Washington, D.C.: Order of Indian Wars of the United States, 1921.

———. "Arms or Tactics." *United Service* 2 (April 1880): 492–98.

———. "Custer's Last Battle." *Harper's New Monthly Magazine* 81 (August 1890): 378–87.

———. "The Leavenworth School." *Harper's New Monthly Magazine* 76 (April 1888): 777–92.

King, James T. "General Crook at Camp Cloud Peak: 'I Am at a Loss What to Do.'" *Journal of the West* 11 (January 1972): 114–27.

Knight, Oliver. "War or Peace: The Anxious Wait for Crazy Horse." *Nebraska History* 54 (Winter 1973): 521–44.

MacNeil, Rod. "Raw Recruits and Veterans." *Little Big Horn Associates Newsletter* 21 (October 1987): 7–8.

Pearson, Jeffrey V. "Nelson A. Miles, Crazy Horse, and the Battle of Wolf Mountains." *Montana The Magazine of Western History* 51 (Winter 2001): 52–67.

Russell, Don. "How Many Indians Were Killed?" *American West* 10 (July 1973): 42–47, 61–63.

Simmons, Clyde R. "The Indian Wars and US Military Thought, 1865–1890." *Parameters* 22 (Spring 1992): 60–72.

Sundstrom, Linea. "The Sacred Black Hills: An Ethnohistorical Review." *Great Plains Quarterly* 17 (Summer/Fall 1997): 185–212.

Trinque, Bruce A. "Small Wars and the Little Bighorn." *Research Review: The Journal of the Little Big Horn Associates* 12 (Summer 1998): 14–42.

Urwin, Gregory. "Was the Past Prologue?: Meditations on Custer's Tactics at the Little Big Horn." In *7th Annual Symposium*, 22–36. Hardin, Mont.: Custer Battlefield Historical & Museum Association, 1993.

Utley, Robert M. "The Contribution of the Frontier to the American Military Tradition." In *The Harmon Memorial Lectures in Military History, 1959–1987*, ed. Harry R. Borowski, 525–37. Washington, D.C.: Office of Air Force History, 1988.

Willert, James. "Another Look at the Reno Scout, with Special References to the Explorations of Tom Heski." *Research Review: The Journal of the Little Big Horn Associates* 14 (Summer 2000): 17–31.

———. "The Sibley Scout." *Research Review: The Journal of the Little Big Horn Associates* 9 (January 1995): 24–31.

Woodruff, C. A. "Historical Sketch of the 7th Infantry." *Journal of the Military Service Institution* 17 (July 1895): 181.

Index